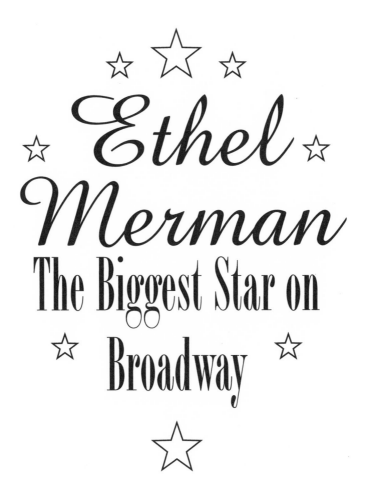

# Ethel Merman
## The Biggest Star on Broadway

Geoffrey Mark

LEGEND

an Imprint of Barricade Books Inc.
Fort Lee, New Jersey

Also by Geoffrey Mark:

*First Lady of Song: Ella Fitzgerald for the Record*

*The Lucy Book*

Published by Barricade Books Inc.
185 Bridge Plaza North
Suite 308-A
Fort Lee, NJ 07024
www.barricadebooks.com

Library of Congress Cataloging-in-Publication Data

Mark, Geoffrey
  Ethel Merman : the biggest star on Broadway / Geoffrey Mark.
      p. cm.
  Includes index.
  ISBN 1-56980-293-9
  1.  Merman, Ethel. 2.  Women singers--United States--Biography. 3.  Motion picture actors and actresses--United States--Biography.  I. Title.

ML420.M39M37 2005
782.1'4092--dc22
                                                                    2005054325

First Printing
Printed in Canada

# Contents

*Dedication*

This book is dedicated to David Little. He died much too young in 1989 (of complications from AIDS) just as his career was taking off. David was an extremely talented singer and comedian and a great inspiration for a teenager just getting started in big-time show business when we first met. It was he who first tapped into the seemingly limitless storehouse of show-business knowledge known as my brain.

He would have loved that I wrote this book, and he would have *loved* that you are reading it!

# *Foreword*

I t was my good fortune, for fifty years, to have Ethel Merman as a good friend. I dearly cherished her, and thought of Ethel as a role model for most of my career. She truly was all the things a good friend should be—encouraging, thoughtful, caring, warm, and, in Ethel's case, so very talented. She used to come to my home when we had our big dinner parties and we'd have a million laughs.

One of my most treasured memories of Ethel involves a gift she made for me. Please allow me to explain. Whenever she appeared in Los Angeles, I would attend at least one of her performances—always with a smile on my face and in my heart for the extent of her genius talent. One time she was appearing at the Shrine Auditorium. I asked the usher who seated me to "please tell Miss Merman that Rose Marie is here." That way, I hoped to be taken backstage to see her after the performance with as little hassle as possible. The usher returned in a short while and said, "Miss Marie, Miss Merman asked that you please come backstage *now*."

I was dumbfounded. Most performers want solitude before going onstage so as to prepare and focus. Also to be very nervous! When I got to Ethel's dressing room, she was needlepointing a pillow and said it was a gift for me in the colors of my dining room (which she had thoughtfully remembered). Here she was, about to perform a show in front of thousands of people, and with no nerves and no fuss, she was thinking about me!

I was so flattered and appreciative. To this day, that pillow sits on the window seat in my dining room.

Ethel and I saw one another through some terrific successes and some terrible tragedies. I think of Ethel so often and miss the wonderful times and friendship we had. I am so happy Geoffrey Mark has written this exceptional book to honor this dear human being.

I loved her very much!

—Rose Marie
September 2005

# *Congratulations!*

Normally in a book like this, there is a very short chapter called *acknowledgments*. It is here that the author gets to thank his agent, his manager, his family, and anybody else who in some way assisted or provided assistance while the book was being written.

In this case, I have decided to call it *Congratulations!* because you were right and I was wrong. Practically everyone listed here has been telling me for years to write this book. Well, *congratulations!* You were right!

Among those who have shared research, audio, or videos with me through the years are: David Little, Tim King, Ron Smith, John Fricke, Stephen Cole, Fred Phillips, Miles Kreuger, Research Video, Shokus Video, Alan Eichler, Dinah Shore, Eric Streit, Sofa Entertainment, Footlight Records . . .

. . . and especially Jeff Sotzing of Carson Productions. Not only did Jeff see to it that I got copies of Merman appearances on "The Tonight Show, Starring Johnny Carson," he paid all the expenses himself. Huge thanks to Mr. Sotzing and the late, great Mr. Carson!

These lovely people took out time from their busy lives to talk with me about Ethel Merman, many have long since passed: Rose Marie, Jayne Meadows Allen, Steve Allen, Milton Berle, Mary Martin, Lucille Ball, Lillian Gish, Maria Karnilova, Michael Stewart, Howard Rogut, Peter Filichia, Carole Cook, Kaye Ballard, Peter Marshall, Lee Roy Reams, David Merrick, Ted Hook, Ann Miller, Milton Rosenstock, Buddy Bregman, Bob Schiller, Bob Weiskopf, Irma Kusely, Maury Thompson, Liza Minnelli, Chita Rivera, Carol Channing, Marty Paich, Billy May, Tom Poston, Harry Zubkoff, Anna Sosenko, Coyne Steven Sanders, Edie Adams, Jimmy Garrett, Donald O'Connor, Candy Moore, Yvonne Craig, Jack Carter, Shelley Berman, Rip Taylor, Lucie Arnaz, Howard Morris, Jerry Orbach.

There are also many more that chose to remain anonymous. They have my heartfelt thanks!

I am indebted to my big-time literary agent, Michael Hamilburg, and am grateful that a man who has shepherded so many best-selling books likes my work. And I must mention my editor at Barricade Books, Allan Wilson. This is the second book of mine Allan has edited at two different publishing houses. His experience is invaluable.

These kind people lent a helping hand, heart, or wallet: Bruce Franklin, Todd Shreiner, Matthew Brooks, Brad and Alicia McClung, Bob and Sabrina Schiller, Ron Carey, Chuck McCann, Louis Nye, Pat Harrington Jr., Jack Riley, Gary Owens, Howard Storm, Chuck Dransfield, David and Howie Morris, Gil and Dee Stratton . . .

. . . and, of course, my so very much-loved mother, Vivian!

# Introduction

**B**eing a performer in show business is damned hard work. Long years of preparation are followed by more years of hard work, paying dues. Tens of thousands of hopefuls migrate every year, like lemmings or grunions, to New York and Hollywood, in an attempt at stardom. Almost all of them are spectacular failures, mythically crashing and burning. They run the gamut from the deliciously untalented to the incredibly unlucky.

Perhaps one climbs the ladder of success and is actually cast as the lead in a show, film, or television series. The day of infamy has come! Thank-you speeches are memorized, shopping is done for chic homes in expensive neighborhoods, and plans are made to make it up to good ole Maw and Paw and Sister Sal (who always stood by through thick and thin). These fantasies end when the reviews are published or the ratings come out.

Many talented performers never appear in a hit. After a couple of flops, their careers are over. If, by some chance, one is truly struck by lightning and actually makes it to stardom, the hard work has barely begun.

Nowhere is that work *harder* than on the Broadway stage. If one is blessed to be in a hit, life totally revolves around being on that stage for three hours of intense concentration, physical exertion, jangled nerves, and heart-pounding adrenaline. This is done eight times a week over a six-day period, going on for two years at a clip with only a short vacation. Holidays only mean an extra matinee. There is no family time, no weekends at the beach, and calling in sick doesn't exist. Very few can handle it, mentally or physically.

The only thing more difficult than being the lead in a legitimate play is starring in a musical. Singing, dancing, costume changes, makeup changes. All are done at breakneck speed while making it look effortless to the audience. Most stars need to sleep until noon to gather their strength. They don't go out shopping or to lunch so as to save their voices and protect themselves from catching illness in the harshness of New York weather.

When someone is starring in a Broadway show, everything revolves around them. If they cannot perform due to illness or stress, everybody else is out of a job. One legendary musical comedy star referred to it as "taking the veil," devoting oneself to the job the way a nun devotes herself to the Catholic Church. There is almost no social life.

There is big money to be earned, but only as long as the show runs. There can be years between significant income. The ego takes a huge battering. If a musical-comedy star introduces even one song that becomes his or her "signature," the star is considered a huge success. The biggest stars are blessed to appear in perhaps three or four hit musicals in their lifetimes.

Ethel Merman starred in fifteen hit musical productions on Broadway. After spending five years trying to make a name for herself in nightclubs and vaudeville, Merman became an overnight sensation in the 1930 production of *Girl Crazy*. Over the next four decades, the indefatigable Ethel introduced more than forty songs on stage that became standards. Although she had costars who sang or danced or told jokes, the shows always revolved around *her*.

The biggest star on Broadway.

Even the fabled Al Jolson did not have such a career. His time in the limelight did not last as long, and his list of hit songs and shows isn't even half that of Merman's.

Tallulah Bankhead and Helen Hayes both claimed "First Lady" of the stage status through the years. Merman had more hit shows than both of them put together. And more hit movies, for that matter.

And what of Mary Martin? For years among Broadway wags, there were two camps (and I *do* mean camp): those who worshipped Merman and those who idolized Martin. There is no doubt that Mary Martin was one of the best stage performers who ever lived. Her hit shows like *South Pacific*, *Peter Pan*, *The Sound of Music*, and *I Do!, I Do!* were wonderful and legendary. Merman had tremendous respect and affection for her. *And* her business management. Martin was richer; Merman was *better*.

There have been three books published about the life of Ethel Merman. The first was a collection of "as-told-to" stories Pete Martin wrote in 1955 for the fondly remembered *Saturday Evening Post*. Titled *Who Could Ask for Anything More*, the book read like the magazine article that it was. Next, Ethel told sanitized parts of her story to George Eels for the best-selling *Merman: An Autobiography* in 1978. According to her, she was

3

able to hang on to her hymen until she was thirty, never took a misstep in her career, and felt that the sordid details of her five-minute marriage to Ernest Borgnine were not worth mentioning. Funny it was—*honest*, it was not.

Soon after her death in 1984, journalist Bob Thomas wrote a biography called *I Got Rhythm: The Ethel Merman Story*. His angle was that she was an alcoholic old bitch with great talent. His tabloid stories were not balanced with any understanding of what motivated her or for that matter, what it was about her as a performer that made her so special. Gossipy and well written it was. *Revealing* it was not.

These books added to the press agentry of Merman's long career. One would think that all she did was point her massive breasts up to the balcony, open her mouth, and while she stood center stage screaming the lyrics of Berlin and Porter and Gershwin and Sondheim, the world fell at her feet. Words like brassy and sassy and tough as nails were used to describe the Merman persona.

Merman herself, in introducing Eels's book, made mention that people didn't think of her as having any of the finer emotions. Unfortunately, the rest of the book showcased this woman who was brassy and sassy and tough as nails, pointing her massive breasts and screaming.

There was a real woman underneath all of the stories. One who loved deeply and was hurt very easily. One who had tremendous self-confidence in her work, yet was deeply insecure as a *woman*.

Ethel wanted to be like her fabled Eadie—to have class. She desperately desired to be a lady. Yet, like Eadie (a hit song "Eadie Was a Lady" was from *Take a Chance*), she frequently showed her class with a capital *K*. She was often gaudy, cheaply dressed, badly coifed, and cursed like a sailor. But that was just on the outside, the mask she wore to protect herself.

Inside, she was an angry woman, fearful of people. She had many friends, but she was mistrustful and lonely. Politically an archconservative Republican, Merman lived a personal life that was much closer to Democratic liberality. Financially, she was an enigma. Although she earned huge sums of money in a very long career and was known to be close with a buck, Ethel's estate came to less than a million dollars.

Romantically, she thought with her vagina. Her suitors were all powerful, muscular, and well endowed. That they had nothing in common with her, were using her for her celebrity and money, or cheated on her constantly were ideas that only occurred to Merman after her lust had been satiated. Once the sex began to wane, only then did she bother to think about her lovers as people. Sounds like many of *us*, doesn't it?

Actually, Ethel Merman *was* like a lot of us—a little bit of everything. She worked hard, she loved, she lost, she knew fairy-tale success and tasted terrible tragedy. She was hysterically funny, she was deeply depressed, loyal to a fault, yet quick to end friendships. A selfless daughter and a selfish mother. Rubbed elbows with very important people, yet was actually quite common.

Until she stepped on a stage. Then she was in a class by herself.

The biggest star on Broadway.

# Preface: We Interrupt This Program

eople buy books like this for several reasons. Perhaps some enjoy reading about famous people. Others want to hear the dirt and know that despite their fame and money, celebrities' lives are often more unhappy than their own. And the die-hard fans want to hear about every song, every appearance, every hairstyle change. Pleasing everybody is impossible, so let me tell you how I am going to please everybody.

In the body of the book, you are going to read everything I know about Ethel Merman's life and the salient points of her career. For those of you who love Ethel, hate Ethel, or have any interest at all in the show business of the twentieth century, I am hoping you will wholeheartedly enjoy the real story of Ethel Merman.

At the back of the book, there are chapters covering her shows, films, recordings, and radio and television appearances. Each and every item is covered in minutiae, featuring cast, crew, dates, and pertinent and interesting information that did not belong in the body of the book. There will be new tidbits and tasty morsels here even for the most jaded of Mermaniacs. Want to know why Merman's hairstyle changed right in the middle of a scene on "The Lucy Show"? Want to know which love songs she privately recorded to woo Ernest Borgnine into proposing? Want to know about the production problems she encountered when she appeared on "The Bell Telephone Hour"? This is the place to find out.

So sit back, grab a snack, and fasten your seat belt because it is my pleasure to drive you through the life of Ethel Merman.

The biggest star on Broadway.

At the turn of the twentieth century, the sidewalks of New York were populated by the biggest collection of immigrants the world had ever seen. The Irish lived in the neighborhoods surrounding the Brooklyn Navy Yards. Jews lived on the Lower East Side of Manhattan in tenements that were a huge improvement over the pogroms of Europe. The Germans lived on the Upper East Side of Manhattan, re-creating the beer gardens of their homeland. Harlem was still mostly a bedroom community for white businessmen. African Americans did not make it their home until after the New York subway system was finished and white businesspeople relocated to Brooklyn, the Bronx, and Connecticut. The Bronx was a mixture of Swedish, Danish, Norwegian, Polish, Italian, and Jewish immigrants who had made enough money to escape the tenements of their recent past. Staten Island was a wasteland and largely uninhabited.

Queens, recently made a borough of New York City proper, was still considered by most to be a part of Long Island. It had many of the conveniences of the other boroughs and few of the drawbacks. Queens was a quaint collection of neighborhoods containing mostly Christian families who had been in the United States for at least two generations. It was more conservative and much less volatile than its sister boroughs. The new subways still under construction made it an easy commute to the hustle and bustle of Manhattan. Yet, there were acres of undeveloped land and easy access to the Atlantic Ocean and Long Island Sound. Large apartments and homes were being built for the new middle class that lived there.

The neighborhood of Astoria sat right on the edge of the border with Long Island. Under the aegis of New York City, the newest of plumbing, electricity, telephone service, and the amenities of the world's largest city were there for the taking by those who could afford such luxuries. On a summer's day, a salty ocean breeze kept the streets relatively cool in the time before air conditioning. Organ grinders with their little monkeys amused children on tree-lined streets while parents threw pennies. Vendors in horse-drawn carriages and pushcarts sold fresh fruit and vegetables direct from the nearby farms. Ice-filled wagons proffered fresh fish from the Fulton Fish Market in Manhattan, as well as seafood from Long Island Sound.

The well-dressed matron wore full skirts and a bustle with a flowery picture hat and high-button shoes. These would soon be replaced by the hobble skirt and high heels, but that was a few years off. The man of the day always wore a starched linen shirt with a celluloid collar, a vest, string tie, and his own high-button shoes. As the ladies changed their styles, men would wear skimpy suits, neckties, spats on their shoes, and bowler hats. The new Americans were *fashionable*.

For entertainment, all well-to-do families had a piano, and

children were given lessons in violin and harp. Families played together and prayed together. There was no radio, no television, and there were no commercial recordings. The exciting new entertainment, motion pictures, was embryonic (and was, in fact, headquartered in Astoria). There were few theaters and even fewer movies to watch. Charlie Chaplin and Mary Pickford were unknown.

The only true entertainment available outside the home was the live performance. Opera, ballet, and symphony orchestras were for the rich and educated. It was vaudeville and the Broadway stage that entertained the common folk. Irving Berlin was still a singing waiter. Jimmy Durante, Eddie Cantor, George Jessel, Jack Benny, Fanny Brice, Al Jolson, Sophie Tucker, George Burns, Gracie Allen, Groucho Marx, and Milton Berle were all child performers of one age or another (and probably lying about it). The biggest things in show business were minstrel shows (white performers satirizing black people satirizing white people) and operettas (a holdover from Europe).

This was the environment into which Ethel Agnes Zimmermann was born on January 16, 1906. When she made the big time in show business, years were shaved off to make it appear she was a mere wisp of a girl. The future Miss Merman would conveniently lie about her age the rest of her life, clinging to those lost years to give an illusion of youth.

Her parents seemed to be the loving, indulgent, nurturing people that were later idealized on television shows like "The Adventures of Ozzie and Harriet." Ethel was an only child, and Edward and Agnes Zimmermann adored their daughter. A bit chubby as a youngster, Ethel possessed a quick wit, dark flashing eyes, beautiful skin, and the ability to learn a tune before she could talk. She was, indeed, their pride and joy.

The Zimmermann family never had to worry about finances, illness, or social deprivation. Edward earned a very comfortable living as an accountant, leaving Agnes to stay at home and indulge little Ethel. There were grandparents, aunts, uncles, and cousins abounding; the Zimmermanns were surrounded by love. The two families had emigrated from Germany (Edward) and Scotland (Agnes) two generations earlier. There were no funny accents or tenements in Ethel's life, nothing of which to be ashamed. Her family had a big house at 359 Fourth Avenue (neither it nor the street still exists), electricity, a telephone, steam heat, and indoor plumbing. For most Americans, these were still luxuries in the days before World War I.

Like many of their social stature, the Zimmermann family had a piano in the parlor, which Edward played with abandon. When it was learned that she could carry a tune, tiny Ethel was placed at her father's feet where she was encouraged to sing along. The louder she sang, the more Edward encouraged her. The more encouragement she got, the louder she sang. Ethel seemed to get an adrenaline rush from her parents' approval. This would last as long as they lived, and they lived until Ethel was almost seventy.

This approval seemed to give Ethel a confidence uncommon in a child. No matter what she attempted, little Ethel was always certain she would be a conqueror. Failure was not in her vocabulary. Edward and Agnes should have written a book on how to build a child's self-esteem. Much of Ethel's childhood was enveloped in laughter and emotional intimacy. The incredibly healthy ego that grew inside of Ethel would be a boon to her career. However, it would later prove a disaster in her personal life.

The Zimmermann family was definitely spiritual, but confused religiously. Throughout her childhood, Ethel had

Christian learning reinforced by church attendance, Sunday school, and Wednesday evening services that were called "Christian Endeavor." This schedule of churchgoing is fairly common among those who consider themselves born-again Christians. But Ethel had an ax to grind—she would only attend churches that would allow her to sing. She went through Lutheran and Catholic and Methodist and Presbyterian before she finally settled on the local Episcopal church. Her indulgent parents allowed her to church-shop as long as she went *somewhere*. Ethel would identify as an Episcopalian the rest of her life.

The only ugliness Ethel was exposed to in her early life was anti-Semitism. It was very common in those early days of the twentieth century. Those of German and Scottish backgrounds often looked down on Jews with anything from mild disdain to outright hatred. It was what they had been taught in their homelands, and they brought their prejudices with them along with their scones and strudels.

In Ethel's case, she was taught the mild variety. The only Jews she ever became close to were the ones she met professionally like George Gershwin and Irving Berlin. And even then, the relationships were warm, but kept at a mostly professional distance. One husband would be Jewish, but he converted at her insistence. Only once did Ethel allow a Jewish man to get close to her heart, and she ended up being spurned for a younger woman. And once Ethel allowed a Jewish *woman* to get close to her heart, and that relationship has always been shrouded in rumor and mystery. Have I aroused your curiosity? Good! But you are going to have to wait fifteen chapters until we get there.

Throughout much of her career, people assumed that Ethel Merman was Jewish. She always politely, but vehemently, denied it.

From the time she was a small child, Ethel's favorite times were when her parents took her to see vaudeville. Female singers like Fanny Brice, Blossom Seeley, Helen Morgan, Sophie Tucker, and Ruth Etting were her inspiration. Certainly, she was exposed to the work of Al Jolson, the only person critics claimed she might have imitated. She was fascinated by the music and the energy of the performances. Although never an intellectual, when it came to what she saw on the vaudeville stage, she was like a sponge. Ethel missed nothing. Not unlike Barbra Streisand thirty years later, she absorbed the work of all the stars that had come before her and then amalgamated it into something totally original.

Ethel also noticed the adulation of the audiences. It was like the attention her parents gave her, only amplified a thousand times. She loved the palpable electricity she felt. It was an excitement Ethel found nowhere else.

By the time little Ethel hit puberty, she was already a veteran at appearing in public as an amateur singer. Edward took her to lodge meetings where she sang to the amusement of the half-plastered lodge brothers. Pretty soon, she was singing at all the lodges, as well as for the local chamber of commerce. During the First World War, Ethel was taken to Camp Mills and Camp Yaphank to entertain the boys before they went overseas. Her range wasn't wide, but her tone was clear as a bell. Her voice actually reverberated like a chime. It was unique and easy to hear in the days before microphones.

Ethel approached her singing with such enthusiasm that the audiences would cheer with excitement. Her vibrato was natural and fast, much different than the sound of her adult years. Her New Yorky accent, which always evidenced itself in her work, was also much stronger in her youth.

By the time she hit high school, there was no doubt in her

mind that she was going on the vaudeville stage and would be a star. In one of the few times that her parents put their collective foot down, the Zimmermanns insisted that Ethel take a secretarial course and learn a trade in case show business didn't work out. In those days, girls could skate through high school taking either home economics or stenography without any of the heavy math, science, or literature courses. Ethel quickly agreed. Typing was fun, and she had no interest in anything intellectual, anyway. She scorned chemistry, history, or anything else that was not show business. As long as Ethel attended school as directed, Agnes Zimmermann was pleased with her daughter. For the most part.

One thing that *did* bother Agnes was Ethel's rough edges. By today's standards, Ethel could not be called a wild youth. However, she was a product of the Jazz Age. Even as a teenager, Ethel preferred the slang-talking, hard-drinking, Charleston lovers among her peers. She kept late hours and learned to enjoy cigarettes and liquor before she was eighteen. Her language was not only becoming peppered with the slang of the day, but with the four-letter words that no lady of Agnes's generation would have ever allowed to escape from her lips.

And boys. Ethel learned *very* early how to be popular with boys. This is one of the great dichotomies of Ethel's life. She truly loved Jesus and felt that she was a good Christian. But when it came to sex, Ethel put her spiritual beliefs aside and got what she wanted. She always felt that sex was a natural bodily function, and despite the church's teachings, she was never shy about her sexual desires. In later years, Merman would brag to Johnny Carson (when asked if she would ever marry again), "Why buy the cow when you can get the milk for nothing?"

She also loved the attention from boys that sex brought and

expected the same sort of devotion from them that she got from her parents. Usually, she was greatly disappointed. Nobody could have lived up to the standards the Zimmermanns had set. Ethel the Coquette expected worship in exchange for her virtue. Most boys had no idea why she got so upset with them after a sexual encounter. Her taste in men was probably usual for a teenager. Ethel liked things flashy and exciting. Her choice of beaus always left her mother concerned and confused.

Then there was the way she *dressed*! One of her friends said, "What she didn't wear, she carried!" Ethel loved dresses that had pleats and sparkles, and wore her first fur pieces regardless of the weather. Agnes had always seen to it that Ethel was dressed in the finest of middle-class fashions. Once Ethel began to work and earn her own money, she would take guidance from no one. Even on a sunny, warm afternoon, one could find Ethel wrapped in fox stoles and gaudy bracelets, wearing pleated chiffon dresses with cloche hats and spectator shoes.

Although her parents had done a fantastic job of raising Ethel to be a well-mannered, God-fearing young lady, the final results were less than successful. It wasn't that the young Miss Zimmermann lacked character; she wasn't a "bad" girl. But she often abandoned Agnes's teachings of eye-batting coyness for the direct embrace of a boy's arms. And it wasn't that she lacked knowledge of the social graces. Ethel knew how to be studiously polite. She just chose to ignore politeness when it suited her purpose. Every gift received was rewarded with a handwritten thank-you note. But if the gift wasn't just to Ethel's liking, it was quickly returned for a cash refund. In later years, she would keep a closet of recycled gifts, each box topped with a typed note describing the contents as well as the giver (lest Ethel give someone a gift they had given to her).

One could get the image that Ethel Zimmermann was a very unlikable young girl. Actually, she was quite popular and had a large coterie of pals. Ethel approached people directly and without guile. Her friends knew exactly who she was because she made no pretense at being anything else. She was energetic, ambitious, and focused. Perhaps she suffered from "only child" syndrome. She wasn't selfish, but she was very self-seeking. Her eyes were always on the prize, and she rarely allowed anything to divert her attention.

For fun, Ethel's tastes could be very simple or quite lavish. Never a coffee drinker, she could enjoy a pot of tea with her girlfriends while they worked anagrams and puzzles together. If Ethel was with buddies with whom she was comfortable, had good music on the Victrola, and had tasty treats like apple pie and cheese and crackers to eat, she was having a good time. She must have had an oral fixation because there seemed to be something in her mouth at all times—a cigarette, chewing gum, cough drops, peanut brittle . . . there was always something.

Other times, the adventuresome side of Ethel would emerge. She would coax her young men to hire a big black car and chauffeur to drive them to amusement parks, ballrooms, fancy restaurants, and speakeasies. She liked to dance, loved to listen to live music, and enjoyed the sideshows and freaks of carnivals and places like Coney Island.

And booze. Ethel's age was not just the Jazz Age, but the bathtub-gin age. She was rarely found drunk, but she enjoyed having a good time. In one of those ironic twists of fate that would later find themselves into Cole Porter's lyrics, Ethel got quite a kick from Champagne!

Ethel finally graduated from William Cullen Bryant High School in June of 1925. She did not get an academic diploma because almost all of her courses had been aimed at training her to be a secretary. She could take shorthand (Pittman method, today obsolete) and type at a then-breathtaking sixty words a minute. Although her speech patterns were filled with syntax and grammatical horrors, Secretary Zimmermann knew how to write a perfect business letter. That's all there was to it back then. There were no electric typewriters, computers, word processors, spreadsheets, presentation software, fax machines, paper shredders, or sophisticated telephone systems. If your telephone had a dial, it was state of the art.

Miss Zimm had also developed well physically. Blessed with fascinating breasts, she also had very shapely legs and an infectious smile. Dressed in short skirts, long pearls, and cloches, Ethel was cute, flirtatious, and efficient. She gave *great* boss.

Ever the promoter, Ethel couldn't sit idly by with just a day job. At night, she sang in local boîtes, eventually graduating to some of the smaller clubs in Manhattan. She worked out a great system for herself. She would sing until two in the morning and take the subway home to Queens. After getting perhaps five hours of sleep, Ethel would tiptoe into the office at ten. If the boss was there, her fellow secretaries would cover until her arrival. If, as often happened, he was not in the office, then Ethel would slip into the executive ladies' room where there was a cot, remove her dress, and take a nap until lunchtime.

All of this sounds very cute until one stops to think. How could Ethel's boss, Caleb Bragg, the head of a large concern that made vacuum brakes, have been so blind as to not see what was going on under his nose? The answer is he wasn't. If he was blinded, it was by the attentions of his sexy secretary. Ethel played him like a violin. She needed the job for the income and to keep her parents off her back. She needed her freedom to work at night at the career she loved. She needed a boss who would look the other way. Ethel made sure she had all these things.

In later years, when men used Ethel in the same way, she found it neither cute nor amusing. Karma is a bitch.

She also made sure to use her boss's contacts. When she learned that her employer's pal, George White, was casting for one of his *Scandals*, Ethel purred in Bragg's ear that she wanted a letter of introduction. She got what she wanted, doing what came naturally. White auditioned her and then offered her a job in the chorus. Ethel politely thanked him, called him an asshole, and told him that she didn't need George White just to be a chorus girl.

Ethel fancied herself a blues singer. She never actually sang things written in the blues idiom. She sang the rhythmic torch songs of the day. Numbers like "Body and Soul" and "Little White Lies" were Ethel's stock-in-trade. She sang what all the other young songbirds warbled. What made her stand out was her voice and physical carriage.

At five feet five inches, she was considered tall for a woman. She wore dresses that accentuated her long legs and full bosom. Ethel never figured out the best way to fix her hair or wear makeup, not even until the day she died. In those days, she wore eye shadow up to her eyebrows, and her hair was "marcelled" into wiry waves.

Ethel was not dainty about her singing delivery. Hands waved, fingers wagged, fists clenched, legs kicked, and hips shook. *Nothing* stood still while she sang.

Her voice was now maturing and was even louder. In those days before microphones, she learned she could garner quite a hand in nightclubs if she could be heard above the noise of the rustling waiters serving drinks and food. Ethel also learned that it could be very effective if every once in a while she lightened up on her singing and allowed herself to be girlish. A separate voice in which to be lovely, if you will. She earned her audience's rapt attention.

Word spread around town about this girl singer, who by late 1926 was calling herself Ethel Merman. Ethel had gone through several names, trying to find one that would sound theatrical and still please her proud father. Ethel Hunter had been her favorite, but Edward Zimmermann could not understand what was wrong with the last name that *he* had given his only child. Finally, they settled on Merman since, after all, it was contained within the longer Zim*merman*.

Notoriety led to Ethel's being booked into a club called Little Russia. In later years, Ethel always claimed that this happened in September of 1929, just before being discovered for

Broadway. She did appear there then for a short return engagement, but it was not her debut. This deception allowed her to cover the discrepancy in her age and the idea that she was a complete unknown in 1930.

It was a step up for Merman, as the club was located in a fashionable neighborhood at 100 West Fifty-seventh Street near Carnegie Hall. It paid more money (Ethel always liked *that*), and celebrities of the day often came by to have a snort and watch Ethel shake it around. One evening, Al Siegel came into the club.

Siegel was one of those Damon Runyonesque characters who thrived in the show business of the 1920s. He was tough, short, well built, took nonsense from nobody, and managed singers. If he had been a movie character, James Cagney would have played him.

He had managed Bee Palmer from an unknown into a star, and now he wanted to manage Ethel. Siegel was struck with how Ethel was received by the audiences. Basically, her onstage persona was that of the hard-boiled dame that would later be played to perfection by Joan Blondell in the Warner Brothers movies of the 1930s. Merman exuded sensuality, yet somehow managed to avoid coming across as cheap or tawdry. Men and women enjoyed her performances equally, and she appealed to both the housewife from Brooklyn and the society matron from Park Avenue.

Siegel, however, didn't like Ethel's musical arrangements and choice of repertoire. He felt that she was singing what everyone else was singing and that there was nothing special about her performance of them except for her voice. After she agreed to be managed by him, he immediately rewrote all the arrangements for her songs. Siegel was a gifted musical arranger and pianist. He made sure that anything up-tempo had rhythms and syncopation that were both original and catchy. He worked with Merman on stealing time, bending notes, taking pregnant pauses during comedy numbers, and singing love ballads with passion and a slight "upper-crust" society accent that was very popular then.

It was around this time that Ethel began using the musical "scoop." It was a device that was being used with some regularity by Rudy Vallee and later Bing Crosby. Ethel would hit a note anywhere from a third above to a full octave above the actual note she wanted to hit and then quickly scoop down to it. In the beginning, it was done lightly, adding cuteness and vibrancy to her numbers. In later years, this scoop would become much more pronounced and the butt of many comedians' jokes.

Al never taught her *how* to sing or how to hold her hands or move on stage. Ethel had discovered all of those things for herself long before Mr. Siegel came along. But he did help her refine the style she had already created. He also began to accompany her on stage every night so there was interplay between the two of them in front of the audience. Their billing read, "Miss Ethel Merman with Al Siegel at the piano."

With Siegel's help, Ethel had her first dream come true. She and Al graduated from nightclubs into vaudeville when they opened at the Ritz Theatre in Elizabeth, New Jersey. Ethel abandoned her day job, as she was now bringing home more money than her father did. Al also got Ethel exposure on the covers for the sheet music of several popular songs of the day. By 1927, Ethel's name was getting coverage in the entertainment and gossip columns of the New York newspapers.

It wasn't that Ethel didn't have an agent. She did, and his name was Lou Irwin. It was Lou who actually did the paperwork for the bookings, but it was Al who knew where to book Ethel and how to market her.

Miraculously, Siegel managed to book Ethel only in night-clubs and vaudeville theaters in the New York metropolitan area. They were able to work for forty weeks in 1928, and Ethel never had to sleep anywhere other than in her own bedroom in Astoria.

Sleeping was one matter; sleeping *with* was quite another. The more popular Ethel became, the more possessive Siegel became. It can never be proven exactly what their private life was like. Siegel insisted until the day he died that he and Ethel had been lovers and that he had taught her everything she knew about singing. Merman insisted until the day *she* died that all Al ever did was write her arrangements. The truth probably lies somewhere in the middle.

In 1929, Al also got her a contract to make talking musical shorts for Warner Brothers. Ethel had a test done and even shot one short (*The Cave Club*), but it only received limited release in 1930. Ethel always claimed she never even got to see it herself. She continued to accept her weekly salary until she realized that they were never going to use her again. Only then did Lou Irwin get her a release from her contract.

Also in 1929, Siegel booked Ethel into the Club Durant (some sources have this happening at Les Ambassadeurs), a speakeasy about to open and run by Jimmy Durante and his partners. It would have been a big break for Ethel, but she developed laryngitis and had to have her tonsils operated on. Ethel did, indeed, work with Jimmy and his pals at Les Ambassadeurs, but that was after their own club failed even before it opened.

There had been rumors circulating at the time that Merman had gotten the job by first singing for Jimmy and then performing oral sex on him and his partners. If that is indeed how Merman contracted her bad throat, it was a very fortuitous batch of blow jobs. After the surgery, her voice returned with even more resonance than it had before. Her vibrato deepened, and she was able to hold very long notes with little effort.

Siegel quickly got Merman out of town and booked her into the Roman Pools Casino and Hotel in Miami Beach. By night, she and Al performed, and by day, she got a tan at the pool. She also made herself a small fortune by standing in the casino in her bathing suit, mules, and feathered jacket, bringing "good luck" to the high rollers. Every time she blew on their dice and they won, she received a percentage. Perhaps they also put a hand around her waist or gave her a kiss. And perhaps she also managed to do a cute jiggle every time they rolled the dice, attracting a crowd to her bouncing bosoms. In no way was Ethel exchanging sex for money, but when she realized which way the wind was blowing, she blew with it. She was earning $500 a week, yet sending home $1,000 in money orders to her mother. Agnes just looked the other way.

The attendant publicity from all of this landed Merman and Siegel into the Brooklyn Paramount Theater in mid-1930. They were now headlining the show at this stage presentation house. Vaudeville was already dying due to the success of radio and talking pictures. Many vaudeville houses were closing or became presentation houses. In these, there would be a showing of a feature film several times a day, and in between the showings of the film, there would be a stage show.

One day, unbeknown to Ethel or Al, Vinton Freedley came to the Brooklyn Paramount to catch their act. Freedley was a Broadway producer who was attached to the shows of the Gershwin brothers, George and Ira. They were writing a new score for a show called *Girl Crazy*, and they needed a sensuous young singer to play the second lead. Ginger Rogers, in her pre-Fred Astaire days, had already been signed as the star of the show. In later years, Ginger claimed that it was her mother, Lela Rogers, who tipped off Freedley to Ethel and sent him to Brooklyn.

Freedley liked what he saw and went backstage after the performance to speak to Ethel and Al. It had never occurred to Ethel to even think about a legitimate Broadway show. Her target had always been vaudeville. But Al knew that vaudeville was becoming passé and that this could be a big break for Ethel.

One day, Ethel, Al, agent Lou Irwin (this was too big for Al to negotiate alone), and Freedley went to see the Gershwin brothers who lived at Riverside Drive and Seventy-fifth Street. As she later enjoyed telling audiences, not only was she in awe of meeting the great George Gershwin, she was in awe of the apartment building. It was an art-deco dream and one of the newest and tallest apartment buildings around. The brothers occupied the whole roof garden—George's penthouse was on one side, Ira's on the other. This was a whole new world to Ethel.

George Gershwin was a gracious host, and over drinks and hors d'oeuvres, the show was discussed. Ethel was asked to sing a couple of numbers from her stage act, with Al playing piano for her. Although Merman always claimed to never suffer from stage fright, on that afternoon, she was nervous beyond belief. She had no idea what this could lead to, how Al would react if she were cast, or what would happen to her life. It was one of the few times in her life that Ethel felt intimidated and clearly in over her head.

Gershwin then sat down and played the three songs that Merman would sing should she be cast: "Sam and Delilah," "I Got Rhythm," and "Boy, What Love Has Done to Me!" All three were rhythmic comedy songs and were right up Ethel's alley. When he was done playing, George told Ethel that if there was anything about these songs she didn't like, he would be most happy to change them. An embarrassed Ethel managed to blurt out, "No, sir, these'll do just fine!"

There was no waiting around for an answer. Ethel was hired on the spot. Although there was no place in the show for Al Siegel, it was agreed that he could play the piano and conduct for Ethel during her numbers. The rest of the band consisted of nobodies like Glenn Miller, Benny Goodman, and Red Nichols. Playing Merman's husband in the show was a young Lew Parker. Thirty years later, he would costar with Ethel again when she appeared in two episodes of the television situation comedy, "That Girl" (Parker played the overprotective father of Marlo Thomas on that series).

By late summer, Ethel was not only in rehearsals for *Girl Crazy*, but she and Al were visited by every vaudevillian's dream—they were booked at the infamous Palace Theatre! Doing the same act they had done at the Paramount, Ethel and Al opened there on September 13, 1930. She conquered vaudeville just as it began to fade, bridging the gap between the minstrel days of Jolson and Blossom Seeley to the more modern show business of sophisticated Broadway, radio, and films.

Between her club dates, film shorts salary, vaudeville dates, and Broadway rehearsal salary, Ethel Merman had earned more than $100,000 from June 1929 to December 1930. That was a huge sum of money in those days, especially for somebody who was not yet considered a star, but a minor celebrity. Ethel later claimed to have been a complete unknown at the time of her Broadway debut. This was far from true.

It was also an incredible figure considering that the Great Depression was less than a year old. Men were selling apples in the street, bread was five cents a loaf, and Ethel Agnes Zimmermann had more money in the bank than most people earned in a lifetime. Taking advantage of prevailing conditions, Ethel's broker was buying up stocks for pennies. She could afford to wait for their value to rise. Merman was twenty-four years old.

There are several myths surrounding the opening night of *Girl Crazy*. Let's examine some of them. First of all, it was rumored that Ginger Rogers hated Ethel for stealing the show from her. This was totally untrue. Ginger got her own chance to enchant the audiences nightly singing "But Not for Me" and "Embraceable You," never mind her energetic dancing. Her success in this show led to her contract with RKO studios in Hollywood and all of those wonderful movies she made. She and Ethel remained good chums the rest of their lives.

Secondly, that it was Ethel's singing of "I Got Rhythm" that first stopped the show. Actually, it was an earlier number, "Sam and Delilah," that made the audience sit up and take notice. Originally, Ethel was brought into the musical to say a few lines and sing her songs. That was the style back then. Many big Broadway female singers were not what they called "talking women." They actually had little to do with the plots of the shows. They came on, said some lines, sang their big number, and then got off. So it was to be with Ethel. However, when rehearsals began, Freedley et al. noticed that Ethel had a great sense of humor and could get big laughs with her few lines. So they wrote more and more comedy dialogue for her.

By the time the show opened, Merman was a comedy figure throughout the first act, but didn't get a chance to sing until almost intermission. The audience didn't have a clue that she even had a singing part. So when Ethel leaned up against the proscenium arch and began to sing, a cappella, "Delilah, was a floozy; she never gave a damn!" in that unique style of hers, the audience went crazy. There was this tremendous whoosh of sound. Ethel wasn't sure what was happening. She thought something was wrong, and perhaps she had lost one of her garters.

Merman got an ovation for that number, which completely blew everybody away. No girl singer received that kind of reaction in a Broadway show in those days. Not a supporting player with a minor song. And a risqué one at that. It wasn't done. Ira Gershwin's lyrics made no bones that Delilah traded sex for power, even if the story was Biblical. And Merman's diction was so perfect that Ira was able to end phrases with rhymes like hootch and kootch, and every word was understood in the second balcony. Not to mention her projection, for which she would become most famous.

It wasn't that no one had ever sung loudly before on a stage. Opera singers had been doing it for centuries. Merman wasn't the only female who didn't twitter a tune. Kate Smith made *her* Broadway debut several months earlier, and the reviewers said that the fat girl sang too loudly. Ethel did not just sing loudly—the word "belt" (too often applied to her) really didn't apply. Ethel Merman sang incisively, hitting her notes like a gong. The sound then reverberated all through the theater. Her voice and style were perfectly matched to the acoustics of nonmicrophoned Broadway theaters. Had she been trained from childhood, Merman could have been an opera singer. It was only in later years, when Ethel traded incisiveness for loudness as she aged, that the word "belt" really applied.

Thirdly, that when Ethel Merman sang "I Got Rhythm," she held a high C for the entire second chorus while the band played the song behind her. By all accounts, this is not precisely true, either. After she sang the first chorus, the band then went into double time, playing the song at lightning-fast speed. It was over this rendition of the song that Merman held her note, and it was A flat above middle C. It did, indeed, stop the show, and Ethel had to repeat the number three times before the audience would quiet down.

It wasn't just Ethel's holding of that one note that made the number so extremely successful. It was her style and energy. While singing the words, Ethel was everywhere, moving about the stage, shaking her fingers, clenching her fists, rolling her eyes. As she started to hold the note, she opened her sparkling eyes as wide as they would go, and with both index fingers, she alternately pointed into the air to the rhythm of the orchestra. At the same time, she moved her eyes back and forth, looking at each pointed finger as if *she* was as surprised as the audience as to what was going on. The presentation was unique, electric, and stunning. The audience was spellbound!

In less than five minutes after finishing "Sam and Delilah," Merman launched into "I Got Rhythm." It was the combination of the two blockbusters back to back that drove those first-nighters wild.

"I Got Rhythm" ended the first act. Ethel was ecstatic at the audience reaction, but did not know that it was anything out of the ordinary. After all, hadn't everybody reacted to her that way since she was a baby? While she busy adding more eye shadow and lipstick for the second act, George Gershwin ran up to her dressing room located on the fourth floor. "Ethel, do you know what you've done?" he asked. Ethel just shrugged her shoulders and started chewing on a new piece of gum. "Never do that number any other way, and never go near a singing teacher!" This was one myth that is absolutely true.

Although Ethel had a cute number in the second act, it was her performance in the first act that had everyone raving. The opening-night cast party was held at the Central Park Casino, which was the trendiest nightspot of the moment. When Ethel walked in, the band (led by Eddy Duchin) began to play "I Got Rhythm," and all the patrons gave her another standing ovation. *Now* Ethel began to realize that something special had happened to her. As she was led to the best table in the place, her mind went back to just a few weeks earlier when they couldn't even find a table at which to place her.

Although she'd had a big night, Ethel was up early the next morning. George Gershwin had invited her to lunch, and she wanted to look sharp for this man who had done so much for her. Normally, Ethel didn't enjoy luncheon appointments, but for Gershwin, she made an exception. When she got to his apartment, he asked her what she thought of her notices. Although Merman was not the innocent she later claimed to be who didn't even know that reviews existed, she honestly had not read the newspaper reviews of the show that had been delivered during the cast party. She knew they were good, but hadn't actually *read* them.

In those days, there were eleven daily newspapers in New York. Gershwin laid them all out at her feet, with the page turned to the reviews of the show. Every one of them featured a photograph of Ethel, with glowing reviews about a new star being born. Even Ethel's strong sense of self was overwhelmed. All George could talk about was what a big star she was going to be and how they had to carefully write her next musical to ensure she would have two hits in a row. Merman just sat in her chair, taking it all in.

It would be foolish to say that Ethel Merman and George Gershwin had an *affair*. George was dazzled by Ethel's performance of "I Got Rhythm." It was his personal favorite of all the songs he wrote. On Wednesday or Saturday matinees, George would sneak into the orchestra pit and take over on the piano. Ethel always knew when he was there. She could feel

31

the difference in how the music was played, and she loved it! Here was this great genius playing the piano just for her.

But theirs was hardly a love affair. Ethel felt too constrained by Al Siegel to get that involved with another man, however famous. And Gershwin was too much in love with himself to ever really give himself to a woman. Both had many people interested in spending time with them. Merman and Gershwin shared a season in one another's lives. Despite all good intentions, George never wrote another song for Ethel. By the time he died from a brain tumor in 1937, the two had not been close for years.

Merman was overjoyed at her success and plunged into her work with abandon. Before 1930 was over, she would appear in *Girl Crazy* every night from 8:30 until 11:20 (with matinees on Wednesday and Saturday), appear as the headlined singer at the Central Park Casino from midnight until 2 A.M., appear in the feature film, *Follow the Leader*, make her radio debut singing "I Got Rhythm" on Louis Calhern's eponymous series, *and* begin the filming of several shorts for Paramount Pictures.

Ethel got into *Leader* due to her friendship with Ginger, who was the female star of the film. Ed Wynn was the comedy star, and Merman really did no more in the film than stand up, sing "Satan's Holiday," and sit down again. The film received moderate reviews, but she had her Paramount contract to keep her happy, ensuring her film work into 1932. There seemed to be no stopping her incredible energy or thirst for success.

The only thing that even remotely marred this period for Ethel was Al Siegel. During dress rehearsals for *Girl Crazy*, Siegel had become ill. Ethel's rehearsal pianist, Roger Edens, took over for Al in the orchestra pit from then on. While Al was recuperating, Ethel went to see him and asked him to write the arrangements for her Central Park Casino stint. He said he would for one half of her earnings in perpetuity. Siegel overplayed his hand. He thought for sure that Ethel would be forever beholden to him for the help he had given her in becoming a star. He also figured that as a man, he was irresistible.

Siegel was wrong on both counts. Ethel, incensed but not ungrateful, wrote him a very large check to thank him for his help to that point and never spoke to him again. Ethel spent the rest of her life denying their personal relationship and denying that he ever did anything for her besides writing some superior arrangements.

The Merm (that's what they began to call her in the gossip columns) turned to Roger Edens, who wrote Ethel's vocal arrangements for many years to come. They became like brother and sister, as there was absolutely nothing romantic between Ethel and the handsome Edens because he was gay. Since Roger did not have an oversized ego, there was never a problem between them for the next forty years.

During the run of *Girl Crazy*, Ethel made the first of her short subject films for Paramount studios. They ran the gamut from operettalike failures such as *Devil Sea* to the best of the first bunch, *Her Future*.

When *Girl Crazy* finally ended its run in 1931 after forty weeks, Ethel decided it was time to pay some attention to her two best friends, her mom and pop. Ethel had not seen much of her parents in the preceding year. Although she always came home to sleep (sometimes as late as six in the morning), she was hardly at home. Between her work schedule and her abundant social life, Merman's world had completely changed. It wasn't that she abandoned her friends and family for life on the wicked stage. She still saw her girlfriends from high school on her day off (and would do so for the rest of her life). But Ethel was now surrounded by the cream of show business' crop. Everyone wanted to get to know her. Many wanted to use her. Some actually helped her.

A guilty Ethel moved the Zimmermann family (including dog Scrapsie) into a large, airy apartment on Manhattan's fashionable Central Park West with views of the park. She sincerely wanted to provide luxury for her indulgent parents, even though Edward continued to work every day and never accepted cash from Ethel. She also wanted to get out of Astoria so her late-night rides home wouldn't take as long. In later years, Ethel claimed this move didn't happen until much later, perhaps to protect her image as a young girl at the time. However, design magazines show photos of the new apartment in 1931.

There was now daily maid service for Agnes, who then turned all her attention onto her daughter, the star. She and Edward kept meticulous scrapbooks of every mention their daughter got in the press. Agnes was getting more and more concerned about her baby's social life. At least when Siegel was around, there was only one man in the picture. Now there were a parade of men, and she did not think they had Ethel's best interests at heart.

Meanwhile, Ethel was booked for a return engagement at the Palace, with comedian Lou Holtz as the emcee. This time she had twin grand pianos on stage and songwriter Johnny Green as her principal accompanist. Thirty years later, Merman used this same setup in her Las Vegas act. She ran for ten weeks at the Palace and was a smash. It was for this engagement that Ethel changed her singing of "I Got Rhythm." Instead of holding one long note, she held the note three times, interrupting the marathon A flat to sing the words "who could ask for anything more" and to sing the bridge of the song. It was this version that Ethel sang for the rest of her life.

Broadway, vaudeville, movies, Ethel had been working long and hard to become a celebrity. She was tired and unsure of what her next move should be. She decided that a vacation was long overdue. Ethel hired herself a big black car, a chauffeur, and she, her folks, and Scrapsie went off on what was supposed to be a road trip. It did not last long.

Ethel had barely unpacked her clothes in the hotel where they had stopped before she received a telegram followed by a long-distance phone call. Her agent had been trying to track her down at every possible stopping place on her proposed route. George White wanted her. NOW!

Mr. White was Florenz Ziegfeld's biggest competitor. After Ziegfeld became famous for his *Follies*, it was inevitable that competitors would copy him. White was a hack producer who put the last of his money into a revue he called the *Scandals*. Much to everyone's surprise, it became a huge hit. Like the *Follies*, each year, *George White's Scandals* was updated with new stars, songs, and sketches. However, *George White's Scandals of 1931* looked as if it was going to be his first fiasco.

Struggling in out-of-town tryouts, there was not one song or sketch that seemed to work. What George White needed was a big boost from a hot young star. Ethel's agent thought that if she could go into the show at the last moment and score another hit, it would be proof that Ethel Merman was all a show needed to be a success.

Merman left her folks and dog in upstate New York and immediately joined the show. The idea that Mr. White, who a few years earlier thought of her only as a chorus girl, now needed her to save his show was extremely appealing to Ethel. She hated what was written for her and demanded that a new song be composed especially for her. This was the beginning of the myth that Ethel Merman was a demanding bitch who was difficult.

Of course, Ethel was right. Although the show boasted Rudy Vallee and Alice Faye (and Ethel always resented that Vallee passed her by in the bedroom department in order to boink beautiful Alice), it was flat and unspectacular. After they added some new comedy sketches for Ethel and a new song, "Life Is Just a Bowl of Cherries," the show became a hit. All of Broadway was sitting up and taking notice. In two years, Ethel had introduced two standards ("I Got Rhythm" and "Life Is Just a Bowl of Cherries") and saved one show. It was also becoming increasingly clear that Ethel Merman was a comedy force not to be dismissed. She was a double threat, not unlike Fanny Brice. Fanny learned to *hate* her!

And, of course, Ethel was still making movie shorts. It was during this period that she made the best of them, *Roaming*. In it, Ethel sang the infectious "Shake Well before Using." It is probably the closest visual record we have as to what Ethel must have looked and sounded like in her first Broadway shows. Additionally, Ethel did some Betty Boop cartoons, singing standards like "Let Me Call You Sweetheart" while Betty did her animated thing.

Of course, Ethel was not satisfied. She added another stint at the Casino in the Park, chirping nightly after the *Scandals* curtain went down. She was making $1,250 weekly on Broadway and more than $1,500 at the Casino. Add that to her $1,000-a-week movie salary, and Merman was pulling in almost $4,000 a week. My maternal grandfather made $30 a week as a presser in a sweatshop in 1931. And ate well.

Before the end of the year, Ethel made her first, but abortive, attempt at being a recording artist. She went into a studio and recorded three numbers from the *Scandals*, but they were either never released or received very poor distribution. None of my research could find an extant copy.

In 1932, after *Scandals* closed and Ethel briefly toured with it, she once again played the Palace Theatre, this time with Jack Haley. She was, in fact, one of the last big stars to play the Palace before it was converted into a movie theater.

The Palace run took her through most of the summer of 1932. When it ended, the Mighty Merm landed in yet-another Broadway show that was in trouble. *Humpty Dumpty* laid somewhere in-between her two previous shows. It was not a "book" show like *Girl Crazy* had been with plot and characters, but it was also not a glamorous vaudeville show like the *Scandals*. This was a revue, a show featuring Ethel and others in tableaux, sketches, and blackouts all revolving around an historical theme.

Flopapalooza!! *Humpty Dumpty* closed in Atlantic City and never got to Broadway. This would have been Ethel's first professional disaster if not for belief in the show by the producers and the genius of Roger Edens. The cast, minus Merman, was fired, and the engaging Jack Haley (future Tin Man in the film classic *The Wizard of Oz* and her recent costar at the Palace) was brought in to play her love interest. Their new duet, "You're an Old Smoothie," became an audience favorite in out-of-town tryouts, but the newly renamed *Take A Chance* (the producers said, "Let's take a chance and remount it," thus the name) still didn't have the panache of a hit.

Roger Edens was still Ethel's pianist. He found a piece of music that had been discarded from the original production and thought it had great promise for Ethel if it were rewritten. He changed some of the lyrics and added a new bridge and an extra chorus. The producers felt it was just the act of a young musician trying to make some extra money and ignored Roger. Edens begged Ethel to push to have the song added to the show. Ethel was loyal and wise. She threatened to leave the show unless the song was given a chance before a live audience. Once more, Ethel was called difficult and a bitch.

Knowing that without Ethel they *had* no show, a new set was built to accommodate the song. An expensive pailleted gown in blood red and black was made for her, as well as a wig and black boa that seemed to be taken directly off Mae West's back. Walking down a long staircase, swinging her hips, undulating her pelvis, and rolling her eyes, Ethel Merman sang "Eadie Was a Lady" and stopped the show. Not unlike "Sam and Delilah," this was another risqué ditty that straddled the fence of good taste. The number was a paean to a dead prostitute as fondly remembered by a madam.

When the reviews came out, not only did no one take offense, but one reviewer even called the show *Eadie Was a Lady*. He'd been so won over by the song, he forgot the name of the show.

Merman had scored in three Broadway shows, introducing four standards in three years. Her career was on fire. It was at this time that she began her recording career in earnest. Ethel could not interest any recording companies to record (or at least release) her singing "Rhythm," "Cherries," or "Smoothie." Now, however, she signed with RCA Victor on its Bluebird label to record "Eadie" and four songs she did not introduce: "I'll Follow You," "Satan's Lil' Lamb," Irving Berlin's "How Deep is the Ocean?" and Harold Arlen's "I've Got a Right to Sing the Blues."

Ethel also signed with Columbia's Brunswick label. They, too, wanted a version of "Eadie." Merman negotiated out of her Bluebird contract (which had called for sixteen songs) to stay with Brunswick because they paid her more money. It was Brunswick that eventually released "Eadie," as well as Ethel's recordings in 1934 and 1935.

Ethel Merman never became a big recording star. Part of the reason was that early microphones could not accurately record the bell-like sound and intensity of her voice. They either had to pull back their microphone levels so that she sounded as if she were singing under water, or they over-recorded her voice so that all you heard was her vibrato. Also to be blamed were the unimaginative orchestral arrangements foisted upon her. To avoid having to pay large sums to the arrangers of the Broadway originals, recording companies hired less-talented people to make her standard arrangements for recordings. See chapter twenty-eight for a complete listing of all of Ethel's recordings and a critique thereof.

Merman was spotted in the show one night by MGM talent scouts. There was a new film being planned that they felt she might be perfect for, *Red-Headed Woman*. It was the story of a bad girl who was glad of it and allowed nothing to get in her way. She would have been costarred with Charles Boyer, Chester Morris, Lewis Stone, and May Robson, and she would have been wonderful. Unfortunately, Louis B. Mayer thought she was vulgar and assigned the plum role to Jean Harlow instead. It made Jean a superstar.

While in *Take a Chance*, Ethel first tapped into a most

lucrative racket: celebrity endorsements. It wasn't long before ads were appearing in all the best magazines for Ansonia Shoes featuring Merman. "I don't 'take a chance' when I wear Ansonia Shoes—$5.94" was the copy under her photo. Throughout the years, Ethel endorsed everything from beer and cigarettes to dishwashing liquid and cottage cheese.

After many months in the show, doing a short tour with it (she would later claim that she never toured or played nightclubs) and a stint at the Paramount Theatre, Ethel received an offer she could not refuse: Hollywood was really calling!

It was not unusual for the Hollywood of the early 1930s to invade Broadway and snatch its best talents for the movies. Motion pictures needed actors who were trained to speak, as pictures were still learning how to talk. Jolson, Cantor, Brice, Tucker, Rogers, Crosby, and Vallee had already been tapped for movie roles. In a way, it is surprising that Hollywood waited so long to grab Ethel.

In late September of 1933, Ethel and Agnes followed a path already well-worn and took the train to Hollywood. Paramount Pictures had decided that Ethel was ready to graduate from short subjects to full-length films, although she was not signed to a long-term contract. Ethel had been so intent on becoming a movie star that she unwisely did not insist on becoming part of the studio family. Hollywood was not Broadway, and she could not float from one place to another, choosing the best parts for herself. The studio system was in full flight, and only those that belonged to it ever really got anywhere.

Ethel faced two challenges. First, she had to live with her mother. Edward insisted that no daughter of his was going off to the land of sin (Hollywood) without a proper chaperon. Ethel needed a chaperon like Michael Jackson needs another nose job. But Ethel, at twenty-seven, still could not endure her father's outright disapproval. Agnes kept her secrets and often questioned if Ethel knew what she was doing, but Edward was kept in the dark. So, in order to keep peace in the family and the charade of snow-white virginity, Ethel and Agnes broke up their family. It was a very unhappy time for the Zimmermanns. Ethel and Agnes took an apartment in the Ravenswood Building owned by Mae West and located close to Paramount. Ethel had known Mae in New York and admired her honesty and guts.

Her second and bigger challenge was at the studio. Because she was not part of the Paramount family, she was paid little attention. They hated how she looked and put her on a crash diet to become thin. They also cut off her long hair, only to decide they hated it short. So Ethel wore a long black wig throughout the film. They dressed her in dark clothes, which with the awful wig made her look Latina. Merman was embarrassed and disgusted.

Instead of starring in the film, she got third female billing under Carole Lombard and Gracie Allen in *We're Not Dressing*. Bing Crosby was the male lead, but most of Merman's scenes were with Leon Errol, with whom she had zero chemistry. Ethel felt she had little to do in the film, since most of the comedy was being handled by George Burns and Gracie Allen.

She liked her costars, especially Gracie and Carole. These two actresses perhaps personified that dichotomy in Ethel's personality. Gracie was a lady, petite, and gentle. She knew her job and was a complete original. With Gracie, Ethel could discuss shopping, clothes, stagecraft, and the latest show-business gossip from New York. Carole was a different matter altogether. Lombard and Merman both shared a ribald sense of humor and a delight in vulgar language that they were embarrassed to use around genteel Gracie. With Carole, Ethel could swap dirty jokes, discuss who on the set was having sex, and which Paramount star had the biggest penis.

However, Ethel found out that she did *not* like speedboats. Part of the filming was done on nearby Catalina Island, and Ethel spent most of the day leaning over the side of the boat, retching. Again, she was embarrassed. Haircuts, wigs, diets, vomiting—when was the studio going to concentrate on her *singing*?

Ethel filmed two numbers for the film. "It's Just a New Spanish Custom" was a throwaway comedy song, but her big moment was supposed to be a production number called "The Animal in Me." Days were spent while Ethel was filmed singing her song in front of a screen upon which jungle animals of every kind were projected. Elephants, camels, and bears were brought onto the stage to surround her while she sang. Even then she felt awkward because the trainer pulled her aside to explain that his animals were reacting to the smell of her having her period, and she would have to leave the set until it was over. The elephants got to stay, but *she* had to leave. They didn't treat her like this on Broadway!

The final coup de grâce for Ethel and *We're Not Dressing* occurred many months later at the film's premiere in New York. She brought all her school chums and extended family, bragging about this great number she had. "The Animal in Me" had been cut out of the picture, and nobody had bothered to tell Ethel. Although it was later used in the film, *The Big Broadcast of 1936* (and Ethel had to be paid a second time for its use), the entire episode left Ethel greatly unhappy.

Another annoyance Ethel found intolerable was the way the Hollywood press intruded into her personal life. In New York, if Merman wanted to boff all the boys in the chorus for dinner and have three waiters for dessert, it was nobody's business. Al Goetz and Billy Sussman had been named as boyfriends by the New York columnists, but they were just beards, and everybody knew it. In Hollywood, her every coming and going was followed by a ravenous press, who did not understand why Merman didn't play the game. They hated her for her lack of cooperation, and she hated them because she couldn't have any fun.

Also, the Hollywood of 1933 offered little in the way of nighttime entertainment. New York had dozens of nightclubs for Ethel to visit, where she received the red-carpet treatment of a star. In Hollywood, there were perhaps three or four nightclubs. And they made Ethel Merman wait while Joan Crawford, Charlie Chaplin, and Cecil B. DeMille were seated immediately. That made Merman burn!

The only happy time Ethel had in Hollywood was when Roger Edens joined her there. Without Merman in New York, Roger wasn't doing the work he loved, so he thought he would take a crack at movies. The naive Edens soon learned that there are unions in Hollywood and very strong ones at that. He could not get any jobs until months had passed and he qualified to join. Ethel paid for all of Roger's expenses during this time, happy to give him the use of her money at a time when it really meant something to him. Within six months, he was hired by MGM and stayed there as an arranger, songwriter, producer, and mentor to Judy Garland for the next two decades. As soon as he could, Edens paid Ethel back every dime.

In later years, Roger wrote many of Ethel's vocal arrangements. That is to say, he would find out which songs she was to sing at any booking she had and would then record himself singing the song the way he felt Ethel should do it. She would take that recording to an orchestral arranger, who would write out the music for the various parts in the orchestra. Edens never took one cent for this work because he loved Ethel so. She knew he collected anything that had clasped hands, so Merman spent the rest of her life searching the world for these things, giving them to Roger because she loved *him* so. Their relationship was probably the most enjoyable of Ethel's life outside of those with her parents and grandchildren.

Despite Roger's company, Ethel felt fed up with the whole Hollywood scene. Ethel and Agnes returned to New York in April 1934. After another stint at the Paramount Theatre (this time with George Jessel, whom Ethel had to fight off every day as he was determined to have sex with her), Merman left for a vacation in Cuba. She spent almost a month sunning herself, drinking Cuba Libres, and enjoying the passionate men of Havana. As soon as she returned, her agent called to say that Sam Goldwyn wanted her back in Hollywood.

Goldwyn was the premier Hollywood producer. He financed all of his films with his own money, meaning there were no bankers or investors to answer to. It was he who had lured Eddie Cantor away from Broadway for a highly success-ful series of musical films. Now he wanted Ethel to appear in his latest, *Kid Millions*. Besides Eddie and Ethel, Ann Sothern and George Murphy were set to costar. Murphy had been part of a dancing act that had appeared with Ethel at the Casino in the Park in 1930. Ann was a pal from New York.

This time she did not feel like such an outsider. Proper attention was paid to how she looked and the comedy she would perform. Her big number was "An Earful of Music," which caught on enough that Ethel recorded the number for

Brunswick. Ethel had a lot more fun making this film, but still did not like Hollywood. She did, however, walk away with a new pal.

One day, one of the chorus girls (whom Goldwyn called Goldwyn Girls) was clowning around on the set with Ann Sothern. The girl was young, tall, very thin, very blonde, and very bawdy. Ethel immediately noticed her and asked to be introduced. They started talking and realized that they had a lot in common. Both were highly ambitious, devoted to their mothers, and enjoyed a good dirty joke. They began to pal around and pretty soon became buddies. Ethel Merman and Lucille Ball remained friends and mutual supporters for the rest of their lives.

Although *Kid Millions* was a popular film, no one offered Ethel a long-term contract. Once again disappointed by the movie colony, Merman decided to return to the arena where she was loved and appreciated: Broadway!

I f there is any such thing as luck, it surely smiled on Ethel
Merman upon her return home to New York City. Not long
after settling in to her Central Park West apartment (she
had hardly lived there for more than a year), Ethel got a call
from her agent. Cole Porter was working on a new musical,
and the new writing team of Howard Lindsay and Russel
Crouse was writing the book. Already hired were William
Gaxton and Victor Moore, names now forgotten, but who were
big Broadway comedy stars in 1934.

Vinton Freedley, in a wheelchair from a slight stroke, was
producing the show, and he wanted Ethel as the leading lady.
The only part of the plot that was worked out was that some
or most of the action would take place aboard a luxury ocean
liner. With only that much information, all the talent was
signed. It was like that in the Broadway of the 1930s—shows
were short on believable plot, but long on comedy and music.

The show, eventually named *Anything Goes*, provided one

of the best scores ever written for a musical. Almost every song became a hit—"You're the Top"; "I Get a Kick Out of You"; "All Through the Night"; "Blow, Gabriel, Blow"; and "Anything Goes" all became standards. The plot was negligible and hokey. A former evangelist turned nightclub singer (Merman) pursues a man (Gaxton) who in turn pursues a woman (Bettina Hall) onto a ship. Also on board is Public Enemy Number Thirteen Moonface (Moore), who longs to be in the "top ten" of criminals. He is masquerading as a Christian missionary working with Chinese converts. Gaxton has no ticket for passage on the ship, so he ends up rooming with Moonface. Confused yet?

The cast certainly was. The original plot had all of the characters shipwrecked together (shades of "Gilligan's Island"!) until a real-life shipping accident made them change the plot on grounds of good taste. The accident was a windfall for it garnered the show great publicity. However, to this day, there are those who believe that the entire "accident" story was just a publicity gimmick cover-up, and that the ever-changing plot was due to the writers simply trying to make the funniest show possible.

The story was changing daily, with Ethel taking down all the changes in shorthand and then typing them up for everyone by the next day. While the final plot was hardly convincing, opening-night audiences loved it. In those days, people really dressed up to go to the theater. Women wore expensive evening gowns, dripped in diamonds, and exhibited enough expensive furs to drive game-show host and animal-activist Bob Barker out of his mind. The opening night of *Anything Goes* was the premier social event of the season.

It was no longer a surprise that Ethel Merman stopped the show nightly. The musical boasted some of Cole Porter's best songs, and he and Ethel became fast friends. This shocked many people at the time as Porter was an effete snob. His only social contacts were with the absolute upper crust. He hid his homosexuality behind his wife, Linda, who herself was wealthy and a society dame. Cole would hire male prostitutes to satisfy his urgings, and even then, he was a snob and a bigot. The white men could enter through the front door, but the black ones had to use the servants' entrance.

Earthy Ethel seemed his complete antithesis, yet they each saw something in the other that was attractive. Soon, they were socializing on a regular basis. Through Cole, Ethel met the cream of society, who were happy to make the acquaintance of the big star with the wicked sense of humor. She was a breath of fresh air for them, and they helped to smooth out her rough edges.

It was through Cole Porter that Merman made the acquaintance of Sherman Billingsley, owner and host of the Stork Club. Both it and its competitor, El Morocco, became the hottest New York nightspots of the 1930s. Both places clamored to have the biggest stars think of it as a "second home," a place to which they would come after their shows to dine, dance, and relax. Billingsley spared no expense in bribing celebrities to come to his club. Women received gifts of expensive perfume and flowers delivered right to their tables. Men got gold cuff links or cigarette cases. The bigger the star, the bigger the gift.

Sherman sent Ethel beautiful flowers on the opening night of *Anything Goes*, which she had put in the chorus girls's dressing room because of her allergy to roses. With the flowers came an invitation to be his guest at the Stork Club any evening after her show. A few days later, Ethel went with Cole to the Stork, mostly to tell Billingsley never again to send her flowers. Sherman was so courtly, he almost bowed and scraped. Before the evening was over, a huge bottle of Ethel's favorite perfume, Joy, was delivered to the table, along with a magnum of Champagne. Merman was impressed.

The next day, every gossip column in every paper carried a story about Ethel having visited the Stork the night before. Ethel liked the publicity, and Sherman *loved* it. He wasted no time in sending a case of the finest French Champagne (Merman's potent potable of choice) to her dressing room. Again Ethel was pleased, and again all the papers carried the story. Before long, Broadway star Ethel Merman was spending many of her late nights at the Stork.

When she felt energetic, she could dance to whichever popular society orchestra was playing in the main room. If she was hungry, she could be fed a sumptuous supper in the more private Cub Room, which was reserved for VIPs. And after several months, if she was feeling romantic, Ethel could be found in Sherman's private office, in flagrante delicto on his leather couch. Sherman and Merman. Sounds nice?

Sherman Billingsley was a married man with children. Ouch! They tried to be discreet, but rarely is this kind of secret well kept. Agnes begged Ethel to reconsider, once again asking if she knew what she was doing. Ethel became almost obsessed with the attention Sherman gave her. He was the only man who could match the kind of intense affection she got from her parents. And the gifts were constantly flowing: talking parrots, diamond bracelets, alligator handbags and shoes, fur coats, white mice in cages, ostrich feather boas . . . anything that might please Princess Ethel. By the time their romance was over, Sherman Billingsley had given Ethel Merman more than $75,000 worth of diamond jewelry!

For her part, Ethel gave Sherman unbridled passionate sex, constant publicity, and very lively companionship. She convinced herself (with the help of Billingsley's lies) that he would eventually leave his family and marry her. Then she would have her career *and* the Stork Club *and* a husband. This fantasy would go on for years.

Being with Sherman wasn't the only socializing Ethel did during the run of *Anything Goes*. She became very friendly with the William Gaxtons, going with them to Sunday football games where they would sit with mink lap blankets and get drunk on hot toddies. She and Madeline Gaxton remained devoted pals well into old age.

Through her friendships with newspaper columnists like Radie Harris, Dorothy Kilgallen, and Ed Sullivan, Ethel made the acquaintance of FBI chief J. Edgar Hoover. They shared the same ultraconservative politics and superliberal personal lives. Hoover had met and fallen in love with one of his G-men, Clyde Tolson, and when they were in New York, they were inseparable. Ethel already had quite a coterie of gay friends (Porter, Edens, etc.) and readily accepted Hoover's lifestyle and desire for discretion. While Hoover was actually on the shy side socially, Clyde was always the life of the party and never failed to make Ethel laugh.

For many years, Merman, Hoover (she called him John), and Tolson could be found doing the town together. Ethel got a kick out of it, being with this man who was as powerful as the president and yet trusted her to keep his dark secrets. She knew he cross-dressed in the privacy of his home and even helped him go shopping for ladies' apparel at the finest stores.

Ethel also became very friendly with her understudy, a pretty young blonde from Albuquerque, New Mexico, named Vivian Vance. Ethel looked upon her as a protégée, taking Viv with her to photo opportunities and social events. Both Ethel and Viv were disappointed when Vance was overlooked as

Ethel's replacement when she left *Anything Goes*, and they remained lifelong friends. Benay Venuta was the one who replaced Merman in 1935 when she left the show to make the movie version, and they were friends, then enemies, then friends, then enemies, for decades.

In March 1935, Ethel made her biggest radio appearance yet when local station WOR (the flagship station of the Mutual Broadcasting Network) upped its wattage from 5,000 to 50,000 and broadcast a show from Carnegie Hall. She sang "I Get a Kick Out of You," much in the same manner as she would for the next fifty years. This is the earliest recorded example (the tape still exists) of Ethel Merman singing in front of a live audience.

Ethel enjoyed doing the show so much that she demanded Lou Irwin find her a radio show of her own. What she got was *Rhythm at 8*, a half-baked variety series featuring her singing. The program lasted twelve weeks, taking her through the summer of 1935. It would be fifteen years before Ethel would get another crack at a radio series.

Later that year, Merman, Gaxton, and Moore participated in a charity benefit for the Seaman's Church Institute. Appearing at the Starlight Roof of the Waldorf-Astoria Hotel, the three joined Joe Reichman's Orchestra, Xavier Cugat's Orchestra, and variety acts, along with Parisian models brought in on the S.S. *Normandie* to show off the latest Paris fashions. Merman and Gaxton sang "You're the Top," and Ethel did many of the songs she had introduced in the four years since *Girl Crazy*.

7

As wise as Ethel Merman was becoming about being a Broadway star, and despite her enjoyment of almost all aspects of her New York life, she still could not give up on the idea of becoming a big movie star. When Paramount Pictures offered to make a movie version of *Anything Goes* with Bing Crosby and W. C. Fields playing the Gaxton and Moore roles, Ethel withdrew from the Broadway version, finished her radio series, and jumped on the first train to Hollywood.

However, she did make one stop. On Saturday, March 16, 1935, the current edition of the *Ziegfeld Follies* was touring in New Haven, Connecticut, after its Broadway run. It had been the first *Follies* to be mounted after Ziegfeld's death, and it was not a huge success. It was in this show that Fanny Brice first introduced her classic Baby Snooks character to audiences, but that is not what made this date so special.

In the show there were two songs sung by Jane Froman and

later Jean Sargent, "Suddenly" and "Green Eyes." On this particular night, the entire show was recorded from start to finish, the first time in history such a recording was undertaken. And on this night, it was the unmistakable voice of Ethel Merman singing the two songs. It is not known if Ethel joined the show that night because it was being recorded or if it was being recorded because Ethel was in it. All that is known is that the show was about to close, and for at least one night, Ethel Merman was in the *Ziegfeld Follies*.

Ethel never admitted this one-night-only performance to anyone and never claimed the credit in any biography. Being in the *Follies* was not going to further her career; she was going to be a movie star.

She never learned. The first thing she found out upon reaching the Big Orange was that the newly formed Hays office (censors) would not approve of the salty Cole Porter lyrics from the original show. Gone would be "Blow, Gabriel, Blow" and "Anything Goes." And the lyrics to the rest of the songs were rewritten so that much of the humor was gone. Then she learned that the rewriting was pushing the production date back, so she would be cooling her heels for three months doing nothing. Because the production date was changed, W. C. Fields would no longer be available to appear in the movie. He would replaced by Charlie Ruggles and not very well.

Dejected and depressed, Ethel called her Hollywood friends like Lucille Ball and Eddie Cantor to complain. When Cantor heard she was available, he prevailed upon Sam Goldwyn to cast Merman in his next film, *Strike Me Pink*. In this one, Merman basically played herself, a glamorous stage star upon whom Eddie has a crush. Her big number was "First You Have Me High, Then You Have Me Low" (which Goldwyn always referred to as "First You Got Me Up, Then You Get Me Down").

Directed by Busby Berkeley, this was one of the best musical moments Ethel ever had on screen. Unfortunately, the movie bombed at the box office as Eddie Cantor's popularity in movies was beginning to wane.

Finally, Paramount was ready for *Anything Goes*. While Reno Sweeney was one of only two stage roles Merman got to re-create in the film version, too much was lost in the translation. The movie became a Bing Crosby vehicle, a successful one, but not for Ethel. History was repeating itself. Again after making a Goldwyn musical and appearing with Crosby in a Paramount film, Merman found herself without a Hollywood contract and retreated to her own medium: Broadway.

Returning to New York, Merman once more appeared at the Paramount Theatre. The Paramount had become her singing home away from home in the middle 1930s, a place to perform in between films and Broadway shows. She was able to demand $3,000 a week and only had to sing for twenty minutes between the showings of the films. By this time, she was using a medley of songs she had introduced on Broadway as her encore, with her pop and film songs filling in most of her act. A medley of this sort would be in Ethel's stage act for the rest of her life.

Ethel had not taken a break since her trip to Cuba, and this time she wanted no phone calls interrupting her rest. She and her parents went to Europe on the S.S. *Normandie*. Ethel enjoyed the fine food, dancing, and rest and could not have cared less about the historical or sentimental value of visiting the birthplaces of her ancestors in Scotland and Germany. That was a gift for her parents. In later years, Ethel denied this trip. It was politically incorrect to admit being in Berlin in the Germany of 1936. Once Hitler began his little game of hide-and-seek with the rest of Europe, Merman simply erased this trip from her memory.

Cole Porter was anxious to write another show for the team of Gaxton, Moore, and Merman. He was embarrassed by what had happened to the film version of *Anything Goes* and wanted to make it up to Ethel. And Sherman Billingsley, who had been sending his gifts to Ethel long distance, happily greeted Ethel with open arms (and an open zipper).

The show Cole came up with was *Red, Hot, and Blue!* Vinton Freedley and Porter went to Gaxton and Moore and described this hysterical comedy being written just for them, with Ethel just having some songs. Then they went to Ethel and described this musical being written just for her, with Gaxton and Moore just doing some comedy. This deception might have worked had it not been for Gaxton dropping in on Ethel at the tail end of her conversation with Porter and Freedley. He listened for a few moments, walked out the door, and out of the show, taking Moore with him.

Freedley wasted no time in finding replacements. Within weeks, Jimmy Durante and Bob Hope were signed on as Ethel's costars. With that kind of talent, it is no wonder that Ethel had yet another hit show under her belt. This time the hokey plot involved siblings separated at birth, a revealing birthmark, and an inherited fortune. It made *Anything Goes* look like *Long Day's Journey Into Night* by comparison. Still, Ethel got several more hit songs to her credit, including "Riding High" and "Down in the Depths on the 90th Floor."

Ethel formed another lifetime friendship (with Durante). She was happy to play straight woman to his wild comedy antics and loved him as a friend. Durante was one of those people that everybody loved. He seemed to have no guile at all and very little temperament. He had already been in show business more than twenty-five years by 1936 and had conquered everything from burlesque to vaudeville to Broadway to radio and films. He always played a version of Durante, and that was good enough for any audience. Whatever their past had been in the 1920s, Ethel and Jimmy were now loving friends.

Even billing had proved troublesome with both the contracts for Merman and Durante giving them top billing. Someone's attorney was asleep at the switch. To avoid a major skirmish, Merman's and Durante's last names were spelled together in an "X" formation, with their names alternating on the marquis and in publicity.

Merman's relationship with Bob Hope was quite another matter. Hope was a newcomer, a brash comedian who was as ambitious as Ethel. Their big number was "It's DeLovely," and Ethel couldn't stand what Hope did with it. Every performance was different, and Merman was getting upstaged. *That* she would not tolerate. She went to the stage manager and told him that if Hope didn't stop his onstage shenanigans, she would take off her shoe and remodel his nose. Hope knew that what he was doing was wrong and didn't really blame Ethel for getting angry. They later became friends. For the moment, a war was avoided.

Ethel almost started a second war when she began an affair with publishing scion Walter Annenberg. Walter, like Cole Porter, came from high society (in this case, the Philadelphia Main Line branch) and would seem to have nothing in common with Ethel Merman. But Annenberg loved show people and had a series of affairs with women like Ethel, Kitty Carlisle, and Mary Martin. He used to call Ethel "East Cupcake" and enjoyed taking her to all the hot nightspots. Except, of course, the Stork Club.

Their relationship was light, fun, and superficial. Ethel enjoyed going out at night as opposed to staying in at the

Stork, and she wanted to make Billingsley jealous. Walter liked Ethel quite a bit, but she was just another notch on his actress belt. After several months, the relationship cooled down.

Ethel also made sure that her pal, Vivian Vance, was once again her understudy. Viv was given a much bigger part in the show this time and should have been happy. Ethel noticed that Viv was often depressed and out of sorts and was concerned for her. Viv was already exhibiting some of the symptoms that would manifest into a complete nervous breakdown several years later.

Although they had not been close in years, Ethel was deeply saddened when she learned of the death of George Gershwin in 1937. In July, she appeared on a radio tribute to Gershwin. In August, she was a featured singer at the George Gershwin Memorial Concert at Lewisohn Stadium in New York. There were more than twenty thousand people in attendance. Although she also sang "The Man I Love" and "They Can't Take That Away from Me" at the concert, the highlight of the show was Ethel's version of "I Got Rhythm." She did the almost impossible vocal trick of singing the number at top volume while being so visibly upset that tears were streaming down her face. Those in attendance said that it was the finest performance of her career. Even the musicians in the symphony orchestra accompanying her gave her a standing ovation with the violinists tapping their bows on their violins in applause.

It was around this time that Ethel's voice began again to change. At age thirty, some of the girlishness was gone from Merman's singing. She became more strident, and her vibrato significantly deepened. Ethel's use of the scoop in her voice also became much more pronounced. This was partly due to her voice maturing and partly to make her sound unmistakable.

There were now all sorts of young lasses in New York trying to imitate Ethel's style, and she *detested* them. Merman wanted to make certain that the only person who could deliver the Merman sound was the original. Unfortunately, Ethel started to lose some of her incisiveness and would sometimes "oversing," vocalizing so loudly that her bell tones came out as a bleat.

Privately, there were some who made fun of Ethel's voice. They were jealous. She was the toast of the town, and they wanted to tear her down. Now Ethel had to deal with the problem that all stars face—becoming a star was one thing, but staying a star was quite another.

*ed, Hot and Blue* had been a big hit and launched
Bob Hope into a lucrative contract with Paramount.
Ethel wanted the same for herself and directed her
agent, Lou Irwin, to entertain all offers. Irwin was moving his
offices to the West Coast anyway and wanted Merman in pictures so he could keep her as a client.

She was not well served by this arrangement. The best offer
came from Twentieth Century-Fox—a three-picture deal at a
salary much higher than Ethel demanded on Broadway. Again,
Ethel was ill-advised. Her three-picture deal was not the same
as being a contract star. They could use her or pay her off at
their whim. There was no security beyond these three pictures.
Irwin was being selfish and shortsighted.

Additionally, Fox was not the best place for Ethel to land.
Their only big musical stars in 1937 were Shirley Temple and
Alice Faye, the same Alice Faye who had been in the chorus
when Merman starred in *George White's Scandals of 1931*. Fox's

musicals were not nearly as successful as those made by MGM. They had neither the performers nor the songwriters to rival Leo the Lion. Had Ethel landed at Metro instead, her entire career might have gone differently. Roger Edens was there, as were Judy Garland, Mickey Rooney, Eleanor Powell, George Murphy, Jack Haley, Ann Sothern, and others who would have made good on-screen pals for Ethel.

Merman was given a star's welcome with a luncheon in her honor and a guided tour of the studio. She was taken to a set where Loretta Young was rehearsing a scene for a film. The set had a long, winding staircase, and Ethel quipped, "Where the *hell* does this go?" Loretta stopped her rehearsal, raised a painted eyebrow, and picked up an empty coffee can. The top was slit and into it went coins anytime anyone used a swear word in front of delicate Miss Young. Once a month, Loretta emptied the can and gave the money to Catholic charities.

"Miss Merman, you said the 'H' word! That'll be twenty-five cents," Loretta informed Ethel. She shook the can so Merman could hear the chinka-chinka-chinka. Ethel had heard all about Young's wild sexual doings from Carole Lombard and found her to be a complete hypocrite. "Tell me, Loretta," Merman intoned, "how much will it cost me to tell you to go *fuck* yourself?"

Ethel was not starting out on the right foot at Twentieth Century-Fox. Loretta Young was its biggest star.

The first picture Fox stuck Ethel into was a Sonja Henie ice show called *Happy Landing*. Her songs were not great, and one was cut before the movie opened. Since everyone in the movie had to ice skate, Ethel was given lessons. She wasn't good, but she wasn't bad, and Merman obediently showed up on the soundstage wearing her skating outfit and white-kid ice skates. The playback began, everyone began to skate, and like a scene out of "I Love Lucy," Merman got whipped around and cut her foot open on someone else's skate. She bled like a stuck pig, and filming had to be held up while Ethel was given first aid and the blood cleared from the ice.

If these indignities weren't enough, the studio was forcing her into an ersatz romance with fellow player, Cesar Romero. It wasn't that Ethel minded because she didn't like Cesar—quite the contrary. She found him handsome, sexy, well mannered, and extremely likable. But Butch, as Cesar was called (*someone* had a wicked sense of humor), was gay and cheap, two things Ethel didn't like in her suitors.

From Fox's perspective, they needed to cover up Romero's lifestyle and Ethel's ongoing affair with Sherman Billingsley. It was commonplace for studios to arrange romances between their stars. It made for good publicity. But Ethel hated to be forced into Cesar's company. She wouldn't get sex out of it, and he didn't bring her nice presents. So Ethel began to retaliate. Cesar would answer his door, and a deliveryman would be there with dozens of pizzas that he never ordered, C.O.D. Or his doorbell would ring, and there would be a chauffeur and a hearse ready to pick up the body. Once Ethel got Lucille Ball to disguise her voice and inform Romero's housekeeper in a very efficient tone that all the water in the neighborhood was being shut off. Cesar came home to find every kind of pot and bowl filled with water.

This sort of "bad girl" behavior stopped when Ethel was assigned to her next film, *Alexander's Ragtime Band*. This was the first of the all-Irving Berlin nostalgia musicals, basing a plot around his catalog of songs old and new. The film starred Tyrone Power, Alice Faye, Don Ameche, and Ethel in a featured role. She looked beautiful and was finally given a chance to do the kind of numbers she had become famous for on the stage. It was an immediate love affair between Merman and Berlin—that is to say, professionally. He wrote two new songs for Ethel (although one would end up on the cutting-room floor), and she was given an opportunity to sing several others from the Berlin songbook. Never was Ethel's talent and personality captured as well as it was in this movie.

The film should have launched Ethel on her way. Unbelievably, Fox next chose to stick her in a grade-B comedy starring the Ritz Brothers. Her only good number was chopped in half. It makes no sense that Merman was not given bigger and better parts. For some reason, Fox did not pick up her option for any more movies. They simply didn't appreciate what she had to offer. It had taken three tries, but Merman was finally convinced that her dreams of movie stardom were a waste of time. Henceforth, Ethel's eyes were only on Broadway.

E thel returned to New York in the summer of 1938 to
bad news. Her dear friend, Cole Porter, had been hurt
in an accident while riding a horse. Both his legs had
been crushed, as well as his spirits. While the sensible thing to
do would have been to amputate and learn to live with it, Cole
was too vain. Instead, he endured operation after operation as
they tried to restore the use of his legs. Many said he would
never write music again. Ethel was devastated.

She immediately plunged into what would be the biggest
radio appearance she ever made. Ethel had been a guest on
several radio shows throughout the 1930s, but this was perhaps the most important broadcast in radio history. Twentieth
Century-Fox reserved an hour on the CBS radio network to
celebrate Irving Berlin's fiftieth birthday and the release of
*Alexander's Ragtime Band*. Hosting the show was no less than Al
Jolson himself, with Eddie Cantor, Sophie Tucker, Rudy Vallee,
Tommy Dorsey, Guy Lombardo, Paul Whiteman, and Connie

Boswell as guest stars. Never before had Jolson, Cantor, and Tucker appeared together on the same program. And who opened the program? None other than movie reject Ethel Merman, socking "Heat Wave" over the ether and hitting a home run.

This is the only recorded moment of Merman and Jolson on the same program, and it is a shame they did not sing together. In fact, they studiously avoided one another. Jolson insisted that the script allow for only a few words out of Ethel's mouth besides her singing. He knew that hers was a talent and presence that could give him a run for his money, and he wanted no part of it.

The last part of the show had Merman taking Alice Faye's place in a radio version of the movie. It is here, and not in the film, that Merman first sang the song "Alexander's Ragtime Band." Although she was only five years old when Berlin wrote it, over the years Ethel claimed this song as her own and sang it in all of her club and concert work.

With Cole Porter ill, Merman had to look elsewhere for her next stage vehicle. Her friend Dorothy Fields, who was a lyricist, writer, and sometime producer along with her brother, Herbert, was writing a show with her newest partner, Arthur Schwartz. Dorothy inquired of Ethel, if she wrote the lyrics, Schwartz wrote the music, she and Herbert wrote the book, Josh Logan directed, and Jimmy Durante costarred, would Merman do their new show called *Stars in Your Eyes*? Merman was appearing at the Strand Theatre in New York, trying to decide what her next career move would be.

Ethel eagerly agreed, mostly on the strength of her pal, Jimmy, being there. Ethel knew that any time Jimmy was on a stage, the audience was convulsed in laughter. If she had some good songs, the show had to run at least a year.

"If" is the biggest word in the English language. Schwartz was a talented man, but he did not understand how to write to Merman's strengths. Her songs were lackluster, and the lyrics dirty instead of saucy. Richard Carlson and Mildred Natwick, talented performers, were given little of substance as costars. Only Mary Wickes shined, and she could get laughs just walking across the stage. The box office was also adversely affected by the New York World's Fair, which opened within weeks of *Stars in Your Eyes*.

To add insult to injury, Cole Porter went back to work without Ethel and wrote a new show for Sophie Tucker. *Leave It to Me* would today be an interesting footnote, except for the enchanting performance of a young gal from Texas of Porter's "My Heart Belongs to Daddy." Mary Martin's star was born, and now Ethel had some real competition. She really needed a big old hit and prevailed upon Porter to write his next show for *her*.

That is how Ethel Merman opened in both *Stars in Your Eyes* and *DuBarry Was a Lady* in 1939. *DuBarry* more than made up for all the *Sturm und Drang* of Ethel's career in the late 1930s. This time Ethel was costarred with that incredible clown Bert Lahr, fresh from his triumph playing the Cowardly Lion in *The Wizard of Oz*. The plot had Lahr as a men's-room attendant in love with a nightclub star. He accidentally drinks a Mickey Finn cocktail he meant for her lover and dreams that he is King Louis XIV and she is the temptress Madame DuBarry. The Porter songs were excellent, and Merman and Lahr stopped the show nightly singing "Friendship."

Lahr was a brilliant, but neurotic comedian who was always certain that at any moment he might faint. Doom seemed to follow him like a dark cloud. He was convinced that Ethel was funnier than he and that his performance was a flop. He didn't get one moment's pleasure from the show.

It is an interesting footnote to consider what might have happened had Ethel taken another show offered her instead of *DuBarry*. Producer Theresa Helburn of the Theatre Guild came up with an intriguing notion that she felt was a surefire winner. How about having Rodgers and Hart write a musical version of the ancient sex farce, *Lysistrata*, with Merman in the lead role? It is inconceivable what these talented people could have done with such raunchy material, but it might have been brilliant. Alas, we shall never know.

Ethel, however, was riding high. After spending five years trying to be a movie star, Merman was back as tops on Broadway in *DuBarry*. In nine years, she had introduced more than a dozen songs in her shows that became standards. While her movie career had not taken off, at least a couple of them had been well received. All was well in Ethel's well-ordered world.

And then the roof caved in on her private life.

One morning in the spring of 1940, Ethel was having her morning tea and toast with cream cheese while reading the paper. She shrieked! Agnes could not imagine what could upset Ethel so. Her daughter was dissolved in tears and cursing a blue streak. Ethel handed her mother the paper, and there in Walter Winchell's column was the story that Mrs. Sherman Billingsley was expecting another child.

Now Agnes knew why her baby was so upset. Sherman had been telling Merman for years that he and his wife did not have sex and that they were married in name only. Ethel and Agnes both heard rumors to the contrary, but Ethel was in love and believed the lies that Sherman fed her. Now she realized that for years she had been a laughingstock, slipping up to Sherman's office for sex while everyone snickered behind her back.

Ethel felt totally humiliated and crushed. She wondered how this seemingly wonderful man could have been such a rat. It never occurred to Ethel to question her own judgment. That was a holdover from her childhood. Failure was not in her dictionary, so Ethel was not known for introspection. When things went wrong, it had to be other peoples' fault.

Merman had given almost six years of her life to Sherman, and now she didn't know what to do. For a while, she shunned all offers to socialize and stayed in her apartment licking her wounds. But Ethel was a survivor, and soon she broke through her depression and began to go out with abandon.

Not unlike the days after Al Siegel, soon Ethel was going through men like water. Sometimes, it was almost anonymous. One cold wintry night, she happened to get into the elevator of her apartment building with a fellow tenant, a young man who was in a new Rodgers and Hart musical. He was young, devastatingly handsome, and happened to notice she was shivering. And that's how Ethel Merman and Desi Arnaz ended up having a one-night stand. Many years later, she and Lucille Ball would laugh about it. Well, *Ethel* laughed about it. But that's a story for another chapter.

Even in the early 1940s, shows didn't run for more than one season. So when *DuBarry* closed in the summer of 1940, Ethel and Cole already had her next show lined up. By that fall, Ethel would have a new hit show and her first husband.

During the summer, rehearsals began for *Panama Hattie.* Buddy de Silva was producing, and this time he put the name of Ethel Merman right over the title. No more costar, she. From now on, whatever show she appeared in, it was "Ethel Merman in . . ." This thrilled Merman to no end and helped her to deal with the sorrow of her failed romance.

In this one, she played yet-another dame from the wrong side of the tracks who is in love with a handsome widower with a young daughter. Complications included a conniving competi-

tor and espionage. Mermsky also had a great supporting cast—
Rags Ragland, Pat Harrington (no, not him, his *father*), Betty
Hutton, Frankie Hyers, Arthur Treacher, and little Joan Carroll.
The show boasted several more hit songs for Ethel, including the
enchanting "Let's Be Buddies" with Joan that never failed to
bring the house down. And "Make It Another Old-Fashioned,
Please" was Cole Porter at his best. It was a beguine for an
unhappy lady pledged to sobriety who talks herself into getting
drunk by the song's end. It was both funny and poignant and
gave Ethel a chance to act during one of her numbers.

Ethel also had special affection for Ragland, Hyers, and
Harrington. After years of working with the likes of Durante,
Lahr, Hope, and Cantor, she enjoyed the camaraderie of these
low comedians. Merman even kept a bottle of Scotch under
the skirt of her dressing table for Ragland, who could not perform unless he had a snootful. Ordinarily, such behavior
would have incensed her, but Ethel understood just how frag-
ile comedians really are. She had become a top-flight comedian herself and an excellent straight man for others.

In later years, Hutton would claim that Ethel hurt her
career by having her best moments cut from the show. One
could not prove it by the playbills both out of town and on
Broadway. Hutton's songs were the same. Nor could one tell
from the correspondence between the two of them during and
immediately after the show's run. Betty lavished praise on
Ethel's generosity, including Merman's gifting her with a cocktail ring for being so good in the show. By the 1970s, Hutton
had nothing but animosity for Merman. Need it be said, they
did *not* become lifelong chums?

Ethel did, however, become very close to Arthur Treacher
and his wife, Virginia. Treacher, probably best known playing
the policeman in 1964's *Mary Poppins* as well being Merv

Griffin's sidekick for several years on his talk show, had Merman to dinner one night. One of the guests was a muscular, handsome man name Bill Smith. He and Ethel hit it off, and they began to date.

About a month after *Hattie's* opening, two major events rocked Ethel's world. Her photograph appeared on the cover of *Time* magazine (at a time when actresses were rarely featured) and all the New York papers announced the birth of the latest Billingsley child. Ethel had not even spoken to Sherman since the pregnancy had been announced, and she thought she was over it. Now, old wounds were being opened with rumors that Ethel had been a home wrecker and was still seeing Sherman. Here she was, cover girl of the nation's leading magazine, sole star of Broadway's biggest hit, and was being snickered at behind her back. Ethel's pride could not take anymore, and she asked Bill to marry her immediately.

Smith knew that theirs was not a love match, but that Ethel needed to hide behind the respectability of marriage. They were married in November 1940, days before Lucille Ball married Desi Arnaz and days after her picture appeared on the cover of *Time*. Theirs was a quickie wedding in Elkton, Maryland, attended by Edward, Agnes, and the Arthur Treachers. Ethel cried throughout the short ceremony, knowing she was doing the wrong thing.

Ethel's career was riding high, but her personal life was in collapse. Both she and Bill knew the marriage was a sham. For one thing, he lived in California, and they barely resided together in their apartment at the Pierre Hotel. This was the first time in her life Ethel was not living with Agnes and Edward, and she was very lonely. Her evenings at the theater were filled with some of the best fun she had ever had, but her nights were morose.

In December, Merman dried her tears long enough to attend a party where she was the featured guest. The American Theatre Wing threw a bash to aid the British War Relief Society. Proceeds from the affair went toward purchasing mobile kitchens for victims of the German blitzkrieg. The United States was still a year away from being in the war, but it was becoming obvious that things would change in the near future.

After flying in snowy weather twice to meet Bill in Chicago to talk things over in early 1941, it was mutually decided that Bill would fly to Mexico and get a divorce there on the grounds of desertion. Ethel didn't care that she would be blamed. She had already met her next great love.

I t is difficult to know how to handle a crossroads in one's life. Ethel Agnes Zimmermann had spent almost all of her thirty-three years with one goal in mind: stardom. She certainly enjoyed fame, although not her fans. To her, fame was getting the best table in a restaurant without having to make a reservation. It was living the life of luxury, enjoying the lucrative gifts that fame provided. It was personal enjoyment of the rewards of the hard work that preceded it.

For Ethel, it was never about fan clubs or autographs or how the guy on the street felt about her. And it was certainly not about handsome men fawning all over her because she was Merman. Ethel had felt from puberty that she was a sexy, well-built lady with enough charms to have any man she wanted. Yet, here she was, in her thirties, once badly burned, once married and divorced, and getting the first really bad publicity of her career. She was no longer the great new thing in show business. She was now part of the establishment. With her name over the title, she had reached the zenith of Broadway stardom. The best she could do now was go sideways.

Or she could find her career slipping. Ethel had made some very poor decisions in her personal life. She could not afford to make any in her public life. Movies were out. Ethel couldn't even get them to hire her to re-create her starring roles. In time, Judy Garland did *Girl Crazy*, Ann Sothern did *Panama Hattie*, Lucille Ball did *DuBarry Was a Lady*, Martha Raye did *Red, Hot and Blue*, Ann Miller did *Take a Chance*, Betty Hutton did *Annie Get Your Gun*, and Rosalind Russell did *Gypsy*.

It was with all this on her mind that Ethel attended a publicity dinner for the *New York Journal-American*. It was held at Dinty Moore's, a popular restaurant in the Broadway district. Ethel was invited by Dorothy Kilgallen, a rising young journalist with a column in the *Journal* and a local New York radio show. It was a free dinner and good publicity for *Panama Hattie*. As Ethel worked the press, she was introduced by Walter and Ella Young to another *Journal* employee, Bob Levitt.

On paper, Robert Daniels Levitt had a lot more in common with Ethel Agnes Zimmermann than with Ethel Merman. He came from a working-class Jewish family, although he had never had a bar mitzvah. He liked to work hard at his job, have a few drinks, eat a good steak, and relax. Bob had been in the newspaper game long enough to know how fleeting fame could be and could not have cared less about it. He was smart, earthy, steady, and—oh yes—built like a football lineman with large biceps.

Levitt and Merman joined the Youngs when they decided to go nightclubbing. When Ethel announced it was time for a working girl to get some sleep, Bob reluctantly saw her home. They had little to talk about in the cab. Levitt had never even seen her perform. He didn't like musicals!

Ethel mentioned that she was out of gum, but Bob made no effort to get her any. When they arrived at Ethel's building, huge snow mounds from a recent blizzard surrounded the cab. Levitt didn't even get out of the car to open her door. Ethel cursed him out under her breath, helped herself over the snow, and was happy to be rid of him.

The next day, a package arrived for Ethel. It was a case of the gum she mentioned along with an invitation to dinner. She demurred, but eventually agreed to join the handsome suitor at El Morocco. Ethel found that she enjoyed Bob's laid-back humor and that he did not particularly care for show business. Soon they were dating, and Ethel found herself doing things she had not done with any other man, like working anagrams, putting together puzzles, and just playing cards.

It is not surprising that Ethel fell in love with Bob. Besides the intense physical attraction between them, Bob Levitt treated Merman differently than had any other man. He didn't revel in her stardom as Sherman Billingsley had. He didn't look upon her as a sister the way her gay friends did. He didn't treat her like a titled lady the way Walter Annenberg did. Bob treated her like a woman and was perhaps the first suitor to do so. He liked her sense of humor, her lack of intellectual pretension, and her earthy dialogue. Bob Levitt enjoyed dating Ethel Zimmermann. She could leave Merman at the door and enjoy his company. For the most part.

Ethel loved Bob's company, but she still enjoyed the night-clubs and late suppers she was used to after a hard night's work. That meant being out until two or three in the morning. Bob was a nine-to-five kind of guy, and their hours didn't mesh. So it was up to Bob to do the adjusting. He would get home from work, immediately go to sleep, and then wake and shower to meet Ethel after her performance. They would enjoy some late-night festivities until Ethel was tired, and then Bob would see her home. He would eventually return to his apartment for a few hours' sleep and then wake and shower for work.

Bob was falling in love with Ethel and in the beginning did not mind making the sacrifice. He knew he could not ply her with diamonds and furs, so he figured all he could give was himself.

Had their romance taken a normal course, Ethel and Bob could have enjoyed a marriage built on a stable foundation. But events intervened that moved their timetable along. When Ethel's *Hattie* costumes all began to get tight, and she found herself fatigued more than usual, she went to the doctor. Some tests were taken, and when the rabbit died, so did any chance for normalcy. Ethel was pregnant, and something had to be done immediately.

Sometime in the fall of 1941, Bob and Ethel eloped to Connecticut. Again she was robbed of a big church wedding, something both she and her loving parents would have greatly enjoyed. The duo would have probably eventually married anyway, but they would have had time to work out the kinks.

To begin with, Ethel did not want to live far from her folks. So she took out a lease on an apartment in the same building as theirs at 25 Central Park West. That was fine with Bob. What was not as fine was the ten-room penthouse Ethel picked out. Laid out on two floors of the building, the apartment featured a huge winding staircase, two large balconies, a library, living room, dining room, den, state-of-the-art (for 1941) kitchen, marble bathrooms, and several bedrooms. The new Mrs. Levitt, the one who so liked how her husband didn't dig celebrity, rationalized that she needed to live like one (as her career demanded).

Agnes helped Ethel hire a staff so that Ethel Merman would have two full-time maids and a cook to take care of things and Ethel Zimmermann didn't have to. She decided that art was the best investment a young couple could make so Ethel and Bob began to build an art collection that could rival a small museum.

Isn't it amazing how far, with good planning, $200 a week can stretch? That was Bob's salary as circulation manager for the *Journal*. In 1941, that was a very large salary, capable of buying a spacious home in a small town and furnishing it comfortably. It was not, however, up to the standards Ethel had come to expect. So it was decided by Ethel that it was OK for her to spend some of her almost $4,000-a-week salary (after his $200 was all gone) to pay for the luxuries she wanted.

Merman always claimed that Bob was fine with this, but their marriage told a different tale. It must have been difficult for Bob, as newspapermen are notoriously hard on one another. He endured hurtful teasing about being *Mr.* Merman and the lifestyle he could obviously not afford and didn't want.

But Bob didn't have much time to ruminate. On December 7, 1941, the United States was plunged into war. Very quickly, almost everything in the country changed, from styles to attitudes to behaviors. The newspaper game changed, too, and so did show business.

People were no longer interested in Broadway shows with little plot and risqué humor. The war made the country very conservative. All of show business was enrolled in bond selling and propaganda. If an entertainer did not support the war effort, that person was considered a traitor.

Ethel withdrew from *Hattie* when her condition became obvious and quickly appeared in her first film in years. *Stage Door Canteen* was the kind of motion picture America devoured during the war years. Part truth, part soap opera, part propaganda, it told fictionalized stories of how the New York Stage Canteen entertained the millions of military personnel who came to the Big Apple from all over the world. Stars such as Ray Bolger, Helen Hayes, Lunt and Fontanne, and Katharine Hepburn would visit almost nightly, either to perform or make sandwiches and wash dishes.

Ethel had made two V-Discs (records made especially for the military) for the war effort and was asked to sing one of them in the film. A slightly pregnant and bloated Merman sang "Marching through Berlin" in the film. Her song took two days to shoot. In reality, Ethel seldom appeared at the Canteen. Her shows ended after the Canteen's nightly closing time, and a pregnant Ethel withdrew from the spotlight.

Bob soon became an officer in the army and happily was stationed in Brooklyn as an attaché to Gen. Homer Groninger. He was now part of the war effort, even if his uniforms were specially made by a private tailor. Being stationed so close to home meant that Bob could see Ethel every day. They were able to spend their evenings having quiet dinners, playing cards, and listening to the radio. For the first time in her life, Ethel was a real *hausfrau*.

Bob often asked Ethel to get her friends to entertain his officer buddies. He owed a favor to a Corporal Zubkoff, the only other Jewish officer in the company. Zubkoff needed entertainers, and Bob needed to find a good tailor for his unhappy general. They used their combined talents to make things easier for one another at a time when being Jewish and an officer in the service was not easy. That both were married to non-Jews didn't matter. Corporal Zubkoff eventually switched to the air force and retired as the full-bird colonel in charge of all of the air force hospitals worldwide. There is a building in Miami named after him. Until the day he died, he never forgot the kindness of Bob Levitt.

Col. Harry Zubkoff was the author's uncle, and his family was very proud of him!

Bob tried to get Ethel to act the part of an officer's wife, but she would have none of it. It wasn't that she was unpatriotic. Ethel's only public appearances during her pregnancy were to sing for military personnel at nearby bases, much as she had done during the First World War. But Merman kowtowed to no one, even if they were a general. Kissing ass was not Ethel's strong suit.

On one occasion, pregnant Ethel unwisely decided to drink her way through what she felt was a dull army evening. Downing more Manhattans than was wise for a woman who was *not* infanticipating, Merman was worse for wear. When General Groninger's wife asked her to sing, her charming response was "Get out of my way, Cuddles, before I spit in your eye!"

At least she didn't tell her to go fuck herself.

In July 1942, Ethel went into Doctor's Hospital to give birth by Cesarean section to her first child. All during her pregnancy, Broadway pundits made jokes about what a terrible mother self-centered Merman would make. "She never forgets a lyric, but she'll probably leave the kid in a cab" was typical of the remarks.

Ethel Merman Levitt made them eat their words. At least in the beginning, Ethel proved to be the most doting of mothers. While she did hire a German nurse and governess to change the diapers, Ethel devoted her time to her namesake, Little Ethel. Bob immediately fell in love with his daughter, whom he nicknamed "Little Bit."

Without a show pressing her to save her energies, she could get up with her husband, send him off to his job in the war effort, and be the lady of the house. With her mom and pop living in the same building, Ethel thought she had finally found the recipe for happiness. She promised Bob that she would not work for at least a year and enjoy her newfound domestic tranquility. Unfortunately, she did not keep her promise.

Vinton Freedley and Cole Porter came knocking on her door with an idea for a new musical. They wanted to do something topical about the war effort and got Herbert and Dorothy Fields to write the book. They were talented scribes and good friends, so that's all Ethel had to hear before signing on. She should have heard more.

Their idea was that several cousins inherit a ranch in Texas, near an army base. They open up the ranch to entertain the troops, but the military thinks they are a house of prostitution and makes the ranch off-limits to all military personnel. This was not much on which to hang almost three hours of music and comedy.

Freedley was not too impressed and bowed out as producer. Mike Todd (later a hugely successful film producer and husband of Elizabeth Taylor), who was such a character that Herbert and Dorothy could have written *him*, came on as producer without even auditioning the material. He felt that with Merman and Porter, he could not lose.

Ethel was sharing her concerns about the show with her pal, Lucille Ball, who had come to New York to publicize her film version of *DuBarry Was a Lady* for MGM. Lucy told her about a strange experience she'd had recently. It seems that Ball was having some dental work done over a period of days. Every time she drove past a certain intersection on Coldwater Canyon in the San Fernando Valley, she heard what sounded like Morse code coming from her teeth! It turned out that her temporary fillings were, indeed, picking up a Japanese transmission, and the traitors were found and jailed.

Merman told this story to Dorothy, and now Ethel's character would pick up transmissions in *her* teeth and save the day! At a time when *Oklahoma* was changing the sophistication level of musicals, Merman's new *Something for the Boys* was very old-fashioned. The plot was slender, her costars were not first rate (although a young Betty Garrett was discovered here), and the score was probably Cole Porter's worst. This was Ethel's first show where, although *it* was a hit, she did not get even one hit song to introduce.

It wasn't that Ethel did not have her moments to shine. She and her leading man, Bill Johnson, dueted on "Hey, Good Lookin'," which seemed to be an audience pleaser. And she and Paula Lawrence had a fine comedy turn in the very risqué "Down by the Mississississississinewah." In this one, Merman and Lawrence play two Native American squaws who are in a three-way sexual relationship with a brave. Perhaps because the show was not the *huge* success of her previous few, Merman was very sensitive to Paula Lawrence's stage deportment.

Lawrence was a fine comedienne who had not yet garnered her own following. During the song in question, Ethel found some business swinging her braids that made the audience laugh. Soon, Paula was swinging *her* braids before Ethel did, stealing her laugh. Then Ethel would lose a moccasin, kicking it into the orchestra pit. Soon Lawrence was losing moccasins, too. When this happened again, Merman complained to the stage manager, who properly instructed Lawrence not to copy Merman's shtick. When it happened again, Ethel filed charges with Actors' Equity, the stage actors' union. Paula was rebuked and eventually replaced by Betty Bruce.

During the run of *Something*, Ethel and Bill Johnson sang several of the songs from the show on radio in order to stimulate ticket sales. It wasn't that the show was unsuccessful, it's just that it wasn't the hit *DuBarry* and *Hattie* had been. Ethel was unhappy and fearful that perhaps her career was beginning to slide.

Also during the run, Ethel filmed a musical movie short for

the armed forces called "Why Do They Call a Private a Private?" It was based on a song written by Frank Loesser, which was in fact, quite funny. Merman had sung it at a bond rally, where it had been recorded as a V-Disc. The saucy lyrics had to be cleaned up for the movie version, which was inexpensively filmed in one day at studios in New York.

Ethel did not look well and wasn't singing at top form. Whether it had been the pregnancy, the strain of a show that wasn't her best, or just age, Merman was losing some of her girlish charm. Her face was getting lined, and she began a battle with weight that she would fight for the rest of her life. She was not yet forty, but Ethel Merman was starting to look middle-aged. And sometimes she sounded like it. When she was a guest on the Andrews Sisters' radio program, they requested she sing "I Got Rhythm." When it came time to hold the extended notes, Merman's throat closed up. She held the notes, but with a bleated waiver instead of a bell. An embarrassed Ethel could hardly read her lines for the rest of the program.

During the run of *Something*, Ethel and Bob had become very friendly with composer/producer Billy Rose and his wife, Olympic swimmer Eleanor Holm. Although Merman had greatly admired Fanny Brice in her youth, the two did not particularly get along, so socializing with Fanny's ex-husband posed no problem. The Roses were the couple the Levitts spent the most time with during this period. When Little Ethel was christened at St. Thomas' church, Eleanor was her godmother.

It was around this time that Bob converted from Judaism to Episcopalian. Ethel always claimed that this had been Bob's idea, but the truth was that she prevailed upon him to convert. She wanted their children to be raised Episcopalian, and she wanted to be able to go to church as a family. She was frankly embarrassed at having a Jewish husband, even one who did not practice his religion. The anti-Semitism of her youth was subtly rearing its ugly head. Merman herself was probably not even aware of it. Soon, Episcopal Bob and his Broadway star wife were worshipping together. It didn't help much.

In early 1944, after the close of *Something for the Boys*, Ethel had a miscarriage. She was devastated by the loss and angry at the failure. Merman was very moody, and with no show to release her creative energies, she became very depressed. Soon, she and Bob were fighting all the time, and eventually, they separated. Ethel just could not understand what was wrong with *him*. It never even occurred to her that she was in emotional distress or that the problem might be hers. From her point of view, Bob wasn't the husband he had been.

Bob was no angel, either. He, too, suffered from depression. Sometimes his black moods caused him to say and do things he later regretted. His career was faltering because he was not the easiest man with whom to deal. Levitt resented working his ass off while his wife opened her mouth and made a fortune. Bob probably never understood how much concentrated effort it took for Ethel to do her work night after night or how much it really took out of her. What he wanted was a wife who would look up to him, lean on him, and let him take care of her.

Unfortunately, Ethel Merman found what most women in show business find. Those that make it to the top in an impossible industry become their own warriors by necessity. By the time they are stars, no man can take care of them as well as *they can take care of themselves*. After decades of being their own personal Muhammad Ali, they cannot and probably should not suddenly hand over the reins of their lives because they marry.

It takes a special kind of man to be happily married to a female star. He either must have self-confidence of steel or be contented to be a kept man. Or worse, he makes his wife's career "their" career. The industry is littered with women like Fanny Brice, Judy Garland, Doris Day, Lucille Ball, Joan Rivers, and Suzanne Somers who tried to "make" their husbands into managers and caretakers. Either the marriages cracked or the careers did.

Because they really did love one another, the Levitts were seeing one another to discuss reconciliation. Within a short time, Bob moved back in with his family. Unfortunately, none of the problems had really been resolved. The Levitts decided that to save their marriage, Ethel needed to go back to work. In September of 1944, Ethel began rehearsing for her next show, *Sadie Thompson*.

*Sadie Thompson*??? What's that you say, dear reader? You never heard of *Sadie Thompson*? You want to know where you can buy the CD? Hang on a minute . . .

This was to be a lusty, lavishly produced musical in the same vein as *Panama Hattie*. In fact, the characterizations were very similar. Merman would play another of her patented bad girls with a good heart who somehow manages to save the day amid much ribald comedy and great songs. Vernon Duke wrote the music and Howard Dietz the lyrics.

However, for the first time Ethel was uncomfortable with the material. It wasn't just one song she didn't care for—she didn't like *any* of them. Merm felt that the lyrics were too precious and over the head of the average Merman theatergoer. After ten days of rehearsals that were more of a battle, Merman delivered one of her famous ultimatums. Either they change the lyrics to suit her, or they could find themselves a new star.

As incredible as it seemed, they chose to get another star. *Sadie Thompson* opened with June Havoc in the role and barely lasted three weeks. Although Ethel felt vindicated in her decision to leave the show (and many columnists supported her decision), her career was at a five-year low. Her last smash hit was in 1940. It was now almost 1946. Ethel was grappling with fears of getting older, not being attractive, and losing her career.

Happily for the Levitts, Ethel found herself pregnant again almost as soon as they reconciled. Merman retreated from the public eye, not wanting anything to harm her unborn child. She was almost forty, which was considered very late to have a child in those days.

Despite her fears, Ethel and Bob enjoyed what was perhaps the last truly joyful time in their marriage. The war had ended, and Bob went back to his work at the *Journal*. The couple was free to enjoy their precocious daughter, enjoy one another, and enjoy being a growing family. When asked by the press, Bob told reporters that he liked Ethel best when she was pregnant. While this raised a few eyebrows, it was very understandable. While she was with child, she was not Merman the star, but Ethel the woman. Her total concentration, which could be intense, was devoted to being a wife and mother. It was the only time Ethel Merman really worked at being a woman. She was free from having to live up to the brassy broad persona and could be a lady.

A lady who checked grocery bills, worried about whether her little daughter was growing properly, and made sure that a tasty dinner was prepared (albeit not by her) for her hard-working husband. A lady who learned how to do needlepoint, even if she never got beyond the first stitch she learned.

A wife who could sit with her husband at night, play cards, eat cheese and crackers, and just relax with being in love. A wife who didn't care about being a STAR. At least until the day her son was born.

On August 11, 1945, little Bobby was born by Cesarean section. Perhaps due to her age, Ethel was very uncomfortable after his birth. She experienced racking gas pains and postpartum depression. Her entire being had been focused on making sure that Bobby was born and healthy. Now that he was, it was almost as if she needed something new to do. She didn't allow herself the chance to enjoy the afterglow of birth and having a new life to care for.

So when Dorothy Fields called Ethel two days later with an idea for a new show, it was the tonic that Merman's depression needed. Although she was still in terrible pain and cranky, what Dorothy offered sounded irresistible. What would Ethel think of playing sharpshooter Annie Oakley?

There are several versions of how this all came together, and all the participants claimed they were there first. But the bottom line was this: Composers Richard Rodgers and Oscar Hammerstein would be the producers; dean of American music Jerome Kern was writing the music; Dorothy was writing the lyrics (and the book with her brother Herbert); and fresh from several years in the service, Joshua Logan would direct.

He had spent the war in charge of teaching others how to entertain the troops. For years, he had been in Paris, greeting his troops with the phrase, "Welcome to Paris, where fornication has replaced the handshake as the greeting of choice!"

Logan had directed Ethel several years earlier in *Stars in Your Eyes*. He had always felt that Merman was an actress and comedian who had never been stretched and was capable of much more than audiences had ever seen.

Josh had seen firsthand the change in the young men through the war years. He knew that the newly returned audience would not support another old-fashioned Merman entertainment where she sang risqué beguines about sex that had little to do with the plot.

Almost immediately, Ethel refocused. Anyone could be a housewife, but only she could be Merman. This was the crucible for Ethel. Despite her love for her husband and children, regardless of the bliss she had enjoyed during her two pregnancies, Merman made a choice for show business. She had tasted the fruit of marriage and motherhood, had in fact longed for it, but found it not as sweet as that of her career. The die was cast. It was a new Ethel Merman.

Bob Levitt was dismayed to find such a change in his wife when he took her home from the hospital. In the blink of an eye, the loving lady he had lived with for the past nine months was replaced by the brassy broad who had a new show. Their marriage never really recovered.

The new show almost never recovered, either. One day, when Jerome Kern was taking a stroll in Manhattan, he had a stroke and died. Without the composer, Rodgers and Hammerstein were no longer willing to produce. Kern's replacement was needed yesterday. There was no time to wait. There were really only two choices that came even close to Kern—Porter and Berlin. Cole was having more operations on his legs. Besides, Logan didn't think he was right for the sort of story Dorothy and Herbert were concocting. He didn't want just another typical Merman score.

That left Irving Berlin. Irving had never really written a

Broadway show where the songs were used to move the plot along. He had spent the last decade writing mostly for films and didn't think he was up to the job. He also didn't think he could write with the country sound needed to tell Annie Oakley's colorful story.

Then there was the problem of Dorothy Fields, who had already been signed as the lyricist. While Kern worked with many lyric writers (and had, in fact, written several hit songs with Dorothy), Berlin always wrote his own. That problem was sidestepped when Dorothy graciously tore up her contract, allowing Irving to be both composer and lyricist. Still, Berlin was not sold. Oscar Hammerstein encouraged him to take the weekend and think about it. He also advised Irving to be him- self and just drop the "g"s at the end of lyrics to imply the country flavor.

Berlin, Rodgers, Hammerstein, and Logan met the follow- ing Tuesday. Berlin had written several songs, including "Doin' What Comes Nat'rally" and "There's No Business Like Show Business." Irving did what he always did, playing the songs on his specially built piano (he could only play in the key of F— the piano had a lever that switched keys for him) and singing in his squeaky little voice.

Dick and Oscar were overwhelmed that Berlin could write so much so quickly. They made him sign a contract on the spot.

Meanwhile, back at the Levitts, Ethel was dieting to lose all the weight she had gained during her pregnancy and giving press interviews while holding Little Bobby and bouncing Little Ethel on her knee. Everyone smelled a tremendous hit in the air, and once again, it seemed like Merman would be on top.

It is really impossible to impress upon anyone just how successful *Annie Get Your Gun* was. In a heartbeat, Ethel Merman was once again the biggest star on Broadway and had crossed over into that rarefied status of legend. This became her longest-running show and gave her more hit songs than any other: "Doin' What Comes Nat'rally"; "You Can't Get a Man with a Gun"; "They Say It's Wonderful"; "I Got Lost in His Arms"; "Anything You Can Do, I Can Do Better"; "I Got the Sun in the Morning"; "Moonshine Lullaby"; and of course, "There's No Business Like Show Business."

Not that there weren't a few bumps in the road along the way. Irving Berlin threw out "Show Business" because he thought Rodgers and Hammerstein didn't like it. Imagine if they had not been able to talk him into bringing it back! A few days before the show opened on Broadway, hanging scenery crashed to the stage, tearing down all of the pulleys that had been holding it up. The cast had been standing there only a few moments before. Dick and Oscar quickly booked the show into an out-of-town theater until repairs could be made.

Little Ethel, who was already a whip with a quip like her mother, just sat there reading a *Wonder Woman* comic book. A few moments before all the brouhaha, Ethel had admonished her daughter against reading in the theater. "Nobody reads while I'm working," explained the mother at the top of her lungs. Little Ethel just shrugged. Hearing her mother holler was something she was used to and greeted with docile disdain.

Merman came up to Little Ethel to explain to her that she would have to be gone for a week. Ethel Jr. barely looked up from *Wonder Woman* long enough to verbally stab her with "Yeah, if the scenery doesn't break again!" Little Ethel was four years old.

Opening night was also a curiosity. *Annie* was in turns hysterically funny, heartwarming, and dramatic. Yet the audience just sat through the first act as if they were drugged. There were few laughs and limited applause. Merman the professional kept going as if nothing were wrong. She knew where the laughs were, she knew the songs were great, and she knew she was great in the part. Ethel did her job and let the audience come to her.

One of the chorus girls asked her how she could keep going to such tepid response. Ethel said, "Inside I'm thinking, 'Screw you, you jerks!' If they were as good as me, they'd be up here, and I'd be out there!"

After the intermission, it was as if the audience held a meeting and decided it was all right to enjoy themselves. The laughter flowed, and every number got an ovation. Ethel received a standing ovation. From that moment forward, with rare exceptions, Ethel Merman received a standing ovation every time she performed.

Ethel had taken lessons during the rehearsal period in how to shoot a rifle and how to ride a motorcycle, two talents she would need during the course of the show. While the motorcycle never failed her, Merman did have a problem with the rifle. Just before she was to sing "I Got Lost in His Arms," Annie Oakley was supposed to shoot the rifle into the air, delivering a dead sea gull to the deck of the ocean liner upon which she was traveling. She would then ask her little brother, Jake, to take the bird to the chef to make her a seagull sandwich. This device got rid of the kid and left Annie alone to sing the number.

During one performance, Ethel shot the rifle, but no seagull fell from above. After waiting for what seemed like a lifetime, Merm simply pretended to pick up a bird that wasn't there and handed it to the kid playing Jake. He just stood there, not knowing what to do. If he'd waited any longer, he would have outgrown the part. Finally, he got the idea and walked offstage.

Another time, Ethel pulled the trigger, but the rifle didn't go off. The bird plopped down on the stage anyway. Without missing a beat, Merman picked up the bird, turned to the audience, and said, "Well, I'll be goddamned! Apoplexy!"

The Levitt household fell into a pattern. Bob, who was having business troubles and needed to really concentrate on earning a living, left the house by eight in the morning. The German governess and Agnes took care of the children while the maid and cook silently went about their tasks. Ethel would awaken between ten o'clock and noon and have tea and breakfast in bed. Resting her voice, she would take no phone calls until late in the afternoon. Merman would peruse the household accounts, pay bills, type letters, and generally take care of business until two. Except for matinee days, the rest of the afternoon was spent playing with her children and returning phone calls.

Never one who liked to perform on a full stomach, Ethel would take a hot bath at five-thirty, followed by a private dinner of steak, baked potato, and a green salad. If Bob came home (and some evenings he didn't—things were getting shaky again), he and Ethel would spend a few moments alone before she limousined off to the theater to make the transformation from Merman to Oakley. After three hours of hard performing (Ethel had never worked this hard in her life—*Annie* was a very demanding show), an exhausted Ethel returned home to a late supper and bed.

Gone were the days of nightclubbing after a show. With the weight of *Annie Get Your Gun* on her shoulders, Merman could no longer afford to squander her energy with nightlife. It wasn't that Ethel and Bob had *no* social life during this time. They became close to Bill Hearst, son of wealthy publisher William Randolph Hearst. Ethel also became a pet of the Duke and Duchess of Windsor. They frequently attended performances of *Annie* and often had Ethel and Bob over to their apartment at the Waldorf Towers.

The Windsors were known for their nonconventional marriage. The duchess' eye often strayed despite the duke having given up his kingdom to marry Wallis. He was a dear little man who loved music and often hummed popular songs under his breath. When Ethel could no longer stand the constant hum and said so to Bob, his retort was, "Maybe the duke is AC, and the electricity at the Waldorf is DC."

Ethel didn't understand their relationship. Once, when the Windsors and the Levitts went out dining and dancing, the duchess spent most of the evening dancing with a man who was little more than a gigolo. When the duke asked Ethel what he should do, she looked him straight in the eye and said, "Why don't you get up off your ass and dance with your wife?"

Another admirer was Dwight D. Eisenhower. He and his wife, Mamie, resided in New York, were enjoying their first real rest after World War II, and came to the show often. Ike admired Merman's talents tremendously and loved the attention she gave him when he came backstage after the show to say hello. At the time, Ike had not publicly declared which political party was his. He didn't feel it was proper for a general to take sides. Whoever was commander in chief was his boss, period. Good old Republican Ethel wanted him on *her* side and later felt that she played a part in his running for the presidency on the Republican ticket. On a shelf in her dressing room, she kept a bottle of Ike's favorite Scotch along with a glass and a sign that said, "General Eisenhower drinks here!"

She did few benefits, and the only outside work was on radio, where she could perform with limited rehearsal and get a large paycheck. She was a frequent guest with Bing Crosby whenever he did his show from New York. Otherwise, her entire life was *Annie Get Your Gun* and her children. This was hardly healthy soil in which a marriage could grow.

Bob was fired from the *Journal* and seemed to drift. He was an adoring father and spent most of his early evenings and weekends heaping attention on the kids. After their early bedtimes, Bob was left alone. His depression returned, and Levitt drank too much. When Ethel returned home from the Imperial Theatre at night, ready to collapse, she often found her husband either not there or pixilated.

Ethel could not understand Bob's behavior. After all, they had two lovely children, a huge apartment, and a hit show. They had everything *she* ever wanted. Why wasn't *he* happy? And how dare he not be there when she got home, breathlessly waiting to hear about every little detail of her evening, the way her parents had done?

Levitt loved his wife very much, but could not reconcile himself with the lifestyle they had. He felt completely emasculated and was dealing with a depression he could not shake. Perhaps if things had been different, Ethel could have seen that her handsome and well-meaning husband was battling mental illness. Merman was single-minded, but loved her family. If only she could have been made to see in how much emotional trouble Bob really was, perhaps she would have used her tremendous persuasiveness to get Bob the professional help he needed.

She, Ethel, was neither the cause nor the cure. Bob needed help that only he could get for himself. But had Ethel been more supportive, more understanding, and less judgmental, things could have been a whole lot different. As Bob's energy and attention slipped away, Ethel found herself having to pick up the slack.

One day off, Ethel decided to take her children on an outing to enjoy her city. Little Bobby and his sister were dressed in their finest, and Ethel was in a mink coat, pearls, very high heels, and a diamond clip in her long wiry hair. From behind, one could hear the quickly paced click of her heels on the concrete as she dragged the kids behind her and screamed, "You don't want to go to the park? You don't want to go to the zoo? What the fuck *do* you want to do?"

*Annie Get Your Gun* was enervating Ethel like no show ever had. After eighteen months, she wanted out. Her very intelligent and precocious children were growing quickly. Her marriage was in trouble, and she was a physical wreck. Her throat was bothering her. The vocal demands of the show were wreaking havoc on her voice. When she was tired or not in good voice, a quaver developed in her vibrato. The long notes were no longer as easy to produce, either. Ethel began eating raw ground steak before shows and during the intermission to keep up her energy level.

Producers Rodgers and Hammerstein would not hear of Ethel withdrawing from the show. Mary Martin, the only performer right for the part who had a big enough box-office name to replace her, was doing the national touring company version. Without Merman, box-office receipts would fall off. After much infighting, with Rodgers publicly blaming Ethel for putting the cast out of work should she choose to leave, Ethel agreed to stay with the show an additional six months IF she would first get a long vacation in order to rest and be with her family. R and H agreed, but Ethel held a grudge. Except for the most formal of occasions, she never again spoke to Hammerstein and only reconciled with Rodgers in 1972 when they both received lifetime Tony Awards.

On the recommendation of friends, a desperately weary Ethel and Bob took the kids for a long holiday to Glenwood Springs, Colorado. The family enjoyed the fresh air, swimming, horseback riding, and wholesome food. For six weeks, she got to rest and get her strength back. One day, scribe Howard Lindsay and his wife actress, Dorothy Stickney, checked in to the hotel. Their living-room windows faced one another, and Howard yelled at Merman that he was already writing her next show, a musical about Perle Mesta. Ethel walked away from the window, thinking to herself, "Who the hell is Perle Mesta?"

After returning to *Annie*, Ethel finished her six months and left. She immediately made her television debut on "The Texaco Star Theater" with Milton Berle in March of 1949. Although she was a tremendous success and literally stopped the show (and it was one of Milton's favorite episodes of all time; see chapter twenty-six about Ethel's television appearances for information on this show in detail), Ethel did not like the small-time nature of early television. She appeared with Milton four times in six months to give it a try, but did not care for it. Tired from her latest Broadway stint, Ethel made one more try for a radio series of her own. She figured that if she could make a radio success, she could work one-tenth as hard for $1,500 a week and stay home with her family, keeping normal hours.

"The Ethel Merman Show" debuted in the summer of 1949 on NBC and fell flat. At first it was a sitcom about a singer named Ethel, her mobster boyfriend, and a producer who were both trying to make her a star. Even though it was cowritten by Joe Stein (one of the brains behind *Fiddler on the Roof* fifteen years later), the shows weren't clicking. After a couple of months, they dropped the ongoing plot, and it became a straight variety show. Either way, not enough people listened, and the show was canceled by October.

Since radio didn't work, Ethel put her eye back on the Broadway beat. Producer Leland Hayward wanted Ethel to do that show Howard Lindsay had mentioned to her so many months earlier: a fictionalized version of how society hostess Perle Mesta became an ambassador. Irving Berlin was happy to write another show for Merman.

However, Ethel wasn't all that thrilled with the prospect of another Berlin musical so closely on the heels of *Annie*. By now, she knew her marriage was in deep trouble and didn't want to miss watching her kids growing up. Ethel was enjoying her freedom. After twenty-five years in show business, the forty-four-year-old Merman was tired of pressure. She was enjoying a rich social life and did not relish giving it up for another heavy-duty musical. In an attempt at changing her image (and perhaps shaking up her husband), Ethel dramatically changed her hairstyle, makeup, and wardrobe. She knew this was the Levitts' last chance.

The makeover only made her look more matronly and tired. Without a steady income, Ethel had to dip into her capital to pay the bills. Bob was nonresponsive, and Ethel was losing patience. The Levitts tried traveling, with Ethel following Bob to places like New Orleans and San Francisco while he tried to get some stable work.

Backtracking a moment, in 1946 Ethel had signed an exclusive, long-term contract with Decca Records. Decca had recorded the original cast album of *Annie Get Your Gun*, as well as an album in 1947 of her earlier hits called *Songs I Made Famous*. Decca was a "personality" company. That is to say that they only signed singers who were also performers, either on the stage, screen, or radio. Ethel was in good company, along with Bing Crosby, Judy Garland, the Andrews Sisters, Ella Fitzgerald, Martha Raye, Danny Kaye, and many others. In 1950, they brought Merm into the studio to record a duet with Ray Bolger of "Dearie." It was the most restrained Ethel had ever been on record, and the recording was charming and funny.

In the days before long-playing records, "Dearie" sold more than 100,000 copies in a matter of weeks. Bing Crosby even had Ethel on his radio show so that he could sing it with her. Unfortunately, while Decca had all this talent, quite often they didn't know what to do with it. In the following few months, they had Ethel and Ray and Ethel and Jimmy Durante record another series of duets, but none of them clicked as "Dearie" had. Then they tried Merman singing other women's hits, like "Diamonds Are a Girl's Best Friend" and "The World Is Your Balloon." Finally, they figured what better marriage than Ethel Merman and Hawaiian music.

15

With radio behind her, television in front of her, and her new recording career a flash in the pan, Ethel decided to return to Broadway in *Call Me Madam*. This time she would play Sally Adams, a fictionalized version of Mesta, who gets appointed as the ambassador to the fictional Lichtenbourg (*Lichten*stein and Luxem*bourg* put together). Everything was first-rate, lavish, and beautifully produced. Instead of the usual mountain of tenor-singing muscles as a leading man, Hayward hired the charming Paul Lukas, star of so many wonderful Warner Brothers dramatic films.

Ethel wisely allowed herself to age in this show. Annie Oakley was the last young girl she played. Mrs. Sally Adams was a widow, and her romantic eye was cast on a decidedly middle-aged man. Also cast in the show was Russell Nype, a juvenile lead and a charming stage performer. During rehearsals, it was suggested that he cut his long hair into a flattop and wear his tortoise-shell glasses on stage. It was with Russell that Ethel had one of her biggest hit songs.

During the out-of-town tryouts, it was obvious that the show needed a new number for the second act. When Ethel suggested that Berlin write a number for herself and "the kid," Irving went into his old bag of tricks for a counterpoint song. While Nype sang one melody and Merman the other, "You're Just in Love" stopped the show nightly. Opening night, they had to repeat the number for the appreciative audience.

*Call Me Madam* was a big success, but not the kind of hit *Annie Get Your Gun* had been. Only three numbers became hits ("Hostess With the Mostes' on the Ball" and "It's a Lovely Day Today" were the others), and Ethel was not given the same chance to stretch her acting muscles. Financially, however, it was a much bigger boon. Merman was paid $6,000 a week plus a percentage of the profits because she and Bob had invested in the show as silent producers. That meant that Ethel would also make money from the original cast album, as well as any future movie sale. An additional boost was Ethel's winning the Tony Award as best actress in a musical.

This was Ethel's first nomination for a Tony. She hadn't won it before because they didn't *have* it before. Although Merm would be nominated twice more, this was her only competitive Tony win.

The *Call Me Madam* original cast album. A paradigm in idiocy. RCA had also been an investor in the show with the proviso that they would get the right to record the original cast album. However, Decca would not release Ethel from her exclusive contract long enough for her to record for RCA. Each company thought they had the upper hand, and both lost. RCA recorded an album with the original cast and musical arrangements, getting Dinah Shore to replace Ethel. Decca put out an album of Ethel singing the songs from *Madam* with Dick Haymes replacing Russell Nype and Gordon Jenkins providing the music. Imbecility! Ultra moronity!! Neither company got a successful recording, although Ethel did receive 10 percent of the profits from both albums.

Between Perle Mesta and the Duchess of Windsor (who was quite taken with Russell Nype, although it is unknown if they actually had an affair), all of high society backed *Call Me Madam*. Women were wearing their hair in a horse's tail like Ethel did, and every young businessman in New York had a crew cut, tortoise-shell glasses, and flannel suits like Russell.

Ethel did not have an understudy for *Madam*. Instead, she had what was called a standby. That is someone who is good enough and well-known enough to cover for the star should she become incapacitated. Ethel chose Elaine Stritch, a sexy girl with a deep voice and a way with words. All Elaine had to do was be available a half hour before curtain time and make sure that Ethel was going on. Then she was free to do what she wanted and got paid well for doing nothing.

Elaine did not *want* to do nothing. She wanted to go on. Every night, she would knock on Ethel's door and inquire, "I gather you're well!" When Merm would answer in the affirmative, Elaine would answer with something sweet like "eat my snatch" and depart. Ethel never missed a performance of *Call Me Madam*. It was from this that the legend grew that Merman had never missed a show in her life, but that was just apocryphal.

Merman was once again the reigning Queen of Broadway musicals at a time when her competition included Mary Martin (*South Pacific*), Carol Channing (*Gentlemen Prefer Blondes*), and Gertrude Lawrence (*The King and I*). Merman's face could be seen in magazine ads for beer, cigarettes, and stockings. Everything was coming up roses!

Too bad . . . Ethel was *allergic* to roses. Her marriage was over, disintegrating in front of her eyes. She was incapable of the type of deep introspection required to help Bob, and she was unwilling to give up her career to focus on him. Bob was emotionally ill, and a frustrated Ethel released him with love. After nine years of marriage, the couple divorced with little fanfare.

Levitt began dating Hollywood star Linda Darnell, who expressed an interest in meeting Ethel since she would be spending time with the children. Darnell sent word through a mutual friend, who asked Ethel what she would do if she saw Darnell. "I'd kick her in the ass!" was her generous reply.

Ethel wasted no time in getting back in the saddle, either. Besides spending much of her time with high society through the duke and duchess, she started an affair with Charlie Cushing. Charlie was an investment banker who was at least ten years older than Ethel. Cushing was not Merm's usual type, but he was courtly and loaded. He gave her the same sort of rush Sherman Billingsley had given her almost two decades earlier: expensive gifts, expensive dinners, and trips to the Hamptons on Long Island (and even Palm Beach, Florida) on her day off. *Madam* was not as tiring a show as *Annie* had been, and without the stress of a bad marriage, Ethel Merman was quite the playgirl.

Merman also became a semiregular on Tallulah Bankhead's radio success, "The Big Show." It was easy for Ethel. The show was broadcast live on Sundays (her day off) at 6:30 P.M., and required minimal rehearsals. Ethel appreciated Bankhead's quirky behavior and loved to have Taloo regale her with the ribald stories of her bisexual love life. This truly was a time of "anything goes" in Ethel's life, and she tried to cram in as much fun as possible.

Merman thought that this would be her last Broadway

112

musical. Between her investments, her income from *Madam* in perpetuity, and the money she could make from radio and television appearances, Ethel thought she would be on easy street and do what she wanted when she felt like it.

There is an old Yiddish expression that translates into: *Men plan while God laughs*. If that is so, the Lord must have had quite a chuckle when Ethel Agnes Zimmermann Levitt met Robert Six.

On the first anniversary of *Call Me Madam*, the producers and cast threw a press party at a restaurant called L'Aiglon. The entire purpose was to promote ticket sales for the show at a time when it was no longer the newest game in town. Then as now, trends come and go in New York. Everyone rushes to see/hear/eat the latest thing, and then they move on. As one of the producers, Merman wanted to make certain *Madam* ran as long as possible.

Charlie Cushing wasn't available to escort Ethel that evening, something he would live to regret. She never dated him again.

A pal, "Doc" Holden, took Ethel to the party, along with some of his friends from out of town. Merman didn't know any of these people and was a little put off at having to glad-hand strangers. When they all arrived at the restaurant, Ethel sat with the cast and producers while the interlopers were sent to tables in the back. Ethel *had* noticed one guy because he was six feet four and built like a football player (shades of Bob Levitt!). Merman definitely had a physical type, and Robert Six from Denver filled the bill.

Although he came with a date, Six was happy to abandon her and ply his charm on the preoccupied Ethel. She really didn't have time for flirtation as it was her job to work the crowd and get as much publicity as possible. Somehow, Six made his way to Ethel and caught her interest.

He was a smart operator. First he laid it on thick, complimenting her on how much he had loved her in all of her shows. Then came the coincidences. Six had done his research. It seems every nitery he enjoyed was also a favorite of Ethel's. And what a coinkidinkie! Both had separated from their mates the previous May.

Six played her like a violin. By the time the party was over, he was having a hamburger alone with Ethel in an all-night restaurant. He told her that he was chairman of Continental Airlines, which greatly impressed Ethel. She liked money and stature almost as much as big biceps and oversized anatomy. Six had all of these.

What he did not tell her was that Continental was struggling. It was his wife's money that had gotten Bob into the airline business, and that money had run out. Continental was not making enough dough as a regional airline to keep Six in the lifestyle he wanted. The airline needed a major publicity boost and a chance to play with the big boys like TWA and American Airlines. Romancing the biggest star on Broadway was the best way to get Six's name into all the columns in one fell swoop.

It was six in the morning (or *Six* in the morning, depending on how you look at it) before Ethel arrived home. Bob had successfully made his conquest.

At least Ethel didn't have to learn a new first name to scream when she had an orgasm.

Ethel and Bob were soon inseparable. Much attention was made in print to how much money he had ("The Colorado Mint") and how big he was ("sech muscles!"). Bob was in love with the publicity, and Ethel was in love with the idea of being in love. After her recent marital disaster, Ethel needed to prove she was a desirable woman.

When Ethel closed in *Madam*, she agreed to open the show's national tour in Washington, D.C. This was not unusual, as Merman had done limited tours with several of her shows. Ethel would come to deny this because never having toured made for a better story. But this time, there was a special reason to tour.

The National Theatre in Washington, D.C., had been closed for several years. Not because it didn't do business, but because it was a segregated theater. Actors, often being on the side of the underdog, refused through Actors' Equity to play in the theater until the policy was changed. Finally it was agreed that if Merman would open the play there, the theater would be open to anyone who could afford to buy a ticket. It was a joyous triumph for civil rights, and Ethel was proud to be a part of it.

Robert Six threw an enormous bash for Ethel at the Mayflower Hotel on opening night, all of which was bankrolled by Continental Airlines. Everyone who was anyone in Washington was invited, as well as the usual suspects from Broadway. The Chinese Ballroom was converted into a French boîte, and the Champagne flowed like water. Even Sherman Billingsley had never made this large a gesture on her behalf. Ethel Merman was sold. Bob Six was now her man. If only Ethel had taken her time and opened her eyes, she could have avoided a lot of pain.

Ethel left the *Madam* tour to make the movie version. Not only did Ethel participate in the movie sale as one of the producers, but she made certain that this was one movie role she would not lose. On the way to Hollywood, Ethel flew to Juarez, Mexico, and got a quickie divorce from Bob Levitt.

I t must be mind-blowing when one's fondest dream comes completely true. Ever since 1929, Ethel Merman had dreamed of being a movie star of the first magnitude. She wanted to be able to snap her fingers and have her most minuscule desire be fulfilled instantaneously. At least, that's what she read in the movie magazines of the late 1920s. Now it was September 1952, and that is exactly how she was treated.

"Oh, welcome to Hollywood, Miss Merman! Yes, yes, we are certain you will be a smash hit in the film version of *Call Me Madam*! Oh, no, Miss Merman, don't worry about the hazards of filmmaking. You just deliver Ethel Merman, and we'll do the rest.

"No, Miss Merman, this way. The limousine and chauffeur are at your disposal as long as you are in Hollywood. We hope you like the mansion we rented for you, at company expense, naturally. We've hired a full-time maid and cook, and we're sure you'll find them satisfactory. As soon as you are settled, we'll send for your children and their governess. She's German, isn't she? The chauffeur already knows how to get to a good German delicatessen!

"If there is anything you need, Miss Merman, anything at all, night or day, you just call us. We'll do anything to make you happy, Miss Merman. We at Twentieth Century-Fox hope you are with us for a long, long time!"

The above conversation is apocryphal only that it did not take place all at one time. The contents are completely true. Ethel felt that this treatment was a bonus for all the years of hard work she had spent paying her dues on Broadway. Now, she was being treated like a lady. And she loved it! Who wouldn't?

Perhaps because she was a middle-aged mother, the Hollywood press no longer seemed to care about what she did. Bob Six was a frequent visitor to Ethel's California casa, but no one wrote about it. While Merm was required to do the usual amount of photo shoots and publicity, she was pretty much left free to concentrate on making the film.

With Donald O'Connor replacing Russell Nype and George Sanders subbing for Paul Lukas, the cast was excellent. Ethel was thin and beautiful, but definitely looking middle-aged. She had begun wearing her hair in an upsweep with lots of little curls, and it was not flattering. Hollywood could make her look good, but it could not make her look *young* anymore. She was in good voice, enjoyed her work, and it showed on the screen. The film version of *Call Me Madam* was a huge success! Ethel Merman won a 1953 Golden Globe award as best actress in a musical or comedy film.

By the end of the filming, Merman and Six were practically living together. It was Bob's idea that they sneak across the border to Mexicali, Mexico, on March 9, 1953, and get married immediately. For the third time, Ethel cheated herself out of a big church wedding. Neither her children nor her parents came to this one.

Oh, and by the way, Bob Six wanted their marriage kept a secret.

This should have been a huge red flag for Ethel. Bad enough it was a quickie wedding (her life was full of quickie weddings and divorces), but Ethel should have smelled trouble from Bob's request. Instead, she felt that nothing could harm her now-perfect life and just shrugged it off.

Six was maneuvering. He wanted to get the biggest publicity bang possible out of the announcement of their marriage and so was waiting for just the right moment. Even when the newlywed Sixes traveled to Miami for the world premiere of *Call Me Madam*, they clumsily dodged questions about their impending marriage since the ceremony had already taken place. It was only when the Colorado press picked up that Six was negotiating for an estate in Cherry Hills Village (near Denver) that he finally admitted he was a newly married man.

Bob made the most of the moment. The press carried stories about Continental Airlines, only briefly mentioning that his wife the star was going to start filming another musical in June 1953. Ethel was mildly annoyed, but rationalized that Six was the man in the family and should get the most attention. Although Ethel would never admit to having made any mistakes in her marriage to Levitt, she did not want the same problems again. She felt, based on the misdirection Six fed her, that he was such a big man in his field that her stardom could not possibly overshadow him. Harrumph, harrumph.

Fox was so pleased with Ethel's performance in *Madam* that it wanted to star her in another musical right away. To that end, Ethel rented a house in Beverly Hills that could be her home away from home in California. She now saw herself as a wife, mother, and movie star, who would live in Denver with her famous husband when she wasn't filming hit musicals for Fox. It was going to be a great life.

Ethel never learned. No sooner did she sign a long lease on the house than she was informed that director Walter Lang was ill and would not be available to direct her next picture. Merman was so certain that part of her success in *Madam* was due to Lang that she asked if they could wait until he was better. The studio wanted to keep her happy and acquiesced, but it was a mistake. They should have struck while the iron was hot. The movie was put off for almost twelve months. Ethel was stuck for the cost of a house she would rarely occupy.

It is not that Ethel was without work while she waited. She received a call from Leland Hayward that he was producing a two-hour television spectacular for the Ford Motor Company on the occasion of its fiftieth anniversary in business. Ford was buying two hours of time on both CBS and NBC, and the show would be broadcast on both networks simultaneously. Edward R. Murrow and Oscar Hammerstein were going to be the hosts, and they wanted Ethel to sing "Alexander's Ragtime Band" on the show. They promised she would have total creative control over every aspect of her performance.

And by the way, wouldn't it be fun for her to do a number with Mary Martin?

Leland was a cagey man. He went to Mary Martin and more or less sold her on the same scenario. Each lady thought they were wanted as the main star of the evening with the other being a guest star. There were plenty of other people on the show from Wally Cox to Eddie Fisher to Kukla, Fran and Ollie. But their duet was to be the highlight.

Both ladies eagerly agreed and flew to New York to begin rehearsals. Ethel and Mary figured they would do some of the numbers they had made famous on Broadway. Then Mary remembered that when she was a young girl singer trying to make a name for herself, she would often sing one number while her musicians played another behind her, just for fun. Ethel thought this sounded great, and pretty soon a ten-minute medley was put together for them.

They rehearsed for weeks, as the orchestrations were complicated and the rhythms were tricky. They had Ethel's favorite conductor, Jay Blackton, leading the band, and Mary's favorite pianist, Johnny Lesko, accompanying them. Ethel and Mary knew that this medley was going to be something special.

Two hours before airtime, all hell broke loose. Somebody finally figured out that Blackton and Lesko were not members of the television union and could not appear on the broadcast. The ladies tried the medley using other people, but it just didn't work. While this was going on, a messenger brought a huge bouquet of flowers to Ethel and told her to enjoy it for ten minutes. Ten minutes??

It seemed that Mr. Ford's secretary made a mistake, and instead of ordering a bouquet for each woman in the show, there was one bouquet they all had to share! Now Ethel started to laugh at the ridiculousness of it all. While she and Mary shared a chuckle over the flowers, Merman made mention of her creative control on the show. Now Mary wasn't laughing. She told Ethel that *she* had creative control.

These two show-business veterans looked at one another and realized they had been had, but good! Now they were laughing hysterically, almost out of control. Just then, Clark Jones (the director) came backstage to tell them that all the union problems had been settled and the show could go on.

The duet was simply staged with the two divas seated on bar stools for almost all of it. Television dueters sat on stools for the next twenty years because of Ethel and Mary. Just as they were about to make their entrances, Ethel turned to Mary and said, "Betcha I can sing louder than you can!"

Both were in top form. Ethel especially seemed to burst with energy. That she was pleased with her magnificent performance showed all over her face. This was the night Ethel Merman became a superstar. All of America was watching her show them what she *couldn't* show them on film—what a tremendous showman she was!

When it was over, the ovation from the studio audience was deafening. Jones didn't know what to do. He couldn't proceed because the audience was going nuts, but he couldn't let his *live* show get behind schedule. So he sent word to the stage where Fran Allison and her Kuklapolitans were waiting to go on and instructed them to begin talking about the medley as soon as the red light went on. At least this way he would have a transition. He had to fade between the two stages twice before the applause died down enough for anyone to even be heard.

Decca recorded the medley while it was on the air and immediately released it. This record also sold more than 100,000 copies in just more than a week. The medley between Ethel Merman and Mary Martin stands, to this day, as the greatest moment in television variety history. It is the hallmark to which the debut of Elvis and the Beatles and Michael Jackson's "Motown 25" appearance are compared. It has never again been shown on television.

Ethel and Bob spent the rest of the summer in Denver trying to get the title to the house they wanted. It was in an exclusive neighborhood, and the gentried folks there did not cotton to having Robert Six as a neighbor. Once they finally agreed, it seemed that Six's cash was all tied up, so Ethel had to provide the entire down payment for the twenty-eight-room house. Ethel's eyes were very slowly opening to the reality of marriage to Robert Six.

Ethel loved the Denver house and felt that it was a wonderful place to raise her children. Both kids had taken a liking to Six and had adjusted to their stepfather much faster than Ethel could have hoped. Although she missed her parents in New York, she felt that a good wife would live where her husband's work was. In fact, she turned down a new musical Irving Berlin wanted to write for her called *Last Resorts*.

Ethel also loved being the lady of the manor. It was surely the biggest house in which she would ever live and made her ten-room duplex in New York (which she gave up) look like a closet. There were maids, cleaning women, a chef, two gardeners, a butler, a secretary for Bob (stenographer Zimmermann still refused to use one when she could type herself), and a nanny for the children. Ethel insisted on comfortable guest rooms for such visitors as (singer and MGM consultant) Kay Thompson, Roger Edens, Benay Venuta, her old pals from Astoria, and of course, her mom and pop. Little Ethel loved country living with its fresh air, horses, fresh soil, and gardens. Bobby was more of a city boy, but enjoyed romping with the dogs on the manicured lawns.

If the Sixes entertained at home, it was usually a barbecue, with Six tending to the meat himself. The chef would make hors d'oeuvres and tasty side dishes, while Ethel liked to shop for interesting desserts. After dinner, guests might be taken to a fancy hotel for dancing, or they might stay chez Six and play cards. Rarely if ever did Ethel sing at her own parties.

It was an easy commute to Hollywood on Continental Airlines, although Ethel was sent a bill every time she traveled. In fact, every month, Bob's secretary sent her a bill for all the household expenses Ethel was expected to pay. The bills were itemized, down to individual tubes of toothpaste. Merman was dismayed, but still hopeful for a happy future. In the summer of 1953, she did a concert in Denver, as well as one at the Texas State Fair for extra income.

She also signed with NBC to star on two "Colgate Comedy Hours" in January and February of 1954. On one of them, she starred with Frank Sinatra and Bert Lahr in a truncated version of *Anything Goes*. Ethel's performance was nothing less than brilliant. She was happy that she was able to give her friend Frank (whose career was in a lull) a job when he really needed the exposure. This was also the only time Ethel and Bert Lahr worked together on television, revisiting their "Friendship" duet from *DuBarry Was a Lady*.

But first she flew to Washington, D.C., in November 1953 to take part in a television show, produced by the B'nai B'rith Anti-Defamation League, honoring President Eisenhower. Merman did a hits medley and was congratulated for desegregating the National Theatre.

Also on the bill was the cast of "I Love Lucy." As Ethel was waiting to go on, Vivian Vance slid in next to her and said, "This is the first time I've waited to go on stage with you that I didn't wish you would drop dead!" Viv was, of course, referring to the years she was Merman's understudy and was dying to go on in her place.

It was obvious as 1954 rolled around that Merman was gaining weight. Her face was bloated, and her midsection was expanding. She immediately had to crash diet because her next film was ready to go before the cameras. Ethel was wary of this movie from the start.

To begin with, she was not the top-billed star. For *There's No Business Like Show Business*, Mermo had to share credit and screen time with no less than Dan Dailey, Donald O'Connor, Marilyn Monroe, Mitzi Gaynor, and Johnny Ray.

Everyone involved was fighting for predominance. In order to placate the stars' egos, Johnny and Marilyn were each given two solo musical numbers. Dailey couldn't sing, so his numbers were limited to three duets with Ethel. Merman had more numbers in the movie than anyone else, but only one solo.

The movie never quite figured out what it was. The plot had about as much direction as a break dancer on a hot rock. While everyone got a chance to shine, it was just too much and yet not enough. None of the songs had anything to do with the plot, which had Merman alternately doing slapstick with O'Connor and crying over Ray's decision to become a priest within the space of three minutes. Merman and Dailey were about as believable a couple as Richard Simmons and Mae West. And Johnny Ray seemed to be in a different musical altogether. Ethel was overweight and not in good voice.

But it wouldn't be fair not to tell you that Ethel detested working with Marilyn Monroe. Marilyn's marriage to Joe DiMaggio was falling apart, and she was taking it out on everyone around her. Monroe often showed up late for work or not at all. It was obvious she was on some sort of medication and taking too much of it. DiMaggio hated Marilyn's part in the film (as did Marilyn) and felt she was dressed like a whore for her numbers. The only time he came to the set, he told all the press that his favorite performer was Ethel Merman!

Merman and Monroe had good reasons not to like one another.

Despite tremendous press and a Cinemascope release, *There's No Business Like Show Business* was not the hit *Call Me Madam* had been. Fox did not pick up Ethel's option on another film. Once again Mermo had to face the fact that she was not going to be a diva of the silver screen. Things were not going the way she planned, and Ethel couldn't figure out what went wrong.

For the next year, Ethel decided to concentrate strictly on television work on both coasts. Appearing on variety, dramatic, and panel shows, Merman could be seen at least once every three weeks on the tube. She was able to command between ten and twenty-five thousand dollars per show.

Her performances had mixed success. Ethel could not control her weight gain and was not looking well. She had worn her hair shortened into a severe "poodle" cut that made her look hard and unglamorous. It was becoming obvious that Ethel Merman was not a happy lady.

History was repeating itself. Ethel and Bob began fighting over money, and soon they were fighting over Six's womanizing. Bob was unhappy that Ethel was letting herself go and was disappointed in her movie career. Her stardom was not shining as big a spotlight on *him* as he wanted. Merman felt that Bob was spending way too much time in New York away from her and not fulfilling his job as a husband or father. Both kids wanted to take the last name Six so they could be one, big happy family, but Bob never adopted them.

Ethel also began to feel she was being drained financially. For the second time in her life, Merman had to dip into her hard-earned capital to pay her bills because her husband wouldn't. Only this time, the dip was deep. The income from sporadic television appearances (however well paying) could not pay for the upkeep on what was essentially a baronial mansion with servants, private school for her children, the luxury apartment her parents lived in, commuting to both coasts, and the expenses incurred in her career. Ethel watched in horror as the fortune she had worked so hard to build up was being methodically drained.

Six paid for nothing he didn't have to and often defaulted to Ethel to pay all the bills. In the beginning of her marriage, she accepted this as part of having a partnership, but once there were other women, Merman balked.

And Merman had one of the loudest balks in the business.

As if she had not done the exact same thing ten years earlier, Ethel decided that returning to the Broadway stage would save her marriage. If she had a show, she would have the needed income and be able to replenish her capital. She would also reside in New York and be able to keep an eye on her husband. As much as she loved her children, she took them out of the life they had only just settled into and shuttled them to New York.

Writers Lindsay and Crouse came up with what they thought was the perfect Ethel Merman vehicle: a satire of the Grace Kelly-Prince Rainier wedding. It was the biggest thing of 1956, and they were sure Irving Berlin or Cole Porter would be happy to supply the score.

They were wrong. Neither Cole nor Irving wanted any part of it. Both felt hurt that Ethel had turned them down when they last asked her to star in a show, and they (rightly) felt that the plot was too slim.

Jo Mielziner was producing, and Abe Burrows (father of television *wunderkind* James Burrows) was directing. There were several top-notch composers in 1956 who would have loved to write a Merman show, including Jule Styne, Harold Arlen, Comden and Green, Johnny Mercer, and (despite acrimony) Rodgers and Hammerstein. In a surprising turn, Mielziner hired two young composers named Harold Carr and Matt Dubey (one was a dentist!) instead. Ethel should have walked out right then and there, but she had already relocated her family and she needed the income. Besides, she was still smarting from the experience of walking away from *Sadie Thompson* and did not want a repeat performance. So Ethel agreed to appear in *Happy Hunting*.

Once the creative team was in place, they had to find Merman a suitable leading man. This was not the easy job it had once been. Ethel was now fifty and looked it. Although she valiantly dieted down to a size eight, she could not reasonably have romantic scenes with a thirty-year-old. The man needed to be fortyish, handsome, sing loudly enough to be heard in duets with Ethel, and be able to handle comedy. But he couldn't be too old or Ethel's vanity would be bruised.

Fernando Lamas was a good, but not necessarily logical choice. He had a fine singing voice, was devilishly good looking, and in need of work. MGM had recently let him out of his contract, and he wanted to segue his career onto the stage and nightclubs.

The first day of rehearsal, the cast sat at a table and read the script out loud. Then they picked up their scripts and began "blocking," figuring out the physical movements while on their feet. After a few moments, Lamas was perturbed and spoke up. "Is this the way it's going to be?" he asked. "I deliver my lines to her, and she delivers them to the audience?" Fernando was referring to Ethel's habit of playing every scene directly to the audience.

"Mr. Lamas," Merman intoned looking him right in the eyes, "I'll have you know that I have been delivering lines on Broadway this way for twenty-five years!" Fernando should have kept his mouth shut, but he didn't. He answered her in his charming accent. "Miss Merman, that does not mean you are right, it just means you are *old*!"

Ethel was horrified! In one sentence, Lamas had verbalized her worst fears and insecurities. This sexy younger man had successfully cut her off at the knees, and that was foolish. Besides being his leading lady, and a much bigger star than he, Ethel Merman was also one of the producers. She and Bob had invested through their corporation Mersix. He had not just been cruel to his coworker, he had been thoughtless to his boss.

Merman never again spoke to Lamas except when she was in character. Fernando was cocky and often let the audiences know his disdain for her by wiping off her kisses on stage. Ethel had to go to the union to get him to stop.

Meanwhile, Ethel had to deal with a mediocre score. It was as if Dubey and Carr had listened to every song she had ever sung and rewrote them for this show. There were only two songs in the entire score that were really any good, "Gee, But It's Good to Be Here" and "Mutual Admiration Society." The rest were so forgettable that Merman prevailed upon her friend, Roger Edens, to write two new ones long after the show had opened.

*Happy Hunting* was not a flop—it ran for a year. It was at least as successful as *Stars in Your Eyes* and *Something for the Boys*. But it was the least enjoyable for Ethel of all the shows she had ever done. She referred to it as a Jeep among limousines. The original cast album on RCA (Merman was finally out of her Decca contract) showed Merman in superb voice singing a very flawed score. Merman was nominated for a Tony Award as best actress in a musical, but did not win.

Merman made the cover of *Newsweek* just as the show opened on Broadway, which gave the show one of the strangest reviews ever published. It admitted that the show and the score were mediocre at best, but that every time Ethel Merman walked out on stage, she made the audience believe it was great. Almost as if she practiced mass hypnosis, everyone who

saw the show loved it. Only afterward did people ask themselves why. Ethel Merman was magic.

On top of her other duties, La Merm was named hostess of
the 1957 New York City Summer Festival. On July 20, she
joined the mayor and other dignitaries by singing "Gee, But It's
Good to Be Here" at the opening ceremonies. The publicity for
*Happy Hunting* was just what the show needed in the dog days
of summer.

Although it did bring in some needed dollars, *Happy
Hunting* didn't solve her marriage problem. Six had moved his
philandering to Denver and Los Angeles now that Ethel was
tied to New York. It was a relief when the show closed in
December 1957. Ethel did not feel relief for long.

The next month, Bob Levitt asked if he could have the kids
for a long weekend. They had spent Christmas and New Year's
with Ethel, and he wanted some time alone with them. Ethel
always gave Bob as much time as he wanted with the children
despite his depressions and personal problems. Levitt had
recently remarried and was out in East Hampton, N.Y., with
his bride and Paul Getty Jr.'s wife. A good time was had by all,
and then Bob sent the kids and the women back into New
York. After the kids left, he carefully took off his expensive
watch and jewelry, wrote a note, and committed suicide by
overdosing on pills.

Ethel and the children were grieved beyond belief. No one
had suspected he was in such a desperate state. Although she
hated to admit it, Merman was feeling guilty that she had not
been a better wife to Levitt and helped him more. It was an
impossible task for her to explain things to their children that
she didn't understand herself.

Levitt left that expensive watch to Ethel, and she rarely
took it off. She took his other jewelry and had the pieces made

into a charm bracelet. In later years, she always claimed that Levitt had been the love of her life. It really is difficult to say who was number one, Bob Levitt or Sherman Billingsley. However, it is easy and unfortunate to say that Ethel Merman never loved a man happily.

It took Ethel quite a while to get over the shock of Bob Levitt's suicide. She could not understand how he had done this to her and their children. No matter how she tried to deal with it, Merman felt as though this was something done against *her*, as opposed to something Bob did because of his own emotional problems. Ethel could not understand having such problems, but she also could not help blaming herself and wondering what she could have done differently.

Although she had not spoken well of Bob since their divorce, after his suicide, Ethel looked back upon their marriage and wished they had never separated. She reasoned that if they had stayed married, none of this tragedy would have happened. And part of that tragedy was her current marriage, which was tearing her apart.

Ethel Merman never really dealt with getting older. Until the last couple of years of her life, she felt and acted as if she were thirty-five and still in her prime. Losing Levitt, watching her kids become teenagers, dealing with Lamas's offensive but truthful comments, and battling a husband who was using her to further his own goals was running riot with Ethel's image of herself. It was that very image, the always conquering, nothing is impossible, "I will always come out on top" feeling that gave her the confidence to tackle show business so successfully. But in private life, it was providing a screen from reality that kept her from dealing with things as they were, as opposed to how she wanted them to be.

In 1958, Ethel once again devoted her efforts to television, visiting the shows of Dinah Shore, Perry Como, Frank Sinatra, Eddie Fisher, and others. She was marking time, because producer David Merrick brought an idea to her that was intriguing.

Comedian/actress/singer/ecdysiast (that means stripper) Gypsy Rose Lee wrote a memoir that spent many weeks on the best-seller lists. All of the book focused on her childhood in show business, dealing with her pampered sister, June Havoc, and her bear of a stage mother, Rose. Merrick thought the book was great fodder for an adult musical, the kind of which had really never been seen on Broadway. Times had once again changed, with shows like *West Side Story* and *Damn Yankees* bringing much more sexual and sophisticated themes to the Great White Way. However, a musical about a monstrous bitch of a mother openly enjoying a sex life outside of marriage, her daughter who marries at twelve, and her other daughter who was a stripper was pushing the envelope.

Merrick got Arthur Laurents to write the book of the show, which went through myriad changes before finally hitting Broadway. Merrick wanted newcomer Stephen Sondheim to write the entire score (it would have been his first), but after Ethel's experience with *Happy Hunting*, she wanted someone with a track record. So Jule Styne (*Gentlemen Prefer Blondes*,

136

*Above:* Ethel the glamour puss, 1933 (author's collection). *Right:* Ethel the film starlet, 1932.

*Above:* Merman the coy chanteuse, 1934 (author's collection). *Right:* Clowning with Frank McHugh, Bing Crosby, and Charles Butterworth on the radio, 1934.

With Eddie Cantor and Duke York, 1934 (courtesy of J. C. Archives).

Ethel's first great love, Sherman Billingsley, owner of the Stork Club (courtesy of Photofest).

Merman and her mom and pop, a true mutual admiration society, 1936.

*Left:* Sexy, sultry Merman, 1936. *Below:* With husband number one, Bill Smith, 1940 (courtesy of Photofest).

*Something for the Boys,* 1942 (courtesy of J. C. Archives).

With husband number two, Bob Levitt, 1944 (courtesy of Photofest).

A tender moment from the original *Annie Get Your Gun*, 1946 (courtesy of J. C. Archives).

**Why ETHEL MERMAN recommends ARRID**

"Why let perspiration ruin your clothes—or your reputation, when you can use Arrid and be protected?

"I use Arrid deodorant cream every day and I wouldn't think of going anywhere without it. I have personally recommended Arrid to loads of people because I like it so much."

*Ethel Merman*

Star of Broadway
Musical Hits

Ethel sold everything from shoes to cottage cheese; this is from 1947.

Publicity photo for the film version of
*Call Me Madam*, 1952.

Irving Berlin coaches his star during rehearsals for
*Call Me Madam*, 1950.

With husband number three, Bob Six, 1953 (courtesy of Photofest).

With great pal Jimmy Durante, rehearsing "The Colgate Comedy Hour," 1953 (courtesy of J. C. Archives).

A rare photo of EM smoking while at a party with Jane Wyman and her husband, Fred Karger, 1954 (courtesy of J. C. Archives).

*Above:* A greatly airbrushed Ethel attempts youthful glamour in a publicity pose for *Happy Hunting*, 1956. *Right:* During a break from filming *There's No Business Like Show Business* with children Bob Jr. and Ethel Jr., 1954 (author's collection).

*Above:* Hugging Jerome Robbins after rehearsing
*Rose's Turn*, 1954 (courtesy of Photofest). *Right:*
With Sandra Church and Maria Karnilova in
*Gypsy*, 1959 (courtesy of J. C. Archives).

*Above:* Belting *Blow, Gabriel, Blow* during her 1960 television special, "Ethel Merman on Broadway." *Left:* With namesake daughter, Ethel Jr., 1959 (author's collection).

*Above:* Ethel, always a welcome guest on TV variety shows of the 1950s and the '60s, rehearses in 1962 (courtesy of Photofest).
*Right:* Ethel's favorite photo of herself, 1961 (courtesy of Carole Cook).

Husband number four, Ernest Borgnine, 1964 (courtesy of Photofest).

It's Lola Lasagne! "Batman," 1967 (author's collection).

Publicity photo with Bruce Yarnell from the 1967 television version of *Annie Get Your Gun* (courtesy of David Sinkler).

Singing *You're Just in Love* on "The Mike Douglas Show," 1971 (courtesy of Rose Marie).

Out on the town with Peter Marshall and Tammy Wynette, 1975 (courtesy of Peter Marshall).

Out to dinner with Carole Cook, 1979 (courtesy of Carole Cook).

Vacationing in Cape Cod, 1977 (author's collection).

*Left:* Surrounded by handsome friends: Jim Russo, Tom Troupe, and Tony Cointreau, 1982 (courtesy of Tom Troupe). *Below:* Her last film role in *Airplane*, 1980—a battle fatigued soldier who thinks he's Ethel Merman! (courtesy of J. C. Archives).

With pals Rose Marie and Richard Deacon, 1981 (courtesy of Rose Marie).

Belting *Everything's Coming Up Roses* in her favorite dress, 1980 (courtesy of Photofest).

*Peter Pan, The Bells Are Ringing)* wrote the music. Ethel admired Jule greatly as he had produced some of her television work in the early- and mid-1950s. And although he was far from her type physically (he was Jewish, short, and squat), he was brilliant, funny, and well endowed. Ethel decided she was going to have an affair with him, to ensure proper companionship and to ensure that all of the best music went her way.

The best music did go her way, but she never got to consummate the affair.

The auditions for Louise, the daughter that eventually became Gypsy Rose Lee, produced a beautiful girl named Sandra Church. She landed both the role and Styne, who was immediately smitten with her. Sandra got what Ethel wanted, so naturally Ethel couldn't stand her. Merman's dislike for her went as far as fantasy. When Ethel did her second autobiography, she declared a very alive Sandra Church as having passed away in obscurity!

Ethel got back at Jule in a very sly way. He invited his STAR to his home for a Passover Seder, and she accepted. Although she was polite and congenial, she made no bones about being bored by the ancient Passover rituals. Finally, it came time to eat the meal. Ethel refused any food offered, reached for her purse, and pulled out a sandwich wrapped in wax paper. It was a ham sandwich! Everyone at the table stared at her in disbelief.

Jule inquired, "What the hell do you think you're doing?" Ethel's retort was, "Well, I don't know anything about Passover except that the food is lousy. So I brought my own!" Another brave soul piped up, "But Ethel, that food isn't even blessed!" A gutsy Merman made the sign of the cross and bellowed, "It is now!" as she stuffed the sandwich into her mouth.

Meanwhile, back at the ranch, things were not too happy, either. Ethel Jr. decided that she wanted to attend and graduate from high school in Denver, so Ethel reluctantly allowed her daughter to live in the Denver mansion with the supervision of the staff and the occasional visit from her stepfather. Merman noticed that her daughter was restless and unfocused, and it concerned her. But with *Gypsy* revving up, Ethel had no time to take her daughter in hand. Merman was about to embark on the most difficult role of her career.

Ethel no longer trusted Bob Six and so did not invest with him (as a partner in Mersix) in *Gypsy*. Had she simply invested on her own, she would have been set for life. But despite her marital woes, Merman felt it unwise to so boldly go up against Six. She knew it would have meant the total end of her marriage.

Meanwhile, *Gypsy* moved forward. Styne and Sondheim were writing the music and lyrics, and Arthur Laurents was wrestling with taming the meandering memoir and turning it into the plot for a musical. A leading man was needed for Ethel, and this time he really needed to act. *Gypsy* was no musical fluff. The story would have been a marvelous straight play without the music. That said, none of the usual musical leading men were right for the show.

Jack Klugman was a marvelous character actor who was making quite a name for himself on Broadway and in television dramas. He was good looking without looking like a leading man, and he could certainly act. However, he was almost twenty years younger than the fifty-three-year-old Ethel, couldn't sing, and had little experience with comedy. While Klugman knew he could play the part, he was very unsure whether he could play opposite Merman.

By this point in her career, Ethel had quite a reputation (mostly unearned) for being a difficult person with whom to work. Her confidence, experience, and enormous talent intimidated those with lesser lights. She never asked anyone to do any more than she did herself, but what she did was enormous.

If you did your job well, were on time, acted professionally, and were polite, you had no problems with Ethel Merman. If you were greatly talented and dedicated to the job on hand, Merman would even be a booster. BUT! If you showed up late, didn't know your lines, didn't give your all while performing, or had bad stage manners, Ethel could be your worst nightmare. She was a thorough professional and demanded the same of everyone around her.

It finally came the day that Jack Klugman had to audition with Ethel Merman. He was so nervous that he threatened to walk out if Ethel steamrollered him and he could not be heard. Merman was no dummy. She knew Jack was extremely talented and really wanted him in the show. When they did a duet together, she sang so softly that her voice cracked!

Ethel was show-wise. She knew that *Gypsy* was nothing like anything she had ever done. Although she would be onstage almost constantly and would indeed sing three-quarters of the score herself, this time she would have to be an *actress* to carry the show. And she needed great actors onstage with her. Merman and Klugman would remain affectionate friends until the mid-1970s.

As rehearsals shaped up, Merman and *Gypsy* got a lot of press. Some said Ethel was crazy to play such an unlikable character, while others praised her courage. Many didn't think that Ethel had the acting chops to carry it off. Actually, the only problem Ethel and *Gypsy* had was that there was too much show. Several numbers had to be tossed out because the show ran too long, and the book of the show had to be condensed.

Before the show left town for out-of-town tryouts, a special rehearsal was held for an invited audience. Dressed in street clothes, and with limited props and scenery, the cast put on a performance of *Gypsy* that some say was never topped. It must have been a very large theater. Everyone in show business I have ever spoken to claims to have been there. Ethel, dressed in a silk suit, stood onstage the entire time, acting when it was her turn, leaning against the proscenium, and beaming at the cast when she wasn't in the scene.

After a short tour where more material was axed, *Gypsy* opened on Broadway in May 1959. To say that it was a hit is to say that children like candy. Reviewers fought over one another trying to find new superlatives to heap on Ethel and the show. Immediately, "Everything's Coming Up Roses," "Small World," "Some People," and "Together Wherever We Go" became standards. When the original cast album was made several days later, it became a top seller even though Ethel was not in top voice the day of the recording.

There wasn't even a title that could be bestowed upon Ethel. She had now outstripped star, superstar, legend, First Lady. With her thirteenth consecutive hit musical, Ethel Merman was now the biggest star on Broadway that ever was or will be. Her competition at the time were ladies like Julie Andrews, Judy Holliday, Gwen Verdon, Chita Rivera, Carol Burnett, and of course, Mary Martin. And still she remained supreme.

Ethel trusted very few people with her music. She felt that without the proper musical director to conduct, even she could get lost. Her favorites through the years included Roger Edens, Al Goodman, Jay Blackton, and her own personal conductor for her concerts, Eric Knight. For *Gypsy*, she had Milton Rosenstock, and she relied upon him heavily. The musical cues, interludes, reprises, and opening vamps were complicated and difficult. Most people have no idea how truly hard it is to sing in a Broadway show. The loud orchestra plays everything *but* the melody, and if the rhythm is the least bit off, a singer can get lost as if in quicksand.

Milton did his job extremely well, something Ethel always admired. So she liked him. After several months in the show, she noticed that Milton seemed edgy and unhappy. She found out that Milton and his wife were having marital problems. Being the sort of no-nonsense person she was, she offered Milton a ride home in her limousine one cold New York winter's night. When Milton got out, Ethel got out, too. "I gotta pee," she said. What could Milton do but take his star up to his apartment and let her use the facilities.

Merman marched into his flat (one wag once said that when Ethel strode down a hall, one could hear her balls clank) and introduced herself to Mrs. Rosenstock. "Listen, Honey," Ethel started, "I know you guys are fighting. Now you sit down here and work this out between you. I need Milton happy. I'm gonna go pee, and then I'm gonna make you some tea!"

In December 1959, Ethel got to do something she had wanted for a long time—her own special on television. She had been a guest on other peoples' shows many times and even guest-hosted a few times, but this was her chance to do a show exactly the way she wanted. When NBC made the offer, she immediately contacted Roger Edens to write the show for her. In this case, loyalty may have done her in. Edens had spent the 1950s producing at MGM and writing special material for Judy Garland's concerts. His presentation tended to be old-fashioned, and he overindulged in medleys.

Had Ethel been allowed to sing a half dozen of her best songs concert-style and had guests like Frank Sinatra, Garland, or Dinah Shore, "Ethel Merman on Broadway" might have been a hit and the pilot for a variety series of her own. Instead, they decided to hire Tab Hunter, Tom Poston, and Fess Parker as her guests and have Merman prerecord all of her numbers and lip-synch them for the cameras.

The special was a lot like the film *There's No Business Like Show Business*—too much and not enough all at the same time. There was no chemistry between Merman and Parker (who couldn't sing well enough to shine alongside of Merman), and Tom Poston was given precious little material to show off his hysterical dry wit. The only sketch that worked was one between Tab as a newly graduated psychiatrist and Merman as his jaded first client. The special ended with a medley of Merman's hits that was overproduced with every sort of scenery and prop imaginable. The critics hated the show, which was not a ratings success. Strike one!

While all of this was going on, Ethel was spending every last erg of her energy doing *Gypsy* eight times a week. It was a much more grueling show than Ethel could ever have imagined. During intermissions, she would sit at her makeup table with her head in her hands, trying to relax and muster up the incredible energy for the second act. As many of you may know, the show ends with "Rose's Turn," a number that is more operatic aria than song. Ethel had to have a nightly nervous breakdown while doing this number, twice on Wednesday and Saturday, emoting from the bottom of her heart and projecting from the bottom of her diaphragm.

Ethel continued to make other television appearances, as long as they could be taped on her day off. Merman needed the extra money because she was about to once again get a divorce. Bob Six wasn't just womanizing anymore. He had found one particular woman and was meeting her in Hawaii every few weeks. Not that Ethel had been totally faithful either, but had Six been a husband, then Ethel would have been a happy and loyal wife.

First, Ethel took a day off from *Gypsy* to attend her daughter's high-school graduation. It was a whirlwind twenty-four hours as Ethel and Bobby had to fly to Denver, attend the graduation, and spend some time with Ethel Jr., and then fly back to New York so as to miss only one performance. Merman should have missed more performances and paid more attention to her daughter. Little Ethel, not so little and no longer a child, was exhibiting some of the same emotional problems her father had. She was often depressed, ill at ease, and unable to focus on her future.

If Ethel was unaware of her daughter's problems, she was aware and indignant that she lost the 1960 Tony Award to Mary Martin's performance in *The Sound of Music*. Ethel loved Mary, but felt that there was no comparison between Momma Rose and Baroness Maria von Trapp. In public, she shrugged it off with the comment, "How can you buck a nun?" Privately, it hurt. She knew this was the best work she would ever do and to be overlooked, made her blood boil.

That summer, Ethel took a month's vacation to travel to Europe with Bobby and Benay Venuta. In fact, Ethel, Benay, Bobby, Judy Garland, and Kay Thompson all traveled to London together. It is here that rumors of Ethel's supposed bisexuality began to surface. Hadn't Kay Thompson taught a younger Judy Garland the joys of Sappho-hood? Wasn't Benay herself a well-known lover of women as well as men? So what were these four women doing together in London, hmmmmm????

All three women were very close friends of Ethel's. Judy particularly idolized her. Early in her career, Merman was Garland's singing hero. She often had to be talked out of doing an impression of Ethel and sing in her own style. And it does happen that Kay and Benay were bisexual women. I have found no evidence that anything even slightly sexual happened on this trip between Ethel and any of these ladies, although Broadway tongues wagged for months.

Ethel simply wanted to get away from stress. Her latest marriage was almost over, *Gypsy* was running Ethel's health into the ground, and her daughter was exhibiting strange behavior. Merman wanted some peace and relaxation. So Bobby and Benay saw the sights while Ethel slept, then Ethel and Benay saw the nightlife while Bobby slept. No one is certain when Benay slept.

By December 1960, things were crumbling. Ethel once again flew to Mexico for a quickie divorce (strike two) and then stopped in Colorado to see her daughter. Ethel Jr. had gotten herself pregnant and married the father of her baby, Bill Geary. By all accounts, he loved Ethel and was happy to be a father. Merman hoped that with a man and a baby, her very intelligent daughter might come down to earth and make a life for herself.

Ethel was never involved in the day-to-day lives of her grown children the way her parents were. In fact, Ethel showered upon her aging parents the kind of affection and attention usually deserved for children. Her mom and pop were still number one in her book, and they always stood by her no matter what. It was the rest of the world with whom Ethel had problems.

In January 1961, Ethel was thrilled to be asked by Frank Sinatra to sing at the preinaugural ball for John F. Kennedy (as she had done for President Eisenhower). Sinatra got David Merrick to close *Gypsy* for one night so she could attend rehearsals and be in the show. She traveled to Washington directly from appearing in *Gypsy* so she would be available for rehearsal first thing in the morning.

During the night, one of the worst blizzards of the twentieth century blew through the East Coast. Washington came to a standstill. Sinatra's troupe, which included Joey Bishop, Milton Berle, Ella Fitzgerald, Nat "King" Cole, Tony Curtis, Bette Davis, Bill Dana, Helen Traubel, and many others, rehearsed at the armory in the afternoon. Afterward, some went back to the hotel by chartered bus, while others took private cars. By nine in the evening, people were doubting whether the performers or the audience were going to be able to make it to see the show, which was directed by William Asher. Finally, by eleven, the show began.

Ethel had never even made it back to her hotel to change. Dressed in a wool suit with a matching long overcoat, she sang "Everything's Coming Up Roses." This is the only visual record made of Merman singing the song with the original Broadway arrangement.

As 1961 progressed, *Gypsy* had been on Broadway for two years and ticket sales were slipping. It was decided to close the show and take the original cast on an extended national tour. Originally, Ethel did not want to go. She'd had two health problems during the run that had really scared her. Once she burst a blood vessel in her throat, making her miss two weeks of performances. Although she healed well, her vibrato had become more pronounced and slightly wobbly. Even though Ethel gave up smoking cigarettes, it did not help. She also developed a back problem that would follow her the rest of her life.

With no husband, a married daughter, and a son about to enter college, Ethel agreed to make the tour. She needed the money. Her marriage and divorce from Robert Six had cost her a fortune. She had to provide for her retired parents, Bobby, and Ethel and Bill Geary, who were really still kids themselves. So Ethel toured in *Gypsy*, playing the show in almost every large city in the United States well into 1962.

She loved the adulation from the audiences (especially in San Francisco where they gave her standing ovations after every number), but was very lonely. She had no husband and was away from her folks and her kids. In order to kill the pain of solitude, Ethel began to drink too much. One night she was at the Ritz-Carlton hotel, drinking with Rosemary Clooney, who was also touring the country. The two women got so plastered that they thought the RC on the bathmat would make a wonderful monogrammed stole for Rosie.

This was a very unhappy time for Ethel. The house in Denver was no longer hers, so she literally had no permanent address. The *Gypsy* tour was killing her health and her voice, and privately Ethel had decided that this would be her last musical no matter what.

By the time the show hit Los Angeles, Ethel thought she was a shoo-in for the movie role. While performing as Momma Rose in L.A, she received word that Rosalind Russell had sewed up her part in the film. Strike three!

Producer Mervyn LeRoy was counting on Russell's box-office name to push a movie that would be fraught with censorship problems. He was shortsighted because Ethel would have been excellent, and without her, the movie flopped. But Ethel was crushed nonetheless, and her drinking increased.

Another watershed year for Ethel was 1962. She had originally planned to play *Gypsy* in London for six months. At the last minute, Jack Klugman and several members of the cast got movie work and couldn't go. Rather than do the show with a British cast, Ethel canceled. Not a wise move. The English loved her and had never had a chance to see her in a musical on stage. Had she done *Gypsy* there, Merman would have had a built-in audience. In Europe, unlike America, once you are a star, you remain a star the rest of your life.

Instead, Ethel was cast in a movie. Perhaps Warner Brothers didn't think she could carry the film version of *Gypsy*, but Stanley Kramer thought she would be perfect as the bombastic Mrs. Marcus in the all-star *It's a Mad, Mad, Mad, Mad World*.

Kramer's stock-in-trade was the dramatic blockbuster. Previously he had starred Spencer Tracy in *Inherit the Wind* and *Judgment at Nuremberg*. Both men wanted to do something lighter and decided to make the world's biggest screwball comedy. The cast included Tracy, Merman, Milton Berle, Phil Silvers, Jonathan Winters, Mickey Rooney, Buddy Hackett, Sid Caesar, Edie Adams, Jimmy Durante, and Dick Shawn, with smaller parts going to everyone from Jerry Lewis to Zasu Pitts to the Three Stooges.

Ethel played the mother-in-law from hell, a woman with a mouth that barked and a body that promised to bite. Merman practically stole the movie, which was one of the greatest comedies ever filmed. Although the folks that hand out the Oscars never recognized comedy films in those days, today Ethel Merman would have been a shoo-in for a best supporting actress Academy Award.

Almost immediately, Ethel and many other large names were talked into providing the voices for a cartoon musical sequel to *The Wizard of Oz*. Liza Minnelli was signed to play Dorothy in one of her first real show-business bookings. Merman would play the Wicked Witch, and buddies like Milton Berle, Danny Thomas, Peter Lawford, and Paul Lynde would provide the other voices. Ethel had three songs in the film, and she was very pleased to be making two pictures back to back.

*Return to Oz* never saw the inside of a theater. It was so badly written, drawn, and edited that it was never released. In 1974, the SFM Holiday Network finally released it to syndicat-

ed television at Christmastime, and original soundtrack albums have shown up from time to time. Once again, Ethel had a disappointing movie experience.

After filming and recording was over for both films, Merm appeared on two Bob Hope television shows and planned to make her Las Vegas nightclub debut. Ethel was determined not to return to Broadway and had to find a way to make a living as a variety artist. Frank Sinatra had signed her to his Reprise Records label, and Ethel made a dazzling album of her songs from the 1930s with swinging Billy May arrangements. With the success of Judy Garland's landmark live recording at Carnegie Hall, it was decided to also record Ethel at the Flamingo Hotel in Las Vegas and release it as a live album.

Unfortunately, Ethel was too old-fashioned for Las Vegas. She sang *at* the audience as she did on Broadway, but did not stop to *include* the imbibing revelers in her fun. Had Ethel been less stiff, less formal, and allowed her ribald sense of humor to come out, she would have been a big hit. But Merman had spent too many years on Broadway to change her style, and audiences were left sated as she sang more than fifteen numbers and a long medley in less than an hour.

The live album, which was the second in a planned series for Reprise that would have given Merman a large, moneymaking catalog of records, was troubled from the word go. Ethel would not use a handheld microphone to sing her songs—she felt it hampered her style. Instead, she wore a body mike at her chest with a battery pack taped to her inner thigh. This was in the early days of wireless mikes, and it did not always record every note as she maneuvered around the stage. Additionally, it picked up and amplified every possible imperfection in Ethel's voice.

The live recording was a ruin. Rather than try it again at a later date, Reprise decided to have Ethel come into the studios in Burbank and rerecord her voice over the recording made in Vegas. She did it in one take without taking a rest. The final album was a shambles, as one could hear both voices singing at the same time. It was a complete flop. Ethel's contract with Reprise was not renewed.

Moreover, Ethel did not enjoy singing to crowds that were smoking, drinking, and eating while she performed. Instead, her agents put together *The Ethel Merman Show*, which was her club act only played in theaters, concert halls, hotel showrooms, and state fairs.

Without a current Broadway success or hit record or film, Merman was allowing her star to descend. She did not do capacity business. Timing is everything, and Ethel was trying to transition her career at a time when nightclubs, theaters, and hotel rooms were closing all over the country. Las Vegas was the ticket, but Ethel had failed there.

The only bright spot of this period was the birth of her granddaughter, Barbara Jean. Merman sent out telegrams saying "Call Me Grandma" and proffered photos of the pretty baby to anyone who wanted them. Merman felt a lot better about her daughter's future and felt she was making a good mother.

So Ethel turned once again to television. She desperately wanted her own show, either a sitcom or a variety series. Merman knew she needed the exposure of television to keep her career going if she was not going to appear on Broadway. And she had offers.

David Merrick came to Ethel again and begged her to do his next show, a musical version of *The Matchmaker*. Jerry Herman, the latest (and possibly last) of the great Broadway composers, had written the score especially for Ethel. While the whole thing sounded both creatively and financially wonderful, Ethel remembered how difficult it was to do *Gypsy* eight times a week for more than three years. She turned Merrick down. Jerry Herman immediately took two songs out of the score (he felt Ethel Merman was the only person who could ever sing them), and Carol Channing got the part of Dolly Levi in *Hello, Dolly!* If Merman had done this show, there is no doubt she would have solidified her stardom in Middle America, which took the title song to its heart.

Instead, Ethel did "Maggie Brown," a sitcom pilot for her old pal, Lucille Ball, now president of Desilu Studios. Lucy needed a new sitcom hit for her studio, and she was a great believer in Ethel's talent. The sitcom was like many of its time and was, in fact, very similar to "McHale's Navy." Merman played the title character, who owned a saloon in the South Pacific during World War II. She had a beautiful daughter all the gobs wanted to grab and a secret beer machine that made her a fortune during the rationed days of the war.

The characters were cute, and the situation gave Ethel a

chance to sing, but CBS wouldn't buy it. Instead, Ethel did "The Red Skelton Hour," two episodes of "The Lucy Show," and two episodes of "The Judy Garland Show." One of them became a classic, as Merman did a surprise walk-on when Judy had a very young Barbra Streisand as her guest. Ethel had been an early booster of Garland's and Streisand's, and both singers had taken more than a little from Ethel's style.

After Barbra announced her forthcoming Broadway show, *Funny Girl*, the three divas began to sing "There's No Business Like Show Business." After a moment or two, Garland and Streisand realized it was useless trying to steal attention from Ethel, so Judy just egged Ethel on to sing louder while Barbra stood there, clearly in over her talented head for perhaps the only time in her career.

The Merm's booming voice was also heard on the radio across America as she became the singing spokesperson for the new postal ZIP codes announced in 1963. She sang a cute jingle called "My ZIP," which became a fashionable catchphrase with Americans for several months.

It was around this time that Ethel ran into Ernest Borgnine at a party. Borgnine had starred in a string of heavy dramas in the 1950s, including *The Catered Affair*, *From Here to Eternity*, and *Marty*, for which he had won a best actor Oscar. In 1963, Ernie was filming his first television series, a comedy called "McHale's Navy."

Borgnine was not classically handsome, but he was solidly built, robust, Italian, and full of life. He dumped his first wife, Rhoda, after the Oscar win and divorced his second wife, Katy Jurado, after a tempestuous, violence-filled marriage. Although Ernie was at least ten years younger than Ethel, he enjoyed her good-natured personality and her foul-mouthed humor. Merman had recently dieted down to her thinnest in years and was looking better than she had since *Annie Get Your Gun* with the help of a face-lift and a new hairstyle. She had become what men call a handsome woman.

All of Hollywood was surprised when they began to date. They were downright shocked when Ethel announced that she and Ernest Borgnine were engaged and would marry in 1964. In fact, in Hollywood, it made the front page of all the trade magazines. Joe Flynn, Borgnine's costar on "McHale's Navy," held up one of the headlines at rehearsal and joked in a very fey way, "I get the pick of the litter!" It was weeks before Ernie would forgive him.

Ethel thought she was playing it safe by giving herself a six-month engagement period. No quickie marriage this time! But Ethel spent most of the six months traveling the country doing her shows and appearing on television. She really didn't know Ernie any better than she had known any of her other husbands.

When Ethel learned that Ernie had never seen her in a show, she went into a recording studio and with her own money recorded a series of medleys portraying her love for Ernie. The songs were about as successful as the relationship—rushed, badly sequenced, and poorly chosen.

Merman began to have doubts. Ernie had a young daughter, and Ethel would be cast in the difficult role of stepmother. If she married Borgnine, for once and for all, she would have to give up the stage and touring, as Ernie was rooted in Los Angeles doing his television series. Lastly, Ethel would once again have to live away from her beloved parents, who were now in their eighties. And she certainly did not want to make another marital mistake.

Lucille Ball surprised Ethel with a wedding shower right at Desilu Studios. All of Merman's pals were invited, from Ginger

Rogers to Edie Adams and every Hollywood woman she had known in between. Lucy's gift to Ethel was beautiful stationery, engraved in gold leaf with the initials EMB. As silly as it seems, that was what pushed Ethel into her decision to go ahead with the wedding. It was one gift that only Ethel Merman Borgnine would be able to use, and it was not returnable.

That night, Lucille threw a hen party for Merman at her Beverly Hills house. Her husband, Gary Morton, and children Lucie and Desi Jr. were sent away, while Lucille Ball, Ethel Merman, and Vivian Vance spent the evening with several bottles of Scotch. The three ladies reminisced about being young together in Broadway and Hollywood. By this point, Merman had known Vance for twenty-nine years and Lucille a little longer. They had done movies and Broadway together and had just finished filming a two-part "Lucy Show" for airing on CBS.

The more they drank, the freer everyone's tongues got. Merman admitted to her one-night stand with Desi Arnaz in 1939, which Vivian found hysterical. Viv said that if she had known it was that easy, she would have hung out in Desi's elevator until he asked *her*! Miss Ball, meanwhile, was not amused and wondered out loud that Ernest Borgnine must be great in bed at night because he was nothing to look at in the daylight.

Viv knew both ladies very well and knew what could happen if they got into a drunken argument. Trying to defuse the situation, Vance suggested that Lucy do their hair. Ball had always been a frustrated hairstylist (of meager talent) and had a mini beauty salon in a room off her kitchen. Viv knew it would take little coaxing to get Lucy to fire up the hair dryer and curlers.

The three continued to drink, and it really is too bad the Desilu cameras were not there to record a scene that could easily have been written by "Lucy Show" scribes Bob Schiller and Bob Weiskopf. Lucy kept teasing and teasing Merman's hair until it practically stood on end while she spritzed hair spray into everyone's eyes. Vivian ended up with her hair pulled back like the Bride of Frankenstein. Finally, the three dames dissolved into laughter and made coffee. Merman swore that Lucille Ball would never again do her hair, but was grateful to have two such good pals with whom to get over the jitters.

Ethel and Ernie decided that they would live in Borgnine's house once the wedding and honeymoon were over. Ernie gave Ethel a free hand with decorating, so Merman took all of her finery out of storage and moved it to Borgnine's house. It was the first permanent address she'd had since 1961. Ethel had been living in hotels since then.

One would think that people of their age would have discussed all aspects of life together, but it seems that little conversation of any depth took place. On the day of the wedding, Merman knew nothing of the plans for the reception. Her mom and pop had come out from New York and finally had the big wedding they had always wanted for their baby. Half of Hollywood was there, as were both of Ethel's children and Ernie's daughter.

After the ceremony, instead of driving to the reception with her new husband, Merman drove with her agent. Already, this was curious. Why weren't the newlyweds together? She inquired as to who was paying for the reception, and he told her that Edward and Agnes were. Ethel knew that it was she who would end up paying the bill, and it made her see red.

One wonders why. Why hadn't all of this been talked out ahead of time? Why would any bride be surprised by the details of her wedding? Why wouldn't Ethel and Ernie cheerfully share the costs together?

As if this didn't make her angry enough, the planned honeymoon infuriated her. Borgnine had done a series of commercials in Hong Kong, trading in on his "McHale's Navy" success. Part of his payment was first-class travel on a luxury liner to Hong Kong. Ethel thought it was cheap and tacky of Ernie *not* to spend his own money on the honeymoon, but instead use the promised trip.

Somehow, it made Ethel feel as though he didn't really love her if there were not some financial sacrifice on his part. Why they could not have negotiated this, honeymooned elsewhere, and then taken the cruise as a vacation later is unknown and puzzling.

There was a one-day break in between the wedding and the honeymoon. Ethel was already angry about the details, but invited Lucille Ball and her husband Gary Morton and Carole Cook and her husband Tom Troupe. Carole and Tom marveled at the chemistry between the freshly married Borgnines. If one did not know of the genius talent lurking under the surface, it could have been anyone's middle-class aunt and uncle. There was no sense of stardom or polish. Ethel happily showed off the swaying hula girl doll she had purchased for the bar.

When the subject of the honeymoon came up, Ethel dismissed the entire cruise with, "All I know about Hong Kong is it'll be hot as a nun's crotch!"

This next story is something I have put together almost sentence by sentence, interviewing people who would only speak if they could remain anonymous. It is more than a little strange, but here it is.

Merman and Borgnine limousined to the Port of Los Angeles and got on the ship. After helping Ernie to unpack (Merman never unpacked because she always traveled by theatrical trunks, which never needed unpacking), they had dinner and began to drink. Ethel was drinking because she was angry with her new husband, and Ernie drank because his new wife was angry with him and he didn't have the foggiest notion why. And to be fair, they both drank because it was free, and they liked to drink.

The twice-married Borgnine, hardly virginal Ethel, drunken couple got into bed to consummate their marriage. Despite Ethel's experienced ministrations, Borgnine was the worst for wine and could not achieve an erection. Ethel, also crocked beyond the point of no return, looked up at him and said, "You can't get it up? What're you, a *fag*?"

Merman would never say a more expensive sentence in her life. Borgnine's Italian temper reached its zenith almost immediately, and he slapped Merman right across the face. Ethel slapped him back, so Ernie hit her with his fist. The marriage was over.

The couple cohabitated in their luxury cabin until they reached Hong Kong, whereupon Ethel got on a plane and flew back to Los Angeles. Soon Ernie joined her, and the two lived totally separate lives in Borgnine's house for the twenty-eight days it would take to get a divorce without either one suing the other for desertion.

The whole thing was a shame because they really did like one another. Their marriage had literally lasted less than eighteen hours. Two very stubborn, very volatile, very sure-of-themselves people would not and could not sit down and admit they had both been wrong and were probably drinking too much. Both Ethel and Ernie were childish and immature. A good counselor could have mended fences and helped teach them to live together. Instead, Ethel got publicity that was even more embarrassing than that she had received with Sherman Billingsley back in 1940.

The couple's last fight was over the wedding presents. Ethel insisted that she knew almost everyone there better than Ernie did and that she should get to keep the gifts. Perhaps she felt that it was only fair since she had absorbed the cost of moving her things to Los Angeles and the wedding reception. Whatever Merman didn't like was returned for a cash refund. The rest was shipped to New York.

**20**

A dejected and sorrowful Ethel decided that from now on there would be no more marriages and no more upsetting her financial applecart. She moved into an apartment hotel on New York's Upper East Side. The furnishings would all be hers in this one-bedroom-and-den apartment, but she would not own it. The hotel provided daily maid service and room service, which was necessary since Ethel could not cook. In fact, she had the kitchen in the apartment removed, leaving only a refrigerator and a toaster oven for rudimentary eating.

The rest of 1964 found Ethel singing in the show rooms of the Plaza and Waldorf hotels in New York, as well as at the Toast of the Town in London. It was there that her old pal, Buddy Bregman, ran into her. Buddy had done the vocal arrangements for several of Ethel's best television appearances in the 1950s. He was now producing specials in England for

159

the BBC and wanted to tape Ethel's club act for broadcast. They met at an extremely fancy and staid restaurant in London's West End to discuss the show and old times.

Over cocktails, Buddy began to pump Ethel for the real truth behind her romance with Ernest Borgnine. Ethel did not want to discuss it and reminded Buddy that they were in a very upscale restaurant. Buddy kept prodding, and Merman kept demurring. Finally she'd had enough and pulling her two hands about a foot apart, shouted at the top of her incredible voice, "Because he had a *cock this big!*" The entire restaurant stopped in slow motion and stared at Buddy, who couldn't find anywhere to hide. Ethel just dove into her soup and enjoyed Buddy's discomfiture. Her show was, indeed, videotaped and has sadly never been broadcast in the United States.

Before 1964 was over, Ethel once more essayed a movie role. Writer/producer Carl Reiner had written a film for his discovery, Dick Van Dyke, called *The Art of Love*. Costarring with Van Dyke were James Garner, Angie Dickinson, and Elke Sommer. The plot was not new—a struggling artist in Paris pretends to be dead so his work will be discovered. Ethel was given the chance to play Coco La Fontanne, a swinging madam in Paris. She even got to sing one number written especially for the film.

Decked out in wild wigs of many colors and even wilder wardrobe, Ethel's Coco was really just a mature version of all the bad girls with a good heart Merman had played in the 1930s. Ethel's comedy timing was impeccable, and she was wonderful in the film.

Like many of Van Dyke's movies, it was funny, but lacked pacing. It also had very adult themes, so it was not a movie for children (Van Dyke's biggest audience after the success of *Mary Poppins* the previous year). *The Art of Love* did all right with the critics, but was not a huge box-office success. Alas, this was Ethel Merman's last major film role.

Merman kept moving, doing her stage show, and appearing on television. She hosted a "Bell Telephone Hour" saluting Cole Porter, who was on his deathbed. Dean Martin welcomed her on his show, and she was sensational. Ethel appeared on daytime television as well, doing things like "The Match Game," and late-night television with Johnny Carson on "The Tonight Show."

On one Carson visit, Ethel brought her daughter on with her. Confused and now desirous of a show-business career despite being the mother of two small children (Michael had been born the year before), Little Ethel joined her mother on the show. Ethel fille walked on already annoyed by her mother. She antagonized Ethel Sr. so badly on camera that the two women were gone from the show by the second commercial. Merman just shook her head. She could not imagine blowing such wonderful national exposure because of perceived wrongdoings on her part, real or imagined. Again Merman was concerned for her daughter's future.

Ethel decided it was time for another long vacation and took her son, Bobby, with her on another trip to Europe. This time, the duo would also visit Russia. Culture maven Bobby loved to travel, even to some place as bleak as Russia was during the height of the Cold War. Merman, as ever, only cared to rest, eat good food, and see what live entertainment there was to see. She did not at all enjoy Russia and could not wait to leave.

As 1966 rolled around, Ethel again decided it was time for a beauty makeover. She began to wear her hair piled high on her head in banana curls and redid her makeup. Perhaps this was to take away attention from her once again expanding waistline. She was now sixty years old, and her days of wearing a size eight dress were over.

She may not have been the hottest young thing around, but the boys at Harvard thought enough of her to name her the Hasty Pudding Club's Woman of the Year. She was honored to travel to the university and take part in the festivities, including the annual drag show put on by the members.

Merman was booked on an episode of "The Hollywood Palace" hosted by the one and only Fred Astaire. She introduced a doctored-up arrangement of *Some People* and was in glorious voice. Following that, Merman and Astaire did a medley that was almost as successful as the one done by Merman and Martin thirteen years earlier. Their divergent styles made for a delightful counterpoint. Here were perhaps the two most talented musical comedy performers in the world, each in excellent form. Their pairing worked so well that it is a shame they never made a film or any other television appearances together. This was show business magic!

As the spring of 1966 dethawed New York City, Irving Berlin came to Merman with an exciting idea. He wanted her to appear in a twentieth-anniversary revival of *Annie Get Your Gun* at Lincoln Center. At first, Ethel thought he was loony. She was much too old for the role and had made it quite clear that she wanted no part of another long run on Broadway. But the more she thought about it, the better the idea seemed. She was tired of touring with her *Ethel Merman Show* and liked the thought of being in her beloved New York all summer.

Also, there had been rumors that Ethel's voice was waning, and she wanted to prove that she could still thrill a crowd in a show. When Irving agreed to write a new number for her and to delete two of the minor songs from the original, Ethel agreed.

She was surrounded by a stellar cast. In smaller roles, Ethel had her old pal, Benay Venuta, and Jerry Orbach. Jerry had been the original El Gallo in *The Fantastiks*, where he introduced the haunting "Try to Remember." Today he is best known for playing a detective on television. There was one tense moment between Mermsky and co-star Jerry Orbach during the run of the *Annie* revival. Jerry began to get a laugh where previously there had been none. This annoyed Ethel, who asked the stage manager to speak to him. The beleaguered manager inquired of Orbach, who told him he was simply reacting to something Ethel was saying. This was repeated to Miss Merman, who told the stage manager, "I don't react to *his* lines, and he doesn't react to *mine!*" For her leading man, Ethel got the extremely handsome Bruce Yarnell. Although he was almost twenty-five years younger than she, audiences really didn't seem to care.

Perhaps Merm was a tad embarrassed by the age difference. Yarnell was not her favorite leading man. She was used to Ray Middleton's growling version of Frank Butler. In contrast, Bruce Yarnell was a pretty boy. Eth told one musician pal that she wished Yarnell would go to Woolworth's and buy himself a pair of balls!

The revival was a tremendous success. Ethel was really enjoying herself and loved stopping the show nightly with the new song, "An Old-Fashioned Wedding." It was a counterpoint song, similar in style to "You're Just in Love." RCA made an original cast album, and it was superbly produced. Merman was in great voice, and her delight in the material showed. This was probably the best recording Ethel ever made. Her voice is clear as a bell, exciting to listen to, and evidenced Ethel deep in character as Annie Oakley. The album was a big seller and got a lot of radio play, even on stations that were playing the Top 40.

The only trouble during the Lincoln Center run occurred opening night. When Ethel arrived for the performance, the

163

only signage stated *Annie Get Your Gun*. Lincoln Center did not yet feature stars on logos and posters. Ethel stopped dead in her tracks and demanded to see the stage manager. She told him in no uncertain terms that unless everything connected with the show said *Ethel Merman in Annie Get Your Gun*, there would be no Ethel Merman in *Annie Get Your Gun*. Signs and banners were hastily arranged for opening night to satisfy her.

The biggest star on Broadway was not stupid. With this, her fourteenth musical production, Merman was once again establishing her preeminence. She also was not unaware that she was far too old for the part. In order to give a wink to the audience and let them know that *she* knew, Ethel ad-libbed a line on opening night. In a scene where she was sitting at a dressing table, she looked into the mirror, patted herself under her chin, and said (referring to the Buffalo Bill show within a show), "Boy, this show has really aged me!" Naturally, the audience knew she was referring to her part in *Annie* and gave her an ovation. The line stayed in.

Berlin did a cute thing opening night. Aware of Ethel's allergy to roses, he had a gold pin in the shape of a rose made for her as a gift. The card was pure Berlin: *A sweet smelling rose/ makes a run in the nose/ So a Metal . . . Petal . . . for Etal!*

Ethel Merman, the biggest star on Broadway, seemed to have no trouble competing in an arena where names like Angela Lansbury, Barbra Streisand, and Barbara Harris were the new darlings of the critics. Through the years, no matter who else was a success on the stage, Mighty Ethel was always the top!

The revival production did so well that it completely sold out its limited run at Lincoln Center. The show was then taken on a brief tour, until it returned to New York at the Broadway Theatre for another limited engagement. After that, Ethel and the show toured through early 1967 when the show was scheduled to be taped as a special for NBC.

Weeks before the taping, Ethel made an appearance at the University of Southern California to inaugurate the new Cole Porter Library. In a symposium with music, she joined Frank Sinatra, Gene Kelly, Fred Astaire, and Jimmy Stewart in remembering Cole. Roger Edens played piano for everyone concerned—somehow he played best for Ethel. When Merman came to the mike, she sang so loudly she blew it out with her first notes! Frank Sinatra, who could not believe what Ethel had done, shouted out, "Hey, Merm! What're ya singing so loud for? You *got* the job!"

It was a lovely evening, and Ethel seemed particularly sentimental. She considered Cole to be a close friend. Porter returned the favor. In his last days, she was one of the few people he let see him. Despite his agonizing pain, cocktails were always ready in a silver shaker, hot hors d'oeuvres were on a warming tray, and the fudge that he served at every possible occasion was in a silver bowl. Even at his deathbed, Cole Porter wanted to be glamorous for his pal, Ethel.

Back to the revival of *Annie*. Something happened the night of the taping. Whether it was stress, worry over her children and parents, or the problem drinking that Ethel had begun fighting, Merman was not herself. Although the audience was already in line and some VIPs had been seated, Merman declared that there would be no audience or there would be no taping.

Everyone was shocked. Ethel had always worked best in front of live audiences, and the show would benefit from the comedy pacing an audience would give. The show had been cut down from its two-and-a-half-hour running time to fit into a two-hour television time slot with commercials. The timing had been based on having audience reactions. Without them, the show would run short.

Merman was insistent, and time was money. The audience was dismissed, and the show was taped. Ethel was not in good voice, and her comedy timing was off. Because of the hugely successful cast album and publicity, the special scored high in the ratings, but was a critical failure. It has never again been seen on television. There are rumors that the master tape was erased.

Why would Ethel blow a chance like this? It had been years since she'd had her own special or had even guest-hosted on someone else's show. If *Annie* had been successful, it could have led to other specials with Merman re-creating her parts in shows like *Call Me Madam* and *Gypsy*. Instead, she destroyed relationships with NBC, RCA, and Lincoln Center.

Perhaps Ethel was reacting to a blistering story in *TV Guide* that appeared that week. It was originally arranged to publicize the special, but instead spanked Merman soundly. Coworkers anonymously told stories of what a cold bitch she was and how difficult she had been during the run of the show. It was rare for *TV Guide* (at least in those days) to share hurtful gossip about a star of Merman's magnitude. And it does seem like gossip, because no one I spoke with could substantiate the article's claims, other than that Ethel was indeed too old for the part and much older than Bruce Yarnell. One of Ethel Merman's biggest triumphs ended on a sour note.

Nineteen sixty-seven was a year that would haunt Ethel for the rest of her life. With the debacle of the *Annie* special behind her, Merman asked her agents to book her on as many television shows as possible. In the early summer, she did another "Dean Martin Show" and filmed a highly popular episode of "That Girl" that reunited her with Lew Parker, her onstage husband in *Girl Crazy*.

It was also around this time that Ethel entered into a "friendship" that still has historians scratching their heads. According to Benay Venuta, and published after Ethel's death in the *New York Post* by no less than columnist Cindy Adams (who always tells the truth *exactly* as it is told to her), Ethel Merman and novelist Jacqueline Susann were engaged in a lesbian relationship. The two *were* friends, and Ethel had known her since the early 1950s. Venuta is now gone, Susann is now gone, and no one is willing to speculate on the record whether Benay's accusations were true.

There were photos of the two of them taken together (especially when Judy Garland came to New York to publicize her upcoming role in the film version of Susann's *Valley of the Dolls*) with their arms around each other. According to Benay, Ethel was so tired of being hurt by men that when Jackie (who had always worshiped Ethel) made a pass, she decided to try it. Venuta told of seeing them open-mouthed kissing and groping one another.

Adding fuel to the fire was Ethel's friendships with so many gay men. The older she got, Merman replaced old pals with fawning gay men who were happy to worship at the hem of her skirts. And Ethel's drinking, especially in the late 1960s and early 1970s, lost her a lot of old pals.

I mention the Susann thing because it is something that has been published and needed to be addressed in any book about Ethel Merman. If it is true, then it allows us a little insight into what Merman's emotions were like at this time. She was, indeed, fed up with men, their cheating and using her for notoriety and money. Merman had many reasons to be distressed, and if she fell for a beautiful, powerful woman who worshiped her, it would be understandable and a fascinating look at why some people dabble in bisexuality. If it is untrue, then Benay Venuta was a jealous, vindictive liar. Either way, who are we to judge?

Ethel was definitely getting plump again, and that distinctive wobble was even more obvious in her voice. She seemed tired and unfocused. Tragedy after tragedy was taking its toll on her nerves and self-esteem. Merman's drinking was beginning to get the better of her. For a little while in the late 1960s and early 1970s, Ethel Merman was precariously close to being an alcoholic.

It was in this depleted condition that Ethel Merman learned

in August 1967 that her daughter and namesake had died of an overdose of pills and liquor. It seems that Ethel Jr. had incautiously mixed antidepression medication and too much alcohol. She was separated from her husband, Bill Geary, and Bill had retained custody of the children. Just as it happened with her father before her, little Ethel had requested her kids for a weekend visit. Unlike her father, Ethel Jr. had not actually contemplated suicide. It was her young children who found her and went to get help. They were terrifically traumatized.

Merman asked Benay Venuta to accompany her on the plane to get to the funeral. Venuta, who through the years was either Ethel's best friend or worst enemy depending on how they were getting along, got so drunk on the plane that Ethel ended up having to take care of her instead of the other way around. At least it gave her something to do.

It never even occurred to Ethel to fight Bill Geary for the custody of the grandchildren. He had been their primary caretaker for quite a while and allowed Ethel very liberal visiting privileges. By all accounts, Bill Geary was a good guy.

Ethel Jr. was cremated, and Merman kept her ashes in a beautiful Dresden urn in her apartment. For three weeks, she was inconsolable, crying day and night. Finally, just four weeks after her daughter's death, Merman was talked into appearing on "The Ed Sullivan Show." It was done live in New York on a Sunday evening, required no travel, and Ethel had done the show many times before.

Many of her friends expected to see an Ethel Merman in mourning, wearing black and being subdued. What they saw on their television screens shocked them! There was Ethel, dressed in a bright yellow chiffon cocktail dress, singing a medley of "Ridin' High," "Get Happy," "Put On a Happy Face," and even "Happy Birthday"! Here was a woman in complete denial. The psychological implications of her song choices were obvious and sad.

Then, in a complete change of pace, Ethel sat down on a bench and gave a heartrending version of "This Is All I Ask." All of her pain, all of her guilt, poured out while singing this number. Nothing Edith Piaf or Judy Garland ever did was more poignant, as Ethel choked back tears while emoting her grief out.

Eventually, Merman put her daughter's ashes in a mausoleum outside of her beloved Denver. It was time to get back into life.

For the next two years, Ethel fell into a comfortable professional niche. She did television shows like "Batman," "The Hollywood Palace," "Tarzan," "The Carol Burnett Show," and "That's Life," and continued to visit Johnny Carson, Mike Douglas, and "The Match Game." People were warned by her agents not to mention Little Ethel or even to offer condolences lest Ethel dissolve in sobs and be unfocused in her work. One only needs to watch a rerun of "Batman" to see a Merman who is not all there. Her role as Lola Lasagne should have been a tour de force, especially since all her scenes were with excellent Burgess Meredith as the Penguin. Instead, it is obvious that Merman is just walking through it.

In the summers of 1968 and 1969, Ethel and Russell Nype toured summer stock with a revival of *Call Me Madam*. Discovered in the cast was a young Donna McKechnie, who would later rise to fame as a major Broadway star. Tom Hatten, who went on to become a popular Los Angeles television personality, was also in the show.

Merm and Nype would drive between dates in his little sports car. They were close pals and enjoyed both seeing the country by car and one another's company. It was Ethel's job to read the map and be in charge of the snacks that were kept in an ice chest in the backseat. The ice covered a false bottom. Underneath it was another kind of ice, Ethel's more than $100,000 in personal diamond jewelry that she actually wore in the show.

It is not certain why this revival was not brought in to New York, except perhaps that it was a bit old-fashioned and out-dated. "I Like Ike" was hardly an audience pleasing number at a time when one of the big numbers in *Hair* was called "Sodomy." *Promises, Promises*; *Hello, Dolly!*; *Cabaret*; *Mame*; and *Fiddler on the Roof* were all still running, but there weren't many new shows to take their place.

It was not lost on Ethel that the Great White Way was changing. The Broadway she knew was hitting its last zenith and very slowly was fading away. Mary Martin had retired to Brazil; contemporaries like Al Jolson, Bert Lahr, Gertrude Lawrence, Fanny Brice, and Gaxton and Moore were dead. Gershwin, Porter, Hammerstein, and Fields were also dead. Berlin and Rodgers were in semiretirement. So were most of Ethel's leading men, like Jack Haley, Bill Johnson, Ray Middleton, and Paul Lukas. Bob Hope and Jimmy Durante were strictly movies, television, and Vegas. It was getting harder and harder to mount new musicals. Production costs and ticket prices were skyrocketing.

With all of this on her mind, Ethel thought twice before turning down the next show offered to her. Once again it was David Merrick, and once again the show was *Hello, Dolly!* Merrick wondered if Ethel would be interested in joining the Broadway company if Jerry Herman added back in the two songs he had eliminated from the score when Merman originally turned down the show. *That* intrigued Ethel. It was one thing to just step into other actresses' shoes, it was another to have the show redone to suit her. Another factor playing on Ethel's mind was her aging parents. Their health was no longer good, and a run in a Broadway show would keep her in New York and close to mom and pop.

So Ethel agreed to follow Carol Channing, Ginger Rogers, Betty Grable, Martha Raye, Pearl Bailey, Phyllis Diller, Bibi Osterwald, Mary Martin, and Eve Arden from the Broadway, London, and national touring company versions of the show in the role of Dolly Levi. Merrick added Ethel's two songs ("World, Take Me Back" and "Love Look in My Window") to the first act. Nothing was cut. The show simply ran twenty extra minutes.

On Ethel's opening night, the audience reacted in pandemonium rarely seen. Whether it was a sense that this really was going to be Ethel's last Broadway hurrah or that audiences were now often made up of enthusiastic gay men who idolized her, every single song received a profound ovation. Both new songs got standing ovations. And this happened every night. The extra applause alone added ten minutes to the show.

It is true that the addition of the two new songs added much depth to the character of Dolly Levi. Previous Dollies had been cute, clever, cloying, or cantankerous, but Ethel gave her balls. She performed the part (and the new songs) magnificently. Without a chorus, without a bevy of dancers behind her, these two numbers were performed with just Ethel Merman in a spotlight by herself. She was glorious. The biggest star on Broadway was enjoying her fifteenth and final Broadway musical success.

An added bonus was the casting of Russell Nype as Cornelius Hackl. Nype was much too old for the part of a virginal man in his twenties, but his boyish charms were perfect for the part. Through the years, Ethel and Russell had become very close. Yet, in just a few years' time, Russell would no longer speak to Ethel. Her behavior while intoxicated infuriated him, and he could no longer stand to be her whipping boy. A friendship of more than twenty years died in an alcoholic blur.

While in *Dolly*, Ethel received the Actor's Fund of America's commendation for outstanding service and generosity. She had never been one of those performers who ran to benefit after benefit. What she did for others less fortunate than she was usually done in private and not publicized. Merman had made a major donation to the fund and had performed an extra performance of *Dolly* to benefit the fund.

It was a great tonic for the hurting Ethel, who was still grieving for her daughter. Over and over, she would ask her friends why this tragedy had happened to her. There would never be any understanding or acceptance on Ethel's part. The slightest mention of Little Ethel would dissolve her in sobs. Every time she read an article stating that her daughter committed suicide, an angry and confused Ethel would fly off the handle in a bitter and tearful rage.

Merman had little time to worry about the past. Her beloved parents were getting very frail. Her mother had experienced a slight stroke a little while earlier, so Ethel had her mom and pop moved from the apartment they had occupied since 1931 and into a smaller one in her own building with a similar floor plan. She personally arranged the furniture, placing things in familiar positions so her folks wouldn't have to do too much adjusting. Even toothbrushes and medicine bottles were put in their old places so nothing would seem out of place.

Who knows why bad things seem to follow goodwill. Soon after heaping all of this attention on her folks, burglars broke into Ethel's apartment and completely wiped her out of jewelry and expensive keepsakes. Gone were all the diamonds that

Sherman Billingsley had given her. Taken were her wedding rings, minks, chinchillas, ermines, gold bracelets, and 1951 Tony Award. Even the glass Eisenhower drank out of during the 1946 production of *Annie Get Your Gun* was missing. The loss was more than $125,000.

Ethel's reaction was mixed. She was insured for some of it, but did not replace any of it. From that moment on, Ethel Merman only bought and wore costume jewelry and cloth coats. It was like part of her life had been stolen, and she could never get it back. She shrugged it off as yet another bad thing that happened to her. Her heart was getting calloused.

Ethel stayed with *Hello, Dolly!* long enough for it to become (at the time) the longest-running musical in history. All together, Merman spent nine months in the show. She truly enjoyed the cast (which included a young Georgia Engel before her success on television's "Mary Tyler Moore"), but she was tired. The author first met her after one performance, and the only words an exhausted Merman could utter were "thanks, kid!" as I opened the limousine door for her. For once and for all, she declared her retirement from the Broadway stage.

That decision devastated composers Jule Styne and Sammy Cahn. They had written the score for a new musical based on the play, *Lilies of the Field*. Their new work, called *Look to the Lillies*, was conceived and especially tailored for the talents of Ethel Merman and Sammy Davis Jr. When Merman turned it down, so did Davis, and it eventually wound up starring Shirley Booth and Al Freeman Jr. The show ran twenty-five performances.

The first thing Ethel did after *Dolly* closed was to appear on "The Merv Griffin Show," which was then on CBS late night opposite Johnny Carson. Merv asked her to sing the two new songs from *Dolly*, and she agreed to fly to Los Angeles. Also on the program was Ralph Edwards, game-show producer extraordinaire. He had hosted the very popular "This is Your Life" all through the 1950s. Unbeknown to Ethel, he was mounting a new version for syndication. Merv asked Edwards how he surprised his victims. He pulled a book from under his feet, ripped off the paper wrapping, and turned to Ethel, telling her that this, indeed, was her life!

An emotional Ethel dissolved into gushing tears. She cried so hard that the taping had to be held up a half hour for Merman to get her composure. They weren't sure they could continue, so emotional was their star. When they finally calmed her down, Ethel spent a tearful half hour with Benay Venuta, her pals from Astoria, and her grandchildren, Barbara and Michael. There were no celebrities, no Lucille Ball or Ginger Rogers, just people from Ethel's private past.

Also missing were her parents. They were just too frail to fly to Los Angeles. Not long after, Agnes Zimmermann had a heart attack followed by a massive stroke. Immediately, Ethel canceled all of her bookings to be near her mother. Agnes was almost catatonic. She never again was able to communicate with Ethel or her husband, Edward. Merm spent every morning with her mother at the hospital. Only on weekends and late evenings did Ethel get away for a little rest or an attempt at relaxation.

Although this was a lovely daughterly thing to do, looking back in perspective one must wonder why Ethel was so quick to give up her career for her mother when she would not spare the same sort of time for her marriages or her troubled daughter. Would Bob Levitt have survived mental illness if Ethel had retired and helped him to help himself? Would Little Ethel still be alive if Ethel had taken a year off from performing and made sure her daughter had the help and guidance she needed? Naturally, these are rhetorical questions that can never be answered.

They are moot points, but they must have occurred to Ethel. She did not work at all in 1971 once her mother fell ill. Every day, she went to the hospital and sat by her mother's side. For months and months, Ethel gently talked to her beloved mother, soothing her, even singing to her. Mother and daughter had traded places, and now Ethel Zimmermann was her mother's keeper and caretaker. She hired expensive private nurses and made sure that Agnes had the best of care. Ethel also looked after Edward, who seemed lost and alone without Agnes at home. She ate all her meals with her parents, rarely socializing with friends. So as not to get bored, Ethel volunteered as a candy striper at the hospital. That way she would be nearby if Agnes needed her, but gave her a chance to move around and take her mind off her mother's degenerating health.

One day, Ethel was in the elevator at the hospital, wearing her uniform. A couple got on, and the woman said, "Has anyone ever told you that you look like a young Ethel Merman?" Before she could answer, the man said, "Ethel Merman *wishes* she looked as good as you!" Waiting for the doors to open, Ethel said, "I *am* Ethel Merman!" and made a perfect comedy exit. Ethel the trouper continued to do her volunteer work for years whenever she was in New York until her own failing health precluded it a decade later.

Among the only professional work Ethel did in 1972 was to fly to London to record an album. It was an offer she could not resist. Her old alma mater, Decca Records, wanted Ethel to make an album of her biggest hits with a fifty-piece orchestra and chorus. Supposedly, Stanley Black was doing the arrangements, but basically they were lifted from those made for her in the past by Billy May and Roger Edens. In an effort to save money and time, all the orchestral parts were prerecorded, and Ethel sang to a playback.

Although Ethel would have been better served singing to a live orchestra, the album was skillfully marketed. For months, London Phase Four Records (a stepchild of Decca) placed ads in all the best magazines, with a lovely Francesco Scavullo photo of Ethel and the name *Merman Sings Merman*. It became her best-selling pop album and was supposed to be the first of a series: *Merman Sings Kern*, *Merman Sings Styne*, etc.

Ethel would have stayed in London longer if she had accepted her next offer: to do a revival of *Gypsy* on the West End. Merman, although flattered, immediately dismissed the offer. The producers pleaded with her, offering to bring her parents by ocean liner to London with a doctor and nurse in attendance at all times. They arranged to get Queen Elizabeth's personal physician to attend to her folks the entire time she'd be in London. Ethel stood her ground. She was not going to risk her parents' health just to be in another show. Angela Lansbury got the job instead and made a hit with the show both in London and on Broadway, earning her another Tony Award.

There was a coda to this story. After Lansbury opened in New York, a reporter asked Ethel if she would follow Angela into the show. She sweetly answered, "I wouldn't follow Angela Lansbury with a shovel!"

Meanwhile back in New York, the people who put on the Tony Awards decided to give Ethel a special lifetime Tony. Would she consider singing on the telecast?

That simple request turned into a miniconcert. Ethel sang full versions of "I Got Rhythm," "I Get a Kick Out of You," "Make It Another Old-Fashioned," "You Can't Get a Man with a Gun," "You're Just in Love," and "Everything's Coming Up Roses." She was in great voice considering she had hardly sung in more than a year, but she looked as if she had aged overnight. Ethel was now fat, plain and simple, and looked like a retired opera singer. Inevitably, she received a standing ovation.

The other honoree that night was Richard Rodgers. He had run into Ethel at the Sardi's bar a few weeks earlier and asked for a reconciliation. That's all it took. He gave in first, and Ethel was satisfied. Twenty-four years of enmity were wiped away.

**23**

After months of suffering, Agnes Zimmermann quietly slipped away on January 14, 1974. Her death was both a relief and a devastating loss. Like Ethel Jr., Agnes was cremated, and her ashes deposited in a Dresden urn that resided with Ethel. In lieu of flowers, Merman requested that her friends make contributions to Roosevelt Hospital. So much money came in that a garden was planted with a plaque honoring Agnes affixed to the fence.

Edward Zimmermann was in his nineties and legally blind. Ethel hired a nurse/companion for her father and made sure to have a drink with him at 5 P.M. every day. After Agnes's death, Ethel cut way back on her drinking, and switched from Champagne and Scotch to Almaden Chablis. She told friends that her teeth had become sensitive to other forms of liquor, but Ethel knew the hard liquor was affecting her. She never totally gave up drinking, but she adjusted her intake.

Once she was sure her father was settled, the next order of

business was to spend some quality time with her grandchildren. Over the next few years, Grandma Ethel took Barbara and Michael to Disney World, Jamaica, and Colorado. She seemed to have a much easier relationship with them than with her own kids. Ethel's son, Bob, had studied stagecraft and was picking up work as a lighting designer and director in summer stock. Bob had married Barbara Colby, a promising young actress whom Ethel liked quite a bit.

Finally, with her family fairly well settled, Ethel began to take her career in hand again. She had barely worked for two years. In 1973, Ethel signed to appear on two television specials, "Ed Sullivan's Broadway" and "S'Wonderful, S'Marvelous, S'Gershwin." Ethel's finely tailored gowns were now a thing of the past, as she wore less expensive caftans in which to perform. These both hid her thick body and thin bank account. Her marriages to Six and Borgnine had drained her. Two years of private nurses and no income had depleted her. Ethel could not afford to retire. She really needed the money.

Merman flew to London twice more to record two more albums for Decca. For some reason, they abandoned the originally intended *Merman Sings* format for yet another studio album of *Annie Get Your Gun* that was badly done and totally unnecessary. It ended up in ninety-nine-cent bins upon release. The other was an album of songs not associated with Ethel called *Ethel's Ridin' High*. She used this album as a launching pad on the talk-show circuit, visiting Dinah Shore, Merv Griffin, Johnny Carson, and Mike Douglas on their respective shows.

For one "Tonight Show" appearance in early 1974, Ethel should have stayed home. Just before she left New York to fly to the coast, her father had a massive heart attack. Once she was certain he was stable, she flew to Denver to put her mother's ashes next to her daughter's and then flew to Burbank to tape Johnny's show. Ethel looked awful, as if someone had beaten her up. To add insult to injury, both her songs were marred by amateurish technical problems that embarrassed her. But Ethel needed Johnny Carson, so she said nothing.

She spent the summer of 1974 touring summer tents and theaters-in-the-round with Carroll O'Connor of "All in the Family" fame. The Great Ethel was relegated to being his opening act, although she received special guest-star billing. The two also did duets of "You're the Top" and "You're Just in Love." On talk shows, Merm made quite a bit out of how much she adored working with Carroll. Privately, she was agonizing over being *anyone's* opening act, even if he was the star of the number-one show on television.

During 1974 and 1975, this was the bulk of her career. Merman was no longer an "A" name as a television guest star. While contemporaries like Kate Smith and Jimmy Durante still frequented shows like "The Sonny and Cher Comedy Hour" and "Tony Orlando and Dawn," Ethel could not seem to break through. She turned down a job on "The Odd Couple" because they wanted her to play Jack Klugman's mother! It was foolishness to think that she would accept such a job when Jack had played her lover in *Gypsy*. Ethel was never friendly toward Jack again.

On March 9, 1975, Ethel joined a stellar cast in *A Gala Tribute to Josh Logan*. Each performer did something special that reflected their relationship with director Logan. Although Ethel had been directed in two shows by Josh (*Stars in Your Eyes* and *Annie Get Your Gun*), she unwisely chose to sing her hits medley instead of songs directly from either of the shows. She was in terrible voice, and the audience was shocked at both her choice of material and vocal quality.

In the summer of 1975, something happened to totally reignite Ethel's stalled career. She was invited to appear with Arthur Fiedler and the Boston Pops on their PBS television series. Merman was terribly excited to sing with such a large symphony orchestra, and it showed. She looked beautiful and sang fabulously. The show went so well that PBS held it back a year and aired it as part of their bicentennial salute in 1976. Even *TV Guide* made big mention of it, giving the show one of its "close-ups" with a lively photo of Ethel singing.

Soon, offers began to come in from all over the country offering Ethel work to sing with symphonies and philharmonics. She retooled her stage show, eliminating about half the songs and sticking with just her biggest hits. From 1976 until 1983, Ethel Merman was singing somewhere in the United States anywhere from two to five times a month. The pace was perfect for a woman who was seventy, and the money ($10,000 per show plus expenses) kept her from having to dip anymore into what was left of her capital.

The mid- and late-1970s found an elderly Ethel Merman still being able to do what she did best. Her voice was no longer as loud, and it did sometimes have that annoying wobble, but she was still a showstopper. Between her concert work, appearances on talk shows and game shows, record sales, and continuing investment income from *Call Me Madam* and *Happy Hunting*, Merman was financially secure for the first time in years.

This was what Ethel had been longing for ever since *Gypsy*: to be able to work as often as she felt like without being a slave to an eight-performance-a-week schedule. And miraculously, as time went by, her voice got stronger. All seemed to be going well.

Ethel was in for one more tragedy. In late 1975, her much loved daughter-in-law was signed to be a costar on Cloris

Leachman's new series, "Phyllis." Although she and Bob had separated (which infuriated Ethel), the girls remained very close and often spoke on the phone. Two weeks into filming, Barbara was leaving an acting workshop when she and a male companion were gunned down in cold blood. Merman happened to be on the West Coast at the time and was staying at the Beverly Hills Hotel. When she got the phone call, she was once again devastated. It seemed that everyone she truly had deep feelings for was disappearing in tragic ways.

Barbara was a follower of one of the cult religions so popular in Los Angeles at the time. The memorial was held at their house of worship, and Ethel was dumbfounded. Mystical chants were incanted, and half-dressed people were in attendance. Merman was ordered to take off her shoes. Incense burned, and Merman burned worse. Finally, guests were asked to speak. Ethel strode up to the microphone. "I don't know what this shit is all about," she gently shared at the top of her voice, "but when I call her tomorrow morning, she isn't going to be there, and I am goddamned angry about it!"

Ethel had slowly replaced old friendships with three very strong ladies: Rose Marie, Kaye Ballard, and Carole Cook. All of them were very talented, very funny, successful, and understood how difficult it was to be a woman in show business. They shared Ethel's joys and sorrows in the last ten years of her life and loved her in spite of her sometimes difficult personality quirks. On the male side, she just adored Richard Deacon, Merv Griffin, and Tony Cointreau, scion of the liquor family.

Ethel enjoyed spending time with Kaye in her Palm Springs house (originally built by Desi Arnaz after his divorce from Lucille Ball) and lounging in her pool. They both shared a passion for easy conversation, a glass of wine, and the luxury of relaxing out of the public eye. Kaye still has a sign hanging in her cucina that says "Ethel's Kitchen," which Merman had gifted her.

Ethel had met Carole Cook through their mutual friend Lucille Ball. When Carole came East to star in *42nd Street* on Broadway, they saw one another often for dinner. And Ethel had known Rose Marie for decades. Rosie was a survivor, a great talent who had overcome being a child star to become one of the first stars of Las Vegas show rooms (and later Broadway and television). She knew perhaps better than anyone how difficult it was to be a female star over the years. Merman trusted her and often sought her advice. Perhaps of all her friends, Rose Marie understood Ethel best.

It was Rose Marie who helped get Ethel through her mother's illness. Rosie was Mike Douglas's cohost on his eponymous show in Philadelphia. Knowing that Ethel was practically a prisoner at Roosevelt Hospital where her mother was being treated, she asked Mike to invite Ethel down, telling her that Rose Marie needed her. The two ladies dueted on "You're Just in Love." It shook Ethel out of her depression and gave her a needed mental respite just when she needed it most.

Ethel was extremely devoted to Rose Marie. She would often travel all over the country to attend Rosie's performances in nightclubs, summer stock, and benefits. Once, when Rosie was spending time with a man she perceived as a possible new husband, Ethel told him to treat her right or she would cut off his balls.

When Rosie was hired to be the hostess of an Easter Seals telethon in Hawaii, the first person she asked to join her was Ethel. While there, the two broads met a young man who was a former poster child named John. When they heard he wanted to get married, they threw him a wedding in Ethel's suite, paying for everything. Mermo sang "They Say It's Wonderful" with no accompaniment, and everyone cried.

It was during this time that bawdy, down-to-earth Ethel had her one and only encounter with the burgeoning adult film industry. Music and film producer Allan Carr decided it would be a gregarious giggle to invite half of Hollywood to a party at a porno theatre. Providing tickets and lavish refreshments, Carr had his reluctant guests arrive in twos and threes to the now-defunct Pussycat Theatre on Santa Monica Boulevard in West Hollywood.

Merm and pal Rose Marie were escorted by Peter Marshall, as all three had recently finished shooting a week of "Hollywood Squares" together. It was here that a good example of Eth's double-sided morality surfaced. While she reveled in humorous fowl language, bawdy stories, and her own personal sexcapades, she was shocked and indignant at what she saw on the screen.

The film was a Swedish import, very popular in 1975. Half of the film was in Swedish, and half was dubbed in English. After one actress spoke in Swedish while pleasuring a man, she magically switched to English while pleasuring a woman. Peter quipped, "Oh look! She's bilingual!"

Merman laughed so hard she nearly fell on the floor.

Ethel knew that Rose Marie was hired, in 1970, to play Joan Rivers's mother in the Broadway bound play *Fun City*. She flew out of town to surreptitiously catch a performance. The play was dreadful, and Rosie's part hardly existed. The former child star received a message backstage to meet Merman in her limousine directly after the performance. Ro did as she was told and found a furious Ethel wrapped in a mink coat. The biggest star on Broadway shared her anger and horror that Rosie was in such an inferior product. They motored to an apartment Ethel had borrowed from a friend, and Rose Marie found Maureen Stapleton and several other Broadway stars, all there to guide her. Merman had organized the entire thing.

It was Rose Marie who was there for Ethel when her daughter-in-law was murdered and who would vociferously defend Ethel whenever anyone talked badly about her or mentioned the Borgnine or Susann affairs.

Rose Marie was Ethel Merman's devoted friend. It is no wonder that Ethel always called her "Baby," harkening back to the days when Merm was a youthful Broadway star and Rosie had her own radio show and was called Baby Rose Marie.

Ethel's tastes had simplified as she aged. She no longer cared to be fancy just for the sake of fancy. Her food was basic meat and potatoes. She eschewed nouvelle cuisine or anything with rich sauces. Her favorite snacks were yogurt and cheese and crackers, always washed down with tea. She paid for her own meals and did not allow others to "treat" her. As much as she could manage it, Eth wanted control in her life. So much had seemed out of control for so many years.

On the evenings when she had no social plans, the aging Merman heated chicken franks in her toaster oven for dinner and was asleep by eight o'clock. She didn't enjoy reading or watching television. Phone calls were limited to her son and grandchildren unless the caller had some juicy gossip to share. Then she could sit on the phone for hours. She loved to write letters, which were all personally typed by Ethel in her trademark cursive font. If she entertained, she had drinks and hors d'oeuvres delivered, then took her guests to a restaurant. Ethel did not like the new Broadway musicals with their rock-and-roll arrangements and overly microphoned singers. She rarely even went to the theater unless she was invited or a friend was performing.

Ethel's professional life was now confined to concert work

and television. Programs such as "The Big Show," "The Ted Knight Special," "The Muppet Show," and "Steve and Eydie Salute Cole Porter" welcomed Ethel as a guest. Merman made her final cosmetic do-over in 1976, but it was a fiasco. Friends took her to a beauty salon in Bel Air where her shoulder-length hair (she'd worn it in a shoulder-length long flip or pulled back in a horse's tail since *Dolly*) was cut into a modern bob with bangs that was blown dry into place. It took years off Ethel's looks, and she was very pleased.

The next morning, Ethel did not have the skill or the tools to repeat what had been done in the salon. Instead, she did her own hair the old-fashioned way with curlers and teasing. She now *added* years to her looks, but no one could dissuade her. This was her look for the rest of her days.

In early 1977, producer and manager Anna Sosenko came to Ethel with an exciting idea. How would she like to do a one-night-only concert with Mary Martin to benefit the theater collection at the Museum of the City of New York? Ethel was enchanted by the idea, but didn't think Mary would do it. Martin's husband and manager, Richard Halliday, had passed away in 1972, and Mary had shunned the public eye.

Obviously, little Anna was very persuasive. Mary agreed, and the date of May 15, 1977, was set for the benefit. Mary and Ethel rehearsed for almost two months. Ethel was going to do set pieces from her concert show in the first act. It was really Mary who needed to get her solo numbers in order. Much was made of Ethel's insistence on limousines for both of them, as well as freshly made costumes. This was only fair, as both ladies were donating their talents. They were up to their talented necks in publicity and working very hard.

The author dropped a note to Ethel, decrying not having been able to get a ticket to the concert. About a week later, Ted

Fetter (cousin to Cole Porter and the curator of the theater collection) called me. "Hello, Geoffrey? Can you hear them in the background? [Ethel and Mary were rehearsing their opening number.] Ethel felt terribly and wanted me to personally call you and apologize. The concert is so sold out. She couldn't get her best friend in at this point. She hopes you understand!"

Although many of her friends from decades past claimed that Ethel had become an unreasonable bitch in her dealings with them, in all of my (and our mutual friends') dealings with her, I found Ethel Merman to be polite, almost shy, mistrustful of fawning fans and strangers, but extremely courteous and thoughtful of the people around her. She was a lady when it mattered.

The night of the show, which was done at the Broadway Theatre, the crowds jammed Times Square. Every celebrity in town was there, from Mayor Abe Beame to Lauren Bacall to Ann Miller. I have never seen anything like it (obviously, I got in), not even attending major awards shows. The police had to form barricades to hold the crowds back. It was pandemonium. At a time when KISS, Abba, the Bee Gees, and Donna Summer were the biggest musical stars in the world, Merman and Martin practically caused a riot in the heart of Little Old New York!

The concert was sold out in less than thirty minutes after the box office opened. A second concert was discussed, but Mary would only do it once. A television network offered to make a special out of it, but again Mary nixed it. She was terrified at the prospect of performing again and wanted as little pressure as possible.

Sosenko brilliantly routined the opening of the show. The lights came up on two big hoops with paper caricatures of Merman in *Gypsy* and Martin in *South Pacific*. Offstage, their two voices sang, a cappella, the opening lyrics to "Send in the Clowns." When the orchestra joined in, the two old war-horses pounced through the paper to appear in the same costumes and poses as the caricatures. Mary was in her oversized sailor suit as Nellie Forbush and Ethel in her frumpy coat and hair ribbon as Momma Rose (she even carried the little dog!).

Neither woman could say a word for almost five minutes. The standing ovation seemed as if it would never cease. When the pandemonium died down, E and M finished the song and went offstage to change. Cyril Ritchard, Mary's costar in *Peter Pan*, came on stage as the narrator for the evening. The rest of the first act had both ladies singing songs they had made famous. It was obvious that Mary was suffering from stage fright as well as ongoing throat problems, but the audience ate her up. One does not lose star quality! Merman was all MERMAN and quite frankly vocally blew Mary off the stage. Her version of "Blow, Gabriel, Blow" was so powerful that jaded middle-aged performers who should have known better were jumping up and down in their chairs with excitement. I have never seen anything like it in my life.

The second act opened with a re-creation of the title song from *Hello, Dolly!* The waiters were a who's who of Broadway leading men: Larry Hagman (Mary's son), Joel Grey, Burgess Meredith, Yul Brynner, and many others. As both ladies had played the role, the audience was unsure as to who might be coming down the staircase (which was hidden behind a curtain). When the band began to play the music, the curtain rose to reveal *two* staircases. E and M descended down identical staircases, wearing identical gowns.

Once again, nothing could be heard for minutes as the audience literally screamed in delight. Each woman acted as if she were alone on the stage, not even noticing the other.

Finally, Mary looked over at Ethel and sang, "Well! Hello . . . Ethel!" Merman acted as if completely surprised and with a limp wrist and in her gayest voice replied, "Well, hello MARY!" Once more the show was stopped at Ethel's inside joke to all the homosexual men in the audience. The rest of the number was pure magic.

After a short film clip from the 1953 Ford telecast (to give Ethel and Mary a chance to catch their breaths and change costumes), Ritchard introduced them once again to repeat the medley in person. Then the ladies ended the proceedings with an audience sing-along of "There's No Business Like Show Business."

In the back of her mind, Ethel had been losing heart about her ability to please an audience. For the first time, she had even secretly entertained ideas of retirement. But with this concert, Ethel knew she still had it, and seemingly years came off her age. She was going to continue thrilling audiences until she dropped dead, she thought.

# 24

As seemed to always happen in Ethel's life, soon after the concert she had to deal with loss. Edward Zimmermann passed away at the age of ninety-nine. This time, Ethel accepted death as she knew her father had lived a full, long life and had never suffered. His ashes, too, were placed in a Dresden urn and given to Ethel.

Sentimental Merman then acquired the ashes of Bob Levitt, as well as those of Agnes and Ethel Jr., and kept the urns all together in a closet. She got in the habit of talking to the urns as if her loved ones were still there. She would sing to them on their birthdays, as well as Christmas carols during the Yuletide season. She had her mom and pop, best loved husband, and only daughter all together to visit with as she pleased. Some of her friends thought she was off her rocker, but it gave Ethel peace.

Another thing that brought Ethel solace was a publication called *The Daily Word*. It was and is a small monthly magazine containing Christian devotions, prayers, Bible readings, and articles about faith. Merman devoured it monthly. If something particularly appealed to her, she cut it out and pasted it into a notebook she kept near her bed.

A small ceramic Christmas tree was kept on a table near her front door, always lit to remind her of God's grace and love. Angry Ethel was beginning to heal and let love back into her life. She was ready for a new challenge.

To that end, Merman had her agents shop book deals. She wanted another reason to visit talk shows besides just showing up to sing a song or two. And she knew that a well-mounted publicity campaign would only make her star rise higher again. She hired George Eels to write the book for her. Eels had penned a very well-received book about Cole Porter. It was Eels who did all the research, and it was he who recorded Ethel as he interviewed her, weaving her reminiscences into a story.

George was concerned from the first that Ethel was not being very honest about her past. She was blurring dates to hide her age, leaving out interesting and important details in order to protect her image. He really wanted her to tell her side of the marriage to Ernest Borgnine, but Ethel was afraid of being sued. So she came up with the idea of titling a page "My Marriage to Ernest Borgnine" and leaving it blank. It was great fun on talk shows, but didn't do much for the book.

Just before the book was published, Ethel shot a pilot for a television sitcom. At this point, she really didn't want to work that hard every week, but an occasionally recurring role would suit her just fine. Ethel would play Lolly Rogers, a loud, over-bearing Broadway star with a mouse of a son. It seems her daughter had died and left her small son for Lolly to raise. The aggressive mother decided that her son (played by Austin Pendleton) would make a better mother than she and foists the

192

kid on him. Ethel would appear in the show perhaps once a month.

If this does not sound like a very funny scenario for a sitcom, you are right. "You're Gonna Love It Here" only appeared on CBS once, buried in the summer with other pilots that did not sell.

Ethel spent much of 1978 pushing the book, and it sold very well. When the notoriety from that was all used up, Merman looked for a similar project to milk for publicity. Someone got the idea that an album of disco music sung by Ethel Merman would be solid gold. Meetings were held, negotiations made, and A&M records hired Peter Matz to produce and orchestrate a disco album with Merman.

Disco had swept the world in the mid- and late-1970s, although by 1979 it was already showing signs of fading. Punk and rap were just around the corner, and even disco diva Donna Summer wouldn't be on the charts for long. Several stars had already taken the disco plunge with varying degrees of success, and one could buy such songs from Barbra Streisand, Bette Midler, Cher, Liza Minnelli, and other luminaries. Ethel was brought into the studio to sing to piano accompaniment. Musicians and singers would be brought in later to be electronically mixed with Merman's raw vocals. Even Donna Summer herself showed up to give Ethel some help with the disco beat.

Rather than burden Ethel with new material, it was decided she would sing her own songs. *That* was the big mistake. Merman's powerful voice singing "I Will Survive" might have been a spellbinder. Ethel belting out "I Get a Kick Out of You" to a disco beat was something else again.

The album made Merman a laughingstock. Although she was actually in excellent voice, the backgrounds and orchestrations were ludicrous. Despite its shortcomings Merman got tons of free publicity from the album. Ethel appeared on every possible television program, from "The Tonight Show" to "Kids Are People, Too." A record signing was held in New York City at the old Korvette's store on Herald Square. People were lined up for hours to get her autograph, and Ethel was gracious to every single one of them. I was there, as well, and asked Ethel if she would record "Gabriel" on her next disco album. She turned to me and said, under her breath, "You really want to hear *more* of this?"

Some people actually blamed this album for the demise of disco. Ethel had lived through fifty years of show-business fads. She found the whole thing amusing. As soon as every possible drop of notoriety was rung out of the situation, Ethel moved on.

For the next two years, Ethel continued her performing routine with few changes. She continued to play her concerts with symphonies all over the United States and Canada. For reasons she never understood, she was no longer booked on "The Tonight Show," but was seen frequently with Merv Griffin. Merv was a big booster of Ethel's and often built theme shows around her. Griffin encouraged her to sing new material and was able to get Ethel to tell her stories in engaging fashions.

In 1979, Danny Kaye's wife, Sylvia Fine, called Ethel with an offer to appear on a PBS special she was producing and hosting saluting the great musicals of Broadway. She wanted to know if Merman would re-create "Anything Goes" and "I Get a Kick Out of You" with copies of the original costumes, sets, and orchestrations. Additionally, Sylvia would interview her and introduce none other than Rock Hudson to join Ethel in "You're the Top."

Although there was practically no money, Merman agreed because she thought it would be fun to capture the original flavor of the show. She was agreeable and sweet as pie during the rehearsal process, right up until dress rehearsal. When Sylvia began to interview her with the same questions Ethel had heard all week, Merman stopped the proceedings and got very angry with Fine. She accused Sylvia of trying to pull a fast one and embarrass her with new questions she had never before heard.

Fine didn't know what to do. She tried to placate Ethel and calm her down, but Ethel was not having any. When they rehearsed "Anything Goes," again Ethel stopped the rehearsal claiming that she did not recognize the lyrics and that they were not Cole Porter's originals. Now Sylvia was getting worried. Ethel's color was getting gray, and she seemed disoriented.

Despite Mrs. Kaye's concern, Ethel would not see a doctor. She did, however, agree to have Sylvia's masseur come in and help relax her. After an hour of therapy, Ethel's color returned, and she now recognized both the lyrics and the interview questions.

Although her performance ended up being excellent, Ethel's behavior was unusual, to say the least.

Ethel was very loyal to Carole Cook, often going to see her performances over and over. She was Tom Troupe's date for the opening night of *42nd Street* in which Carole had a large part. The evening was an enormous success for all concerned, garnering over fourteen curtain calls. Finally, producer David Merrick stepped on stage to announce the death of director Gower Champion.

There was a stunned silence, both in the audience and on stage. You could have cut the tension with a knife. Ethel, in her loudest stage whisper, turned to Tom and said, "Well, if you gotta go, *that's* the way to go!" The entire audience heard her, shared a laugh and then began to exit the theatre.

More vistas opened up by 1980. Merman became an occasional member of the "Love Boat" cast, playing Gofer's mother, Roz. There was a special two-hour version where Ethel got to sing with the likes of Carol Channing, Ann Miller, Della Reese, Cab Calloway, and Van Johnson. She even appeared in a cameo role in the movie satire, *Airplane*. In it, she played a shell-shocked Vietnam veteran who *thinks* he is Ethel Merman. It was great satire, and Ethel convulsed audiences as she tried to sing "Everything's Coming Up Roses" as attendants restrained and tranquilized her.

One of Ethel's great joys in this season of her life was getting close to Mary Martin. They had always been true admirers of one another's talents and had been friendly. But clashing performance schedules, touring, and filmmaking had left them little time to spend together. Now they had that luxury, but it was almost cut off.

Mary had been visiting her best friend (and some say lover), Janet Gaynor, in San Francisco when the ladies were hurt in a bad car accident. Mary's pelvis was broken, but she was otherwise all right. Janet survived, but eventually died from her injuries.

Ethel Merman was among the first to call the hospital when she heard about the accident. She continued to call Mary every day, offering encouragement and a kick in the behind when it was needed. It took Mary months of excruciatingly painful rehabilitation, but she did learn to walk again and went back to work. She had been hosting the series "Over Easy" on PBS, and almost as soon as she returned to the set, invited Ethel to join her as a guest on the show.

The two old broads had a grand time together, and Ethel

decided to spend several days with her. They found that they had very similar outlooks on life and enjoyed both the superficial fun of shopping as well as sharing their hearts together. After that, whenever Ethel came to the West Coast, she visited Mary, and likewise when Mary came to New York. Once, Mary was joining Ethel and some pals at Ethel's apartment for cocktails. She got there a little late and out of breath, but proud of herself. Mary Martin had actually taken her first public bus ride, all by herself. Ethel could not get over how protected Mary was. She always said that she felt Mary really *was* Peter Pan!

Ethel was seemingly happier and healthier than she had been in years. She was in good voice, working steadily, and spending quality time with the people she loved. She had gotten closer to her son, Bobby, and often he designed the lights and sound for her concerts. The grandchildren were growing up, and Merman was very proud that Barbara had been an exchange student in Europe. All seemed well.

In the summer of 1980, Merman appeared on Jack Jones's syndicated variety show called "The Palace." She looked and sounded great, but had an accident during the taping. Comedian Marty Allen was also on the show, and at the finale, he bumped into Ethel on purpose to get a laugh. There were streamers coming down from the ceiling, and neither Merman nor Allen noticed that Ethel's feet had gotten caught in them. She landed with a thud and momentarily blacked out. The taping was stopped and a doctor called for immediately. She ended up with a bump on her head and was a little dazed for a while.

When she flew to Europe to guest with Patrick Wayne on "The Monte Carlo Show," she ended up in a huge argument with her conductor of almost twenty years, Eric Knight. Ethel began to accuse him of all sorts of wrongdoings, and Eric couldn't make heads or tails out of it.

More and more often, Ethel was complaining of back pain that wouldn't go away. Sometimes she would mix up the words in a sentence or use words backwards. Still, she pressed on, ignoring any signs that something might be wrong.

When the residence hotel she was living in went co-op, Ethel strangely decided not to buy the apartment she had lived in for years. There had even been a spread in *Architectural Digest* on how beautifully the apartment was decorated. Merman seemed to have an aversion to owning anything of great monetary value. Instead, she moved to another residence hotel. Her monthly rent was now $5,000.

In May of 1982, Ethel once again did a benefit for the theater collection for the Museum of the City of New York. This time, she performed at Carnegie Hall the same concert she had been doing since 1975. Although it was obvious she had gained even more weight in the previous few months, the sold-out house gave Ethel Merman a standing ovation that seemed to go on all night. Yet, she forgot some words to her encore, "What I Did For Love," and ignored her conductor, Eric. It was the last time they would work together, as Knight could not forget the slight on such an important evening. And it wasn't like Ethel to forget lyrics.

That September, Merv Griffin did an entire show saluting Ethel Merman. Jule Styne played piano for Ethel as she sang "Everything's Coming Up Roses." Jerry Herman did the same for "Before the Parade Passes By." Composer Hal David gave Ethel the Pied Piper Award on behalf of ASCAP (which had actually been presented to her at the Carnegie Hall concert). But the highlight of the show was when Merv brought on two surprise guests: Lucille Ball and Ginger Rogers!

Both ladies had been sworn to secrecy and were literally sneaked into the theater. Lucy had a cold, but wouldn't have missed it. The three ladies had been friends for fifty years, and they were marvelous fun together.

Ethel was also the special guest star on a new "Texaco Star Theater" special saluting Broadway. While the rest of the show was done by such luminaries as Bernadette Peters, Carol Burnett, and Sammy Davis Jr. without an audience, all the stars gathered together to be Ethel's audience. She was without peer and proved what a powerhouse performer she still was. It was Ethel Merman's final American television appearance, although no one could have suspected it.

In fact, Ethel's star was on the ascendant. By 1983, audiences were again rediscovering her, and she was in demand everywhere. Producers wanted her to star with Ginger Rogers in a concert version of *Girl Crazy* at Carnegie Hall, with Ethel getting top billing over Ginger. Others wanted her to tour with Mary Martin in a play with music called *Legends* (Carol Channing eventually took her place). Another idea was to have Merman and Martin do a musical version of *Arsenic and Old Lace*.

Her voice was heard on radio stations hawking the wonders of sending mailgrams, and she filmed a long series of commercials in New York for Friendship dairy products. An enthusiastic Ethel was happy to report that she was the only person in history to be booked to sing on the Academy Awards in April (an Irving Berlin medley), the Tony Awards in June (a medley from *Girl Crazy*), and on the Emmy Awards in September all in one year.

Merman, still complaining of back pain, continued to do her concerts all through late 1982 and into 1983. Observers on the scene reported an Ethel Merman who seemed to look like a stooped, little old lady backstage, one incapable of performing for an hour or more under hot lights. However, the moment she heard the opening strains of her music, decades of age magically melted off. Her body carriage was suddenly erect, as if someone had turned on the electricity to her body. Out would step Ethel Merman, the biggest star on Broadway.

In November 1982, Ethel traveled to London to appear in a command performance for the Queen Mother. The only thing Ethel sang that night was "There's No Business Like Show Business." That's all she needed to do to stop the show. Merman was a particular favorite of the Queen Mum, who came to her performances whenever Ethel was in London. With that one song, she wiped two hours of other performers from the audience's minds and hearts. She was the best, and she knew it.

After her triumph in England, Madame Merman spent the holiday season in New York. She flew to Florida to appear in concert at the Peabody Auditorium in Daytona on February 18, 1983. It was the last one she would ever do.

Back in New York, Ethel was packing for an extended trip. She was booked to sing with several more symphonies, then she would fly to Los Angeles to begin rehearsals for her Berlin medley on the Academy Awards telecast on April 11. Rather than fly back and forth, she was going directly to California, giving herself a chance to spend time with Mary Martin, Lucille Ball, Kaye Ballard, Rose Marie, and other West Coast pals.

Merman was a meticulous packer, almost obsessive. She always traveled with theatrical trunks, which allowed her to hang dresses wrinkle free and offered drawers for all sorts of storage. Each area was labeled with a typed note for easy retrieval. Most people I know barely fold their clothes before they toss them into suitcases and hope for the best. Not Ethel. She was raised in the vaudeville tradition that a performer was only as good as they looked.

In recent years, Ethel had cut way back on the amount of

money she spent on her stage clothes. Gowns were worn again and again. Basically, Ethel had only four dresses that she wore in all of her television and concert work. Each was made to hide her microphone battery in her cleavage. And they weren't that expensive to begin with. So she had to take good care of them.

When she realized she was almost done with packing, Ethel called down to the lobby to get bellboys to bring down the trunks in advance of calling a limousine to the airport. As the call went through, the biggest star on Broadway had a massive stroke.

To add insult to great injury, no one would be able to help Ethel before she first helped herself. Ever since her great jewelry robbery, Merman had six locks installed on her front door. They were deadbolts that could only be opened with a key or from inside. Ethel had not passed out after the stroke. Although she could not speak and was partially paralyzed, she knew what was going on and what she had to do. Slowly, painfully, Ethel Merman crawled across the floor of her apartment, inch by inch, until she reached her door. With Herculean effort, she raised herself off the floor and unlocked the door. The manager of the building had been alerted and was outside waiting to be let in. As soon as she opened the door and saw him, she passed out.

When Ethel regained consciousness, she was in Roosevelt Hospital and was completely out of it. She was unable to speak—all she could do was make sounds. What she did not know was that brain surgery had been performed to see if doctors could repair whatever damage had occurred. What they found was an inoperable tumor. Brain cancer had caused Ethel's stroke.

It will never be known if Ethel's fall a couple of years earlier had been the instigator for the tumor. It is also impossible to know whether it would have been possible to save her had she paid more attention to her symptoms and seen a doctor earlier. All Ethel knew was that it was impossible that this was happening to her. She had bookings to fulfill and things she wanted to accomplish. In her mind, she was too young to be disabled. Merman was seventy-seven years old.

Extreme therapies were tried, even though doctors were not hopeful. All of Ethel's hair fell out, and her face and head blew up like a bubble. She was almost unrecognizable.

Initially, there was no public mention of Ethel's illness. An announcement was made that she would not do the Oscar show due to a bad cold. Her friends found this curious and became concerned. Finally, Mary Martin got through to Bobby and was told what happened. She immediately flew to New York to see Ethel. When she got to Roosevelt Hospital, she found her dear friend so bloated that she didn't even know it was she. Mary walked out of the room, thinking it was someone else.

Once Mary was told that it was, indeed, Ethel, she broke down in tears. She couldn't believe anyone could change that much so quickly. She was coaxed back into Ethel's room after she calmed down because Merman had seen her and reacted in recognition. Mary sat down next to the suffering Ethel and held her hand. In what was perhaps her best performance, Mary told Ethel that she would get better, that she *had* to get better. *Peter Pan* reminded *Annie Oakley* that she, too, had faced a major medical trauma, and although it was painful, had learned to walk again. Now she, Ethel, had to learn to walk again, too! Mary reminded her that anything she could do, Ethel could do better.

The effect on Ethel was miraculous. Seemingly overnight, she was talking again and asking for a walker to exercise. Within a couple of weeks, Ethel was telling her agents to hold all her bookings until December, when she would be healthy enough to resume her career.

Bobby had come East and took complete charge of Ethel's convalescence. He took her home, where she continued to improve slightly. Friends could come by and see her for short visits. They would find Merman in a dressing gown and wig to cover her still sparse hair. Those who didn't know of the prognosis were hopeful she would completely recover.

Slowly, inexorably, Ethel Merman began to deteriorate. Where once she had been able to speak in complete sentences, now she was only able to muster up phrases. Her energy seemed to leave her, and she became bedridden. Bobby was a totally devoted son who was there to make his mother happy and comfortable. He was almost never out of her sight and was responsive to her slightest desire. In truth, Bobby gave Ethel the kind of "mothering" that he had never received from her.

Mary Martin came East again to visit Ethel. She went into Saks Fifth Avenue to buy Ethel a brightly colored robe in which to receive visitors. Mary being Mary, she simply took the item and left the store. It never occurred to her that she actually had to stop and pay for it. Her husband, Richard Halliday, had kept her that sheltered. Baroness Maria von Trapp was detained by the store security officers until she was identified and let go.

Mary did not allow this embarrassment to stop her and took a cab to Ethel's apartment. She was shocked at how far downhill Ethel had gone since she had last seen her. When Mary shared some gossip with Ethel, something Merman loved to hear, all the once Mighty Merman could utter was "assholes!"

The last time Carole Cook came to visit Ethel, it was in the company of Tony Cointreau and his partner Jim Russo. It was a beautiful day, so they decided to bundle up Ethel and take her to the park. Making certain she was comfortable in her wheelchair, they stopped to hear a band play. Sure enough, the song was Ethel's "Life is Just a Bowl of Cherries." Slowly, almost in a whisper, Merman began to try to sing along. She couldn't enunciate all the words, and her voice was weak, so Carole, Tony and Jim began to sing along with her. Here was the biggest star on Broadway, singing one of her trademark songs, and no one even noticed she was there.

Carole and the fellas felt the tears rolling down their face as the band played song after song made popular by the great Ethel Merman. It was one of the last times Ethel left her apartment.

In the last months before her illness, Ethel had befriended a talented young writer named Stephen Cole (who today is an award-winning lyricist in the theatre). Steve had obtained a mountain of Merman memorabilia, as well as many rarities on videotape. Previously, Ethel had enjoyed spending time at Steve's house, watching her old short films that she hadn't seen in fifty years. Now Steve brought more video for her to watch, hoping to encourage and entertain her. Ethel didn't even recognize herself on the screen.

Ethel Merman was a fighter. Almost from the time she was cogent as an infant, nothing seemed out of her grasp. And professionally, it wasn't. Personally, romantic happiness eluded her, and she lost that fight. Now she lost another one. On February 15, 1984, she lost her battle with cancer.

Five days later, all of the lights on Broadway were dimmed in tribute.

Ethel Merman, the biggest star on Broadway, was gone.

# Radio and TV Appearances

It is impossible to list every single radio or television appearance made by Ethel—alas too many of them have been lost to history. In some cases, all we have are printed references, so information is not complete. Every effort has been made to be as accurate and complete as research will allow.

## The Louis Calhern Show
**December 1930 [30 minutes, Radio, Live]**
**Cast:** Louis Calhern, Ethel Merman
**Performance Notes:** This is Ethel's radio debut. She sings a medley of songs from *Girl Crazy*.

## The Gus Van Show
**NBC Blue, January 4, 1931 [15 minutes, Radio, Live]**
**Cast:** Gus Van, Ethel Merman
**Performance Notes:** Curiously, Ethel is interviewed on this program, but does not sing.

*Live From Carnegie Hall*
**Mutual Broadcasting Network, March 4, 1935 [30 minutes, Radio, Live]**
**Cast:** Bob Dudley (host), Vinton Freedley, Ethel Merman, Victor Moore, William Gaxton
**Concept:** The New York City flagship station of the Mutual Broadcasting Network, WOR, is increasing its wattage from 5,000 to 50,000, making it one of the first superradio stations in the country. To celebrate, a live show is done by remote broadcast from Carnegie Hall.
**Performance Notes:** Just weeks before she leaves the cast of *Anything Goes*, Ethel sings "I Get a Kick Out of You." It is the only recorded example extant of Merman singing the song in the exact manner and arrangement as in the Broadway version. Her voice is clear, and one can hear how poignantly Ethel sang it in its original version.
**Interesting Sidenotes:** Although Ethel is there, William Gaxton sings "You're the Top" as a solo, depriving history of hearing how it originally sounded with Merman as a duet.

They literally made an announcement that WOR was going to stop broadcasting and shut down its 5,000-watt tower and then come back on the air from its 50,000-watt tower. It only took a brief moment, but the difference in clarity was astounding. From then on, WOR could be heard regularly in New York, New Jersey, and Connecticut.

*Rhythm at Eight*
**NBC, May 5, 1935 [30 minutes, Radio, Live]**
**Cast:** Ethel Merman (host), Ted Husing (emcee), Al Goodman (musical director)
**Concept:** Starting tonight and for the next twelve weeks, Ethel Merman hosts a radio variety show. The concept is close to that of Kate Smith's hugely successful series, which has the songstress singing but all of the talking is done by an emcee. It is a summer replacement series, and does not make it to the fall lineup.

*A Gershwin Memorial*
**WHN, July 13, 1937 [60 minutes, Radio, Live]**
**Performance Notes:** Merman's contribution is "I Got Rhythm."

*All-Star Tribute to Irving Berlin*
**CBS, August 13, 1938 [60 minutes, Radio, Live]**
**Cast:** Al Goodman (musical director), Walter Winchell, Ted Husing, Ethel Merman, Al Jolson, Irving Berlin, Eddie Cantor, Sophie Tucker, Ben Bernie, Lew Lehr, the Brox Sisters, Rudy Vallee, the Connecticut Yankees, Tommy Dorsey and his Orchestra, Connee Boswell, Guy Lombardo and his Royal Canadians, Paul Whiteman, Jon Steel, Louella Parsons, Darryl F. Zanuck, Tyrone Power, Alice Faye
**Concept:** A special program honoring Irving Berlin on his fiftieth birthday and plugging the release of the film, *Alexander's Ragtime Band.*
**Performance Notes:** In the first half of the show, Ethel sings "Heat Wave" and "Walking Stick" (two of the numbers she does in the film). In the second half, Ethel takes Alice Faye's place in a radio re-creation of *Alexander's Ragtime Band*, singing the title number.
**Interesting Sidenotes:** This is Merman's first public performance of the song "Alexander's Ragtime Band," but certainly not the last. In later years, Ethel would claim she sang the song in the film (Alice Faye did) and would claim it as her own. The number became a part of her repertoire from the earliest days of television, and she sang it at every one of her concerts until the very last one she gave in 1983. No one sang it better than she!

*The Jimmy Durante Show*
**NBC, 1939 [30 minutes, Radio, Live]**
**Cast:** Jimmy Durante (host), Ethel Merman
**Performance Notes:** Durante and Merman dueted on "It's All Yours."

211

*Keep 'Em Rolling*
**Mutual Broadcasting Network, November 9, 1941 [30 minutes, Radio, Live]**
**Produced by Arthur Kurlan. Musical Direction by Morton Gould**
**Concept:** This was a one-time only broadcast put on by the Office of Emergency Management.
**Performance Notes:** Ethel sang the theme song to the show, "The Flame of Freedom Is Burning" (written by Richard Rodgers and Larry Hart).

**The Chamber Music Society of Lower Basin Street**
**NBC Blue, 1944 [30 minutes, Radio, Live]**
**Cast:** Johnny Johnston (host), Ethel Merman, Dinah Shore
**Performance Notes:** This appearance occurs during rehearsals for *Sadie Thompson*, so Merman plugs a show she will never do. Interestingly, Ethel warbles "The Very Thought of You" rather than one of her hits. It is the first time Ethel and Dinah work together, but certainly not the last.

*The Andrews Sisters Show*
**NBC Blue, October 1944 [30 minutes, Radio, Live]**
**Cast:** Patty, Maxene, and LaVerne Andrews, Ethel Merman
**Performance Notes:** Her song here is "I Got Rhythm." See page 90 for the full story of this appearance.

*Stage Door Canteen*
**ABC, January 12, 1945 [30 minutes, Radio]**
**Directed by Earle McGill. Musical Direction by Raymond Paige**
**Cast:** Bert Lytell (host), Ethel Merman, William Gaxton
**Concept:** A radio version of the nightclub for servicemen with the same name.
**Performance Notes:** Gaxton and Merman reminisce about being in *Anything Goes*, and their duet on "You're the Top."

*Philco Radio Time: The Bing Crosby Show*
**NBC, June 11, 1947 [30 minutes, Radio, Live]**
**Cast:** Bing Crosby (host), Ethel Merman, Alec Templeton
**Concept:** Perennial crooner Bing Crosby hosts a variety show with music and sketches.
**Performance Notes:** Ethel and Cros and Alec do a medley of favorite songs. Her tonsils wrap around snatches of "I Got Rhythm," "I Get a Kick Out of You," "Blow, Gabriel, Blow," "You're the Top," and "I'm an Old Cowhand." Then the group does a complete version of "Anything You Can Do, I Can Do Better."

*Philco Radio Time: The Bing Crosby Show*
**NBC, May 19, 1948 [30 minutes, Radio, Live]**
**Cast:** Bing Crosby (host), Ethel Merman
**Concept:** Perennial crooner Bing Crosby hosts a variety show with music and sketches.
**Performance Notes:** Merman and Bing do a piece of special-material parody of "Your Hit Parade" called Your Flop Parade. The songs, which were originals written by major songwriters just for the show, included "Tears in My Ears," "Boise, Idaho," and "Washday in the Sky." Both were in great voice, and the bit was such a success, it was later repeated with other songs.

*The Texaco Star Theater*
**NBC, March 22, 1949 [60 minutes, Live]**
**Cast:** Milton Berle (host), Ethel Merman, Keye Luke, and variety acts
**Concept:** Milton Berle hosts a live television vaudeville show.
**Performance Notes:** Ethel had just weeks before concluded her long run in *Annie Get Your Gun*. She comes out with her shoulder-length, fluffy hair flowing and dressed in an unusual gown that has one long sleeve and one arm sleeveless.

Merman sings two of her earliest hit songs, "I Got Rhythm" and "I Get a Kick Out of You." This is her television debut, and she is more than up to the challenge. Her powerful voice and personality come right across the airwaves intact. As with many early television shows, the lighting is terrible so Ethel does not look her best.

After her solos, she joins Berle for one of the funniest sketches ever done on his groundbreaking series. The idea was to use a turn-of-the-century couple with their first automobile to lead into a duet of "Friendship." Within moments, both of their cheap costumes begin to fall apart, causing Berle to lose his timing and forget the dialogue. This makes Ethel laugh, and *she* starts to forget the setups to his jokes. Knowing they were in a losing cause, Uncle Miltie cues for the song.

Instantly, he blanks out on both the lyrics and the proper key. Ethel tries to carry on, but Milton's embarrassment causes him to begin to do unplanned shtick with Ethel. He even goes so far as to give her a Moe Howard, Three Stooges-style poke in the eyes. By the time they get to the end of the song, Ethel pushes him and tells him to shut up because it was over.

The entire thing stops the show. Milton could not get the audience to stop cheering. Unfortunately, the loss of time forces Berle to cut short the finale, right as Merman is singing "The Varsity Drag." **Interesting Sidenotes:** Berle was so pleased with the whole thing that he had Ethel on the show three more times in the next six months. Alas, two of the dates have been lost to time. This was Milton Berle's favorite episode of his show.

### *Philco Radio Time: The Bing Crosby Show*
**NBC, March 23, 1949 [30 minutes, Radio, Live]**
**Cast:** Bing Crosby (host), Ethel Merman
**Concept:** Perennial crooner Bing Crosby hosts a variety show with music and sketches.
**Performance Notes:** Only one day after making her television debut with Milton Berle, it is back to radio for Merman. She and Bing reprise the concept of Your Flop Parade. This time the songs are "Rhythmitis," "Grace," "There's a Flaw in My Flue," "On a Rainy Day," and "Silver Coated Moon."

## The Ford Show
**NBC, June 20, 1949 [30 minutes, Live]**
**Cast:** Ethel Merman, Lauritz Melchior
**Concept:** Another attempt at an early television show.
**Performance Notes:** This program airs just as the musical *South Pacific* is becoming an enormous hit. Merman duets with opera legend Melchior on "Anything You Can Do, I Can Do Better," hoping for some of the same magic Mary Martin has with Ezio Pinza. Her solo is "There's No Business Like Show Business." This is the first time she sings this song as a solo number. It certainly will not be the last!

## Thru the Crystal Ball
**CBS, June 20, 1949 [30 minutes, Live]**
**Cast:** Ethel Merman
**Concept:** Originally, fables were supposed to be dramatized in dance. Eventually, it became a straight variety show.
**Performance Notes:** When original host Jimmy Salvo found work elsewhere, Ethel stepped in to host this one episode.

## The Ethel Merman Show
**NBC, July 31, 1949 [30 minutes, Radio, Live]**
**Written by Will Glickman and Joe Stein. Directed by Kenneth MacGregor. Musical Direction by Al Goodman**
**Cast:** Ethel Merman, Allen Drake, Leon Janney
**Concept:** Originally, a girl singer is helped by her agent and mobster boyfriend to become a star. Eventually, the plots are dropped in favor of a straight variety show.
**Performance Notes:** The basic problem with the series is that Ethel is playing a young girl just starting out in show business. She made no attempt at sounding young and girlish, and her strident performances didn't match the plots.
**Interesting Sidenotes:** This was a grade C attempt at a series. In reality, the network never meant for it to be anything more than a summer "filler" series until the fall. Very few tapes of the show exist, which is a shame because during the run of the show, Merman sang almost all of her hit songs.

*The Texaco Star Theater*
**NBC, October 18, 1949 [60 minutes, Live]**
**Cast:** Milton Berle (host), Ethel Merman, Dean Martin, Jerry Lewis, and variety acts
**Concept:** Milton Berle hosts a live television vaudeville show.
**Performance Notes:** Merman comes onstage wearing her new horse's tail hairstyle and looks years older than she had just a few months ago. She sings "Great Day" and a medley of "There are Smiles," "Smile, Darn You, Smile," and "When You're Smiling." She is also featured in the finale as a hillbilly. Ethel is in great voice.
**Interesting Sidenotes:** Although Ethel is billed as the special guest star, Martin and Lewis totally steal the show from her and Berle. Milton was very generous giving these guys so much airtime and so many chances to steal his own material. Like many huge stars, while he could be very protective of his stature, when he came across people he thought were truly talented, he could be their biggest booster.

This was Ethel's last appearance on the show. She decided she did not like television and except for one interview, would retreat to radio and the stage until 1952.

*Philco Radio Time: The Bing Crosby Show*
**NBC, March 22, 1950 [30 minutes, Radio]**
**Cast:** Bing Crosby (host), Ethel Merman
**Concept:** Bing Crosby hosts a variety show with music and sketches.
**Performance Notes:** It is about this time that Ethel's recording of "Dearie" becomes a hit. Here, she and Crosby do it with the original arrangement. It is hugely superior and a shame that the two had not done a series of recordings together, as they were both signed to Decca Records.

*The Stork Club*
**CBS, November 1950 [30 minutes, Live]**
**Cast:** Sherman Billingsley, Ethel Merman
**Concept:** Billingsley would invite celebrities to his famous Stork Club and interview them at table 50.

**Interesting Sidenotes:** Although they had hardly spoken in a decade, Ethel agreed to this interview to promote *Call Me Madam*. She was a married lady, the Stork Club was on the wane, and she felt she had nothing to lose. The show itself was amateurish and awkward. It would disappear as television became more sophisticated.

*The Big Show*
**NBC, November 5, 1950 [90 minutes, Radio, Live]**
**Written by Goodman Ace. Music by Meredith Willson**
**Cast:** Tallulah Bankhead (host), Ethel Merman, Fred Allen, Jimmy Durante, Paul Lukas, Danny Thomas, Jose Ferrer, Frankie Laine
**Concept:** The great Miss Bankhead hosts one of the last of the big radio variety shows. It is broadcast live from New York, and everyone from Groucho Marx to Margaret Truman appeared on it.
**Performance Notes:** On this episode, Merman sings many of her hit songs from *Call Me Madam*. She and Bankhead also enjoyed some very clever, bitchy badinage that was a hallmark of this show.
**Interesting Sidenotes:** Ethel was a semiregular on this series. She usually appeared within the first half hour, which allowed her to split early and enjoy her day off from *Call Me Madam*. Although she did sing other things, for some reason "There's No Business Like Show Business" was repeated over and over.

*The Big Show*
**NBC, March 4, 1951 [90 minutes, Radio, Live]**
**Written by Goodman Ace. Music by Meredith Willson**
**Cast:** Tallulah Bankhead (host), Ethel Merman, Herb Shreiner, Fred Allen, Frankie Laine, Margaret Truman

*The Big Show*
**NBC, April 29, 1951 [90 minutes, Radio, Live]**
**Written by Goodman Ace. Music by Meredith Willson**
**Cast:** Tallulah Bankhead (host), Ethel Merman, Jimmy Durante, Milton Berle, Gordon MacRae, Rosemary Clooney

*The Big Show*
**NBC, October 14, 1951 [90 minutes, Radio, Live]**
**Written by Goodman Ace. Music by Meredith Willson**
**Cast:** Tallulah Bankhead (host), Ethel Merman, Fred Allen, Jimmy Durante, George Sanders

*The Jack Benny Salute*
**CBS, November 9, 1951 [Radio, 30 minutes]**
**Cast:** Ethel Merman, Milton Berle, Ronald and Benita Colman, Mary Martin
**Concept:** A salute to Jack Benny on the twentieth anniversary of his first radio appearance. Simultaneously, Jack is being roasted at the Friar's Club.
**Performance Notes:** Her contribution to the show is a rousing rendition of "There's No Business Like Show Business."
**Interesting Sidenotes:** Although they could not be considered close friends, Ethel and Jack had known one another since the late 1920s. They never really had a chance to work together, but they were a mutual admiration society. Benny sent Merman a note after seeing her in *Call Me Madam*, praising her for her unique comedy timing. Ethel always treasured that handwritten note and read it on "The Tonight Show" not long after Jack's death in December 1974. She had it framed and hanging in her den until her death.

*The Big Show*
**NBC, February 3, 1952 [90 minutes, Radio, Live]**
**Written by Goodman Ace. Music by Meredith Willson**
**Cast:** Tallulah Bankhead (host), Ethel Merman, Fred Allen, Jerry Colonna

*The Big Show*
**NBC, March 9, 1952 [90 minutes, Radio, Live]**
**Written by Goodman Ace. Music by Meredith Willson**
**Cast:** Tallulah Bankhead (host), Ethel Merman, Phil Foster, Richard Eastham, Joe Frisco, Peter Lorre, Fibber McGee and Molly

*The Big Show*
**NBC, April 20, 1952 [90 minutes, Radio, Live]**
**Written by Goodman Ace. Music by Meredith Willson**
**Cast:** Tallulah Bankhead (host), Ethel Merman, Fred Allen, Groucho Marx, George Sanders, Julie Harris, Eddy Arnold

*Toast of the Town*
**CBS, March 29, 1953 [60 minutes, Live]**
Sadly, this program has not survived the sands of time, and there is no information about it. However, the previous week, host Ed Sullivan announced that there would be a salute to the forthcoming motion picture *Call Me Madam*, featuring Ethel Merman. One can assume that she sang something from the score and that perhaps a clip from the film was shown.

*The Ford 50th Anniversary Show*
**CBS and NBC, June 15, 1953 [120 minutes, Live]**
**Produced by Leland Hayward. Directed by Clark Jones**
**Cast:** Oscar Hammerstein II (host), Edward R. Murrow (host), Ethel Merman, Mary Martin, Kukla, Fran and Ollie, Bing Crosby, Frank Sinatra, Eddie Fisher, Rudy Vallee, Wally Cox, Howard Lindsay, Dorothy Stickney, Marian Anderson
**Concept:** The Ford Motor Company celebrates its fiftieth anniversary by looking back at the previous fifty years in American history and culture.
**Performance Notes:** Ethel's first appearance on the show finds her in a mock-up of a jazz nightclub, wearing a dress and feathered headdress from the 1910s. She sings "Alexander's Ragtime Band" for the first time on television. She is in near-perfect voice.

Next, Ethel is a woman disguised as an Army enlistee for a comedy version of "Mademoiselle from Armentieres." Because it is television, the spicy last stanza is excised while Ethel sings, "Cut, or we'll be off the air, inky dinky parlez-vous!"

Ethel and Mary don straw hats and striped summer suits as they lip-synch to a scratchy recording of the Happiness Boys doing an

old routine. This is the least successful of Ethel's contributions to the evening.

Finally, Ethel and Mary do their duet. I believe this to be Ethel's greatest recorded performing moment. Everything comes together perfectly to show the world why Ethel Merman is the biggest star on Broadway.

**Interesting Sidenotes:** This was Mary Martin's television debut. Ethel Merman appeared twenty-five years later on Ford's 75th Anniversary show. See that listing for further details.

*Dinner with the President*
**CBS, November 16, 1953 [60 minutes, Live]**
**Produced and directed by Richard Rodgers and Oscar Hammerstein II**
**Cast:** Ben Grauer, Walter Cronkite, Rex Harrison, Lilli Palmer, Richard Rodgers, Oscar Hammerstein II, Lucille Ball, Desi Arnaz, Vivian Vance, William Frawley, Ethel Merman, Eddie Fisher, Jane Froman, Helen Hayes, William Warfield, Jackie Robinson, Thelma Ritter, Bernard Baruch, David Goldenson, J. Edgar Hoover, Hubert Humphrey, William S. Paley, Gen. David Sarnoff, President Dwight D. Eisenhower

**Concept:** The B'nai B'rith Anti-Defamation League salutes President Eisenhower at a dinner and show that is televised from Washington, D.C.

**Performance Notes:** A thin and tanned Merman, wearing an exceptionally unattractive gown, does a medley of songs. She is in excellent voice and is proud to be there due to her strong admiration and friendship with Ike. That she was also publicly lauded by Rex Harrison for her efforts to desegregate the National Theatre added frosting to the cake.

**Interesting Sidenotes:** This is the only televised occasion when Ball, Arnaz, Vance, and Frawley re-create live both their characters and pieces of business directly from an episode of "I Love Lucy."

"Douglas Edwards and the News" and "The Perry Como Show" were preempted for this broadcast.

*The Colgate Comedy Hour*
**NBC, December 6, 1953 [60 minutes, Live]**
**Produced and staged by Joseph Santley. Written by Charlie Isaacs and Jack Elinson. Directed by Sid Smith. Sketches directed by Charlie Isaacs. Musical Direction by Roy Bargy. Gowns by Beaumelle**
**Cast:** Jimmy Durante (host), Ethel Merman
**Concept:** A weekly variety series featuring a rotating list of hosts from the vaudeville world.
**Performance Notes:** Although Jimmy is the host, Merman is featured as much as he is. The show starts with Ethel and Jimmy on stools doing a very long medley of songs built around the themes of travel and the tune "I Feel a Song Coming On." There is an obvious desire to re-create the magic of Ethel's duet with Mary Martin several months earlier.

There is a dressing-room comedy scene with the two stars, leading into a production number "Everywhere You Go" featuring Durante's de rigueur partner, Eddie Jackson. Next, through the electronic magic of film and live television, Merman duets with herself, singing both parts of "You're Just in Love." This is actually a very difficult thing to achieve technically, requiring a great deal of rehearsal. Ethel should have recorded it this way. It is marvelous!

Next, there is a spoof of Judy Garland's singing of "Get Happy" from the motion picture *Summer Stock*. Merman begins to sing "I Get a Kick Out of You," and then a group of chorus boys (including Durante) come out of the wings. She rips off her skirt to reveal sequined slacks and sings the number with choreography mimicking Judy's. It is very effective, a real audience pleaser.

The show ends with its stars doing a "thanks" medley and a reminder that both Jimmy and Ethel will host future episodes of the series.
**Interesting Sidenotes:** This series was on directly opposite Ed Sullivan's "Toast of the Town" on Sunday nights. Stars who hosted the most episodes include such giants as Ed Wynn, Dean Martin and Jerry Lewis, Eddie Cantor, Bob Hope, Bud Abbott and Lou

Costello, and of course, Jimmy Durante. It was originally planned for Merman to appear approximately every six weeks. However, her shooting schedule for the film *There's No Business Like Show Business* interfered, and she was dropped.

**The Colgate Comedy Hour: The Ethel Merman Show**
**NBC, January 24, 1954 [60 minutes, Live]**
**Produced and directed by Joseph Santley. Written by Charley Isaacs and Jack Elinson**
**Cast:** Ethel Merman, Jimmy Durante, Gene Nelson
**Concept:** Merman hosts an episode of this variety series.
**Performance Notes:** This is the first time Merman hosts a big-time television variety hour. For her appearance here, Roger Edens wrote a piece of recitative called "Just a Lady with a Song." While the lyrics would change through the years, Ethel sang it for the rest of her life in all of her nightclub and concert work to open her show.

Ethel's opening number, a long medley of pop songs, is prerecorded, with Merman lip-synching to allow her to do some fairly fancy choreography. There follows a slapstick pantomime sketch with Ethel as an inept substitute harp player with a symphony orchestra. It tries to be very much like "Lucy," but misses.

Durante and Merman have a long sketch together set in Jimmy's mansion, where Ethel's singing of "I Got Rhythm" shatters all the glass and statuary in the room. She hated doing things that would mock that song or her singing of it, but she was overruled. The two also duet on "When You're Smiling."

The final piece of the show was nothing short of magnificent, and it is a shame Ethel didn't do more things like this one. Using the music from Cole Porter's *Can-Can*, a sketch is built about a lonely, mousy tourist in Paris and her fantasies after imbibing a bit of wine. With the proper dramatic framework, Ethel is allowed to turn from singer to actress and back again. She is nothing less than terrific.

At the end of the show, Ethel is presented with her *Golden Globe* award for her performance in the movie, *Call Me Madam*.

222

**Interesting Sidenotes:** This is the second of several television pairings between Ethel Merman and Jimmy Durante. They worked very well together, and it was always a solid click. As happened on many live shows of the time, the show ran short. Durante came out and played a couple of numbers, one of which wasn't even finished yet!

*The Colgate Comedy Hour: Anything Goes*
**NBC, February 28, 1954 [60 minutes, Live]**
**Produced by Jule Styne. Directed by Clark Jones.**
**Orchestrations by Buddy Bregman and Nelson Riddle**
**Cast:** Ethel Merman, Frank Sinatra, Bert Lahr, Sheree North
**Concept:** This variety program suspends its usual format to present a shortened version of the musical *Anything Goes*. The plot is greatly simplified. This time Merman is a star who is trading her career for marriage to a titled British nobleman. Sinatra is her agent and lover who does not want to lose her. He follows her onto a ship bound for England, as does Lahr portraying the gangster turned clergyman.
**Performance Notes:** This was Merman's first attempt at re-creating one of her stage roles on television. The plot of the show was tremendously trimmed, making room for Sinatra's crooning and Lahr's mugging. Ethel was in tremendous voice, although she was poorly costumed. They did not yet realize that wearing gold or silver lamé made the wearer seem twenty pounds heavier. A thin Ethel looked stout, needlessly.

Here you will find Merman's best renditions of the songs "You're the Top" and "Anything Goes."
**Interesting Sidenotes:** This program was broadcast from the El Capitan theater in the heart of Hollywood. Sinatra was at a point in his career where he was literally having trouble finding work. Merman had him cast as a favor to her friend who was having hard times. They were totally miscast as lovers. Frank never forgot her kindness and repaid her over and over through the years when *her* career needed a boost.

It was decided to have Bert and Ethel re-create their fabled duet of "Friendship" from *DuBarry Was a Lady*. The presentation was almost exactly like the one they did on Broadway. It is the only video of them working together.

### The Best of Broadway: Panama Hattie
**CBS, November 10, 1954 [60 minutes, Live, Color]**
**Written by Ronald Alexander. Directed by David Alexander. Story by Herbert Fields and B. G. DeSylva. Produced by Jule Styne and Martin Manulis. Music by Cole Porter. Orchestrations by Buddy Bregman. Musical Direction by Buster Davis**
**Cast:** Ethel Merman, Ray Middleton, Art Carney, Jack E. Leonard, Neil Hamilton, Karin Wolfe, Betty O'Neil, Joseph Mccauley
**Concept:** Once a month, CBS preempted its regular schedule to present these adaptations of Broadway shows. This time it was Merman's big hit, *Panama Hattie*. As with *Anything Goes*, the plot is simplified and also sanitized. Merman is a loudmouthed saloon singer in Panama, in love with American war hero Ray Middleton. He has a daughter from a previous marriage Ethel wants to impress, and an enemy plots to blow up the canal.
**Performance Notes:** This is her first television appearance since she appeared in the film *There's No Business Like Show Business*. It is also her first appearance with her new, short hair. Ethel had her long hair completely cut off at the neck and slicked back on the sides like a man. On top she wore tight "poodle" curls. The effect was severe and masculine and made her look ten years older. *She* loved it!
**Interesting Sidenotes:** Although broadcast in color, this production was not anywhere near as successful as *Anything Goes*. Only two of her songs from the original ("Let's Be Buddies" and "Make It Another Old-Fashioned, Please") were retained, and both were shortened for time. She also sang "Fresh as a Daisy," which had not been her song in the stage version, and "Ridin' High" from *Red, Hot and Blue*.

Neither Art Carney nor Fat Jack Leonard were very funny. They were given inferior material. Ray Middleton had been Merman's first Frank Butler in the 1946 version of *Annie Get Your Gun*. Middleton was now overweight, and his lack of acting talent was all too obvious.

*Suspense: Never Follow a Banjo Act*
**CBS, December 1954 [30 minutes, Radio]**
**Performance Notes:** It is here that Ethel first sings her arrangement of "Zing! Went the Strings of My Heart." She would repeat it four years later on Frank Sinatra's eponymous series.

*The Shower of Stars: Showstoppers*
**CBS, January 25, 1955 [60 minutes, Live, Color]**
**Produced by Buddy Bregman**
**Cast:** Ethel Merman, Red Skelton, Bobby Van, Jane and Betty Kean, William Lundigan (announcer)
**Concept:** This is an early attempt by CBS to have a color variety series with different guest stars each week. Bill Lundigan is the announcer. This week, Red Skelton hosts a show saluting Broadway showstoppers.
**Performance Notes:** Although Skelton is the host, Merman is the STAR of the show. She sings "Eadie Was a Lady" (with altered lyrics to satisfy the censors), "There's No Business Like Show Business," and "A Little Girl from Little Rock" (with the Kean Sisters).

*The Shower of Stars: Ethel Merman's Showstoppers*
**CBS, April 14, 1955 [60 minutes, Live, Color]**
**Cast:** Ethel Merman, Red Skelton, Peter Lind Hayes, Mary Healy, William Lundigan (announcer)
**Concept:** The first version (see above) was so well received that CBS decided to do another. This time, they gave Ethel top billing.
**Performance Notes:** Among her numbers this time were strange arrangements of "I Got Rhythm" and "Doin' What Comes Nat'rally."

*The Toast of the Town*
**CBS, July 17, 1955 [60 minutes, Live]**
**Cast:** Ethel Merman (host), Russell Nype, Jimmy Edmonson (Professor Backwards)
**Performance Notes:** Her vocal contributions this evening were "Heat Wave," "You're Just in Love" (with Russell Nype), and "That's the Kind of Dame I Am."

**Interesting Sidenotes:**
In the days when his show was live, Ed Sullivan rarely had guest hosts. This is one of the few times someone else hosted "Toast of the Town."

Because of the conflicts between Decca and RCA, Merman and Nype never got to record their famous duet. This is the only video archive of what that duet might have looked and sounded like on stage.

*Person to Person*
**CBS, September 9, 1955 [30 minutes, Live]**
**Cast:** Edward R. Murrow (host), Ethel Merman, Robert Six, Ethel Levitt, Bobby Levitt
**Concept:** Edward R. Murrow sits in a studio in New York while his crew takes live cameras into famous people's homes and he interviews them.
**Performance Notes:** This is the only video extant of the Six family all together at their estate in Denver. Everyone seems to be on edge. The stresses and unhappiness of the Merman-Six marriage are apparent.

*The Chevy Show*
**NBC, December 6, 1955 [60 minutes, Live]**
**Cast:** Robert Cummings (host), Ethel Merman, Jonathan Winters, Tennessee Ernie
**Concept:** A variety show based on Bob Cummings fictional road trip from Hollywood to New York.
**Performance Notes:** Ethel's contribution is set in a fictional Chicago nightclub. Dressed in a lovely gown and backed by twin pianos and a full orchestra, Merman does a special material piece about not doing her usual songs tonight and then does a medley of "I Love a Piano," "The Lady Is a Tramp," and "The Gypsy in My Soul." Next, Ethel does a stunning medley of songs about places in America as a sort of a musical travelogue.

Later in the show, a glamorous Ethel is dressed in a gold lamé gown and does a duet of "Friendship" with Tennessee Ernie.

**Interesting Sidenotes:** Sponsors were highly sensitive and very powerful in those days. Tennessee Ernie could not be billed using his last name because sponsor Chevrolet refused to have a *Ford* on its show.

## Masquerade Party
**CBS, February 1956 [30 minutes, Live]**
**Cast:** Peter Donald (host), Ilka Chase, Mary Healy, Ogden Nash, George de Witt
**Concept:** Stars are disguised in elaborate costumes and makeup while a panel of celebrities questions them, trying to guess their true identities.
**Performance Notes:** Ethel is disguised as a gas-station attendant with the clue being the pump that says "ethyl" on it. Our Lady is on this program to promote all of her forthcoming television work.

## General Electric Theater: Reflected Glory
**CBS, March 25, 1956 [30 minutes, Live]**
**Based on a play by George Kelly. Written by Arthur Arent. Directed by Leslie H. Martinson**
**Cast:** Ronald Reagan (host), Ethel Merman
**Performance Notes:** Alas and alack, this show has been lost to time, and no copy of it exists.

## Max Liebman Presents: The Music of Gershwin
**CBS, May 12, 1956 [90 minutes, Live, Color]**
**Directed by Max Liebman. Produced by Max Liebman and Bill Hobin**
**Cast:** Ethel Merman, Cab Calloway, Alfred Drake, Tony Bennett, Richard Hayman, Toni Arden, Peter Conlow, Harrison Muller, Patricia Wilde
**Concept:** A special devoted to the music of George Gershwin. This was the first of several such specials featuring Merman over the next twenty years.
**Performance Notes:** Her contributions were not large, snippets of

songs like "But Not For Me" and "I Got Rhythm."

**Interesting Sidenotes:** Max Liebman had been the guiding genius behind the groundbreaking variety series, "Your Show of Shows." When star Sid Caesar wanted to control his own show, this series of specials was given to Liebman by NBC. This episode was broadcast from the NBC color studios in Brooklyn.

### The United States Steel Hour: Honest in the Rain
**CBS, May 9, 1956 [60 minutes, Live]**
**Written by Mort Thaw**

**Concept:** This was one of the longest-running anthology drama series on television. Each week, a different cast and crew did a live play for television. This time, it was the story of a middle-aged woman, never married, who has both a new fiancé and a gambling problem. She gambles away all of his savings and nearly loses everything.

**Performance Notes:** Although Ethel had the talent to pull off a dramatic part like this one, the show was clumsily written, and she received bad direction. The script called for her to call herself ugly more than once. To that end, bad lighting and makeup allowed every wrinkle and sag to show on Merman's face. She looked terrible and elderly. Much *too* old to be a virginal woman worried about losing the only man who had ever looked at her.

### The Ed Sullivan Show
**CBS, June 24, 1956 [60 minutes, Live]**
**Produced by Marlo Lewis. Music by Ray Bloch**

**Cast:** Ed Sullivan (host), Ethel Merman, Shelley Winters, Ruth Gordon, Sam Levine, Teresa Brewer, Ronald Reagan, Natalie Wood, Robert Walker, Walt Disney, Lucille Ball, Desi Arnaz, Kate Smith, Jack Paar, Phil Silvers and the cast of "The Phil Silvers Show," Harry Belafonte, Gregory Peck, Louis Armstrong

**Concept:** This is the eighth-anniversary show of Ed's series.

**Performance Notes:** Shelley, Ruth, and Sam join Ethel in singing "Sullivan For Me!"

*See You at the Polls*
NBC, November 8, 1956 [30 minutes]
**Produced by Jack Denove, Hollywood chairman of the American Heritage Foundation**
**Cast:** Bob Hope (host), Anna Maria Alberghetti, William Bendix, Spring Byington, Rosemary Clooney, Bing Crosby, Jimmy Durante, Peggy King, Peter Lawford, Groucho Marx, Ethel Merman, Donald O'Connor, Byron Palmer, Jane Russell, Danny Thomas
**Concept:** Bob Hope hosts a musical show to remind the public of their right and responsibility to (and their heritage of) the vote. Most of the appearances were actually pieces of film donated by the major studios with applause tracks added.
**Performance Notes:** Her contribution here was film of her dueting with Donald O'Connor on "You're Just in Love" from the film, *Call Me Madam.*

*The DuPont Show of the Month: Crescendo*
NBC, September 29, 1957 [60 minutes, Live]
**Written by Peter Ustinov and Leslie Stevens. Directed by Bill Colleran. Produced by Paul Gregory**
**Cast:** John Collicos (host), Rex Harrison, Julie Andrews, Ethel Merman, Diahann Carroll, Peggy Lee, Mahalia Jackson, Louis Armstrong, Stubby Kaye, Benny Goodman, Eddy Arnold, Sonny James, Dinah Washington, Stanley Holloway, Turk Murphy
**Concept:** A wealthy Englishman is introduced to all aspects of American musical styles and performers.
**Performance Notes:** Although Merman joins this stellar cast in a very unusual show, she does not actually sing.
**Interesting Sidenotes:** This was the premiere episode of the series.

*The Perry Como Show*
NBC, October 5, 1957 [60 minutes, Live, Color]
**Directed by Grey Lockwood. Written by George Foster, Goodman Ace, Jay Burton, John Aylesworth, Mort Green**
**Cast:** Perry Como (host), Ethel Merman, Garry Moore, Burr Tillstrom and the Kuklapolitans
**Performance Notes:** No kinescope or video of this episode is in existence, so it is not known what Ethel's contributions were.

*The Perry Como Show*
NBC, December 7, 1957 [60 minutes, Live, Color]
**Directed by Grey Lockwood. Written by George Foster, Goodman Ace, Jay Burton, John Aylesworth, Mort Green**
**Cast:** Perry Como (host), Ethel Merman, Red Buttons, the Everly Brothers
**Performance Notes:** In an unusual choice of material, Ethel does a tribute to Al Jolson, singing many of his signature tunes. Afterward, she joins Perry for a duet of "Red, Red Robin" while he teaches her to sing in his relaxed style. This is a wonderful showcase for her, and Como is clearly thrilled to have her.

*The Chevy Show Starring Ethel Merman*
NBC, March 30, 1958 [Live, Color]
**Cast:** Ethel Merman (host), Jack Paar, Polly Bergen, Andy Williams, Genevieve, Al Kelly, Hugh Downs, Paul Weston and his Orchestra, the Butler Dancers
**Concept:** Ethel Merman is hosting the Chevy Show on a week when regular host Dinah Shore is off. The hour shows the audience how Ethel came to book her guest stars on this program originating from Los Angeles.
**Performance Notes:** This is not Ethel's finest hour. She is overweight, and her gowns by Wilma look like Wilma Flintstone. She opens the show with "You Make Me Feel So Young," interpolating a plug for sponsor Chevrolet into the lyrics. Her first big number is "Get Happy," conceived for her by Roger Edens and orchestrated by Paul Weston.

There is no shortage of high-powered showmanship, but once again, Merman is oversinging and spoiling her vocal quality.

There is a short comedy skit with vaudevillian Al Kelly doing his patented double-talk with Merman, followed by a duet with Polly Bergen on "When the Red, Red Robin Comes Bob, Bob, Bobbin' Along."

After a long sequence featuring Jack Paar and Genevieve, Ethel has her best moment in the show, a cover version of Perry Como's "Catch a Falling Star." She does not copy Como, does not oversell, is enchanting, and manages to make the song her own.

Ethel concludes the hour by spending more time with Polly Bergen. Interestingly, although Andy Williams is a guest on the show, he and Merman do not interact musically at all. Instead, Ethel sings snatches of "Over the Rainbow," "You Made Me Love You," "The Trolley Song," "I Could Have Danced All Night," "My Heart Belongs to Daddy," "I'm Gonna Wash That Man Right Out of My Hair," and "Wonderful Guy" interspersed with Polly singing Ethel's biggest hits. The two close the hour singing "Friendship."

**Interesting Sidenotes:** This live show ran long, so the only credit shown was for Ethel Merman's gowns by Wilma. Dinah Shore appears in a filmed commercial for Chevrolet singing "The Fun Is in the Going."

For weeks before this broadcast, Jack Paar and Genevieve (a regular on Paar's show) promoted the program on theirs, talking up flying to Los Angeles from New York and getting to work with Ethel Merman. Jack and Genevieve were extremely popular on television at this time.

Polly Bergen was also a welcome visitor into American homes. She had her own variety show, was a regular on "To Tell the Truth," and had played chanteuse Helen Morgan in a critically acclaimed television spectacular.

*The Frank Sinatra Show*
**ABC, April 25, 1958  [30 minutes]**
**Cast:** Frank Sinatra (host), Ethel Merman, Jesse White
**Concept:** A variety show hosted by Frank Sinatra
**Performance Notes:** This is one of Ethel's most successful television appearances. She looks beautiful and gets to sing two songs not normally associated with her: "Zing! Went the Strings of My Heart" and "I'm Always Chasing Rainbows."

Sinatra and Merman have a very funny sketch parodying Sinatra's appearance on "Person to Person." It ends with the duo singing "You're the Top."

*The Ed Sullivan Show*
**CBS, June 1958 [60 minutes, Live]**
**Performance Notes:** Ethel is one of a multitude of stars who appear briefly to wish Ed congratulations on his tenth anniversary on television.

*The Dinah Shore Chevy Show*
**NBC, October 19, 1958 [60 minutes, Live, Color]**
**Cast:** Dinah Shore (host), Ethel Merman, Marge and Gower Champion, Danny Thomas, Rusty Hamer
**Performance Notes:** Unfortunately, a tape of this show no longer exists.

*The Perry Como Show*
**NBC, November 29, 1958 [60 minutes, Live, Color]**
**Cast:** Perry Como (host), Ethel Merman, Marge and Gower Champion, Conway Twitty, Hugh Martin
**Performance Notes:** She sings "Taking a Chance on Love," "That Old Feeling," and two Hugh Martin numbers, "Have Yourself a Merry Little Christmas" and "The Trolley Song."

## The Eddie Fisher Show
**NBC, December 1958 [60 minutes, Live, Color]**
**Performance Notes:** Her solo was a rousing rendition of "Seventy-six Trombones." She and Eddie dueted on a medley of "you" songs, parodying the medley she and Mary Martin did of "I" songs on the "Ford" show.
**Interesting Sidenotes:** This is Ethel's first appearance on videotape, recently brought into use by NBC and soon extensively used to replace live performances.

## The Ed Sullivan Show
**CBS, October 11 1959 [60 minutes]**
**Cast:** Ed Sullivan (host), Ethel Merman, Mario Lanza, Larry Blyden
**Performance Notes:** Her contributions to the show are "There'll Be Some Changes Made" and "I'm Glad There Is You."
**Interesting Sidenotes:** The audience reacts strongly to the first number, as well they should. Merman had been singing it for quite a while. It was among the songs Al Siegel had arranged for her back in the late 1920s.

## Ford Startime: Ethel Merman on Broadway
**NBC, November 29, 1959 [60 minutes, Color]**
**Cast:** Ethel Merman (host), Fess Parker, Tom Poston, Tab Hunter
**Concept:** "Ford Startime" was an anthology series. Each week was different from the last, ranging from comedy to drama to variety. This week featured Merman hosting her own variety special.
**Performance Notes:** What should have been a triumph was a disaster. Foolishly, despite years and years of evidence to the contrary, Merman was talked into prerecording all of her songs. As a live singer, she was in a class by herself. As a lip-syncher . . . well, people turned this show off all over the country.

It was on this program that Ethel introduced her concert version of "Blow, Gabriel, Blow." The arrangement was by Billy May, and she sang it this way for the rest of her life.
**Interesting Sidenotes:** The sketch with Tom Poston, trying to

tempt a guard at Buckingham Palace, was suggested by a similar scene that Lucille Ball did on "I Love Lucy" a few years earlier.

### The Bell Telephone Hour: The Four of Us
**NBC, January 29, 1960 [60 minutes, Color]**
**Cast:** Ethel Merman, Ray Bolger, Benny Goodman, Bea Lillie
**Concept:** Four icons of show business meet to discuss a special they will do together. As a group, they decide not to do their signature numbers, but to try something different.
**Performance Notes:** What a difference two months can make. Ethel was nothing short of atomic here, doing a lavish ragtime production number with dancers and singers as she did tunes like "Alexander's Ragtime Band," "When My Sugar Walks Down the Street," "After You've Gone," "Sweet Georgia Brown," and "Way Down Yonder in New Orleans." At the end of the show, she does a truncated version of "I Got Rhythm."
**Interesting Sidenotes:** Happily, this performance has been released on DVD, along with some fascinating outtakes.

### Ford Startime Talent Scouts
**NBC, February 23, 1960 [60 minutes, Color]**
**Created by Irving Mansfield. Produced by William Nichols. Executive Produced by Irving Mansfield and Peter Arnell. Directed by Grey Lockwood. Written by George Foster. Choreographed by Danny Daniels**
**Cast:** Dave Garroway (Host), Ethel Merman, Joan Crawford, Hugh Downs, Maureen O'Hara, Richard Rodgers, Tommy Sands

And their discoveries: The John LaSalle Quartet, Paul Wallace, Colleen Dewhurst, Lester James, Brascia and Tyber, Laurie Peters, Joanie Sommers
**Concept:** The idea of a talent-scouts program began on radio with Major Bowes and came to television with Arthur Godfrey. In this incarnation, top celebrities brought on talent that were not unknown, but had not yet had their major chance at stardom.

**Performance Notes:** Ethel appears in a floor-length, sleeveless dress, wearing a diamond necklace and matching earrings and white gloves. Unlike the other stars, who simply introduce their discoveries, Ethel does a comedy bit with Garroway, pretending she is on "This is Your Life."

Her discovery is Paul Wallace, the talented performer who stopped *Gypsy* nightly with his rendition of "All I Need Is the Girl." Merman considered him her protégée, and he briefly dated Ethel's daughter.

**Interesting Sidenotes:** Jack Paar had originally been scheduled to appear as Lester James' discoverer, but had walked out on "The Tonight Show" that week due to a brouhaha over a water-closet joke. Rather than cancel James, Paar's sidekick, Hugh Downs, took his place.

One night around the time of this broadcast, Merman went out on the town with her daughter and Paul Wallace. Ethel drank too much and accused Paul of trying to use her. To make up for it, she gifted him with a wallet stuffed with money, symbolically wishing him to always have plenty of dough.

Executive producer Irving Mansfield was the husband of Jacqueline Susann, with whom Ethel was reported to be "mighty close" in the late 1960s. These folks had some eye for talent. Colleen Dewhurst went on to a magnificent career as a dramatic actress, and Joanie Sommers had quite a career as a singer of popular songs, recording many albums and appearing on television and in major nightspots.

*General Electric Theater: The Gershwin Years*
**CBS, January 15, 1961 [90 minutes]**
**Cast:** Ethel Merman, Frank Sinatra, Maurice Chevalier, Florence Henderson, Julie London
**Performance Notes:** While Ethel gets to sing such Gershwin favorites as "Embraceable You" and "Somebody Loves Me," her best moments are a duet with Sinatra of "Let's Call the Whole Thing Off" and a long segment of numbers and dialogue from *Strike Up the*

*Band* and *Of Thee I Sing*. Naturally, she ends the show singing "I Got Rhythm."

**Interesting Sidenotes:** Merman's duet with Sinatra was recorded separately from the rest of the show and spliced in to make it look as though he is there in the room with the rest of the cast.

This is the last time Ethel Merman sings "I Got Rhythm" holding the long notes on an "ooooooooh" sound. Henceforth, she will sing "ahhhhhhhhhhh" and hold a lower note, making it easier for her to sing the song. It is sad, but understandable, that Ethel could no longer sing the song exactly as she had more than thirty years earlier.

### The Bob Hope Show
**NBC, Spring 1962 [60 minutes]**
**Performance Notes:** This is another example of a show that has been lost to time. All that is known is that Ethel, Hope, and Fabian did a gangster sketch together.

### The Academy Awards
**NBC, April 1962 [120 minutes, Live, Color]**
**Performance Notes:** Dressed in a flowing chiffon gown, an angry Ethel defies the Hollywood that would not cast her in the movie version of *Gypsy* and sings an Irving Berlin medley that ends with her doing "There's No Business Like Show Business" while walking through the audience. She practically gets in the faces of the people who have rejected her, pausing only once to kiss Florence Henderson on the cheek.

### The Bob Hope Show
**NBC, November 20, 1962 [60 minutes]**
**Performance Notes:** Ethel does the "smiles" medley she had done long ago on Milton Berle's "Texaco Star Theater," as well as a version of "There's No Business Like Show Business" where she forgets the lyrics. The other highlights of the show include a Japanese sketch with Hope, as well as a duet with him of their hit from 1936, "It's DeLovely."

*The Perry Como Show*
**NBC, January 1, 1963 [60 minutes, Color]**
**Performance Notes:** Merman does two of the numbers from her Las Vegas act, "That Old Feeling" and "Got a Lot of Living to Do." She also duets with Perry on "Whispering," a number she would record ten years later in London.

*Vacation Playhouse: Maggie Brown*
**CBS, September 23, 1963 [30 minutes]**
**Written by Wilton Manhoff. Directed by David Alexander. A Desilu Production**
**Cast:** Ethel Merman, Mark Goddard, Marvin Kaplan, Roy Roberts, Susan Watson, Wally Vernon, Walter Burke, Hamilton Camp
**Interesting Sidenotes:** See page 151 for a full description of this appearance. Although this show was filmed in color, it was broadcast in black and white.

*Lincoln Center Day*
**CBS, September 22, 1963 [60 minutes, Live]**
**Directed by Norman Abbott. Music conducted by Alfredo Antonini. Miss Merman's pianist, Lew Kessler. Miss Merman's trumpeter, Dick Perry**
**Cast:** Alistair Cooke (host), Sally Ann Howes, Robert Merrill, Veronica Tyler, David Wayne, Richard Rodgers, the New York City Ballet with Jacques d'Amboise, the Merrill Staton Singers, and special guest star, Miss Ethel Merman
**Concept:** This was a live special from Philharmonic Hall at Lincoln Center honoring the first anniversary of the opening of the center.
**Performance Notes:** Merman helps open the show by appearing with the rest of the cast and singing a bit of "Everything's Coming Up Roses." She wears a long gown with a pleated chiffon skirt and looks lovely.

Later in the show, she and pianist Lew Kessler are introduced and literally come up through the floor to a tremendous ovation. Ethel is wearing the very same dress she wore on the the "Ford 50th

Anniversary Show" ten years earlier, shortened to 1963 cocktail length. She sings "They Say It's Wonderful," followed by a rousing rendition of "Blow, Gabriel, Blow" with Dick Perry as her very own Gabriel.

At the end of the show, Merman again joins the cast onstage and sings a bit of "The Song Is You."

**Interesting Sidenotes:** Lincoln Center was built on the site where much of the film *West Side Story* had been shot. The tenements were torn down to provide space for the New York State Theater, Philharmonic (Avery Fisher) Hall, the Metropolitan Opera House, and the Julliard School.

This was the only time in her career that Merman was billed as "Miss" Ethel Merman. She demanded and received special billing apart from the rest of the performers.

### The Judy Garland Show
**CBS, October 6, 1963 [60 minutes]**
**Cast:** Judy Garland (host), Barbra Streisand, Ethel Merman, the Smothers Brothers, Jerry Van Dyke
**Concept:** Judy Garland hosts a musical variety show.
**Performance Notes:** During Judy's "Tea for Two" segment with Barbra Streisand, Ethel is seated in the audience and begins to sing "You're Just in Love." Judy invites her onstage, where the two legends discuss Streisand, "the new belter." Barbra uses the occasion to announce her forthcoming Broadway musical, *Funny Girl*. After some very female badinage among the ladies about how thin both Judy and Ethel are and some advice to Streisand about getting a good dressing room, the three decide to sing "There's No Business Like Show Business" together. After just a moment, both Judy and Barbra stop singing and allow Merman to be Merman.
**Interesting Sidenotes:** Ethel and Judy had been friends for years. As a teenager, Ethel Merman was Judy's singing idol, someone she wanted to be just like.

Ethel was taping "The Red Skelton Hour" at CBS Television City in a studio just across the hall from where this show was taped. She stopped rehearsals for that show in order to make her appearance here.

Merman was an early supporter of Barbra Streisand's and at this point in her life, considered Barbra a friend. This is the only time Ethel Merman ever appeared with Barbra Streisand anywhere.

*What's My Line?*
**CBS, October 27, 1963 [30 minutes, Live]**
**Executive Produced by Gil Fates**
**Cast:** Dorothy Kilgallen, Allen Ludden, Arlene Francis, Bennett Cerf, Ethel Merman (Mystery Guest)
**Concept:** A panel of four celebrities tries to guess the occupations of total strangers.
**Performance Notes:** Ethel looked lovely and chic. She managed to promote her new film, *It's a Mad, Mad, Mad, Mad World*, her forthcoming appearance at the Persian Room at the Plaza Hotel, and her guest shot on "The Red Skelton Show" all in ninety seconds. When Arlene Francis asked her to sing a few bars of anything, Merman quipped, "At *these* prices?"

*The Red Skelton Hour*
**CBS, October 1963 [60 minutes]**
**Cast:** Red Skelton (host), Ethel Merman
**Performance Notes:** Although it is known that Merman did "That Old Feeling" and a sketch with Red where she tries to teach him to sing, this is another lost episode.

*The Jerry Lewis Show*
**ABC, November 2, 1963 [120 minutes]**
**Written, Produced, and Directed by Jerry Lewis**
**Cast:** Jerry Lewis (host), Sid Caesar, Ethel Merman, Mickey Rooney, Dick Shawn, Phil Silvers, Terry-Thomas, Jonathan Winters, Dorothy Provine, Ben Blue, Barrie Chase, Buster Keaton, Don Knotts, Carl Reiner, Peter Falk, Madlyn Rhue, William Demarest, Del Moore (announcer), Lou Brown Orchestra

**Concept:** Comedian/filmmaker Jerry Lewis hosts the only regularly scheduled two-hour variety series in television history.

**Performance Notes:** She is one of the cast from her latest film *It's a Mad, Mad, Mad, Mad World*, all on here to promote the film. Although Jerry seems a bit put off by the entire concept for this episode and is less than charming to the audience (which is made up of the press, both domestic and foreign), he shows Ethel the sort of respect and admiration that is her due. Using no less than eight cameras to capture her from every possible angle and height, Jerry captures Ethel's first televised performance of her hits medley most effectively. For her part, Merman is in almost-perfect voice. The audience of hard-boiled press gives her a long, sustained standing ovation when she is done.

**Interesting Sidenotes:** Although he worked very hard, Jerry just could not make this series work. It was eventually replaced by a new variety series called "The Hollywood Palace."

### The Judy Garland Show
**CBS, January 12, 1964 [60 minutes]**
**Cast:** Judy Garland (host), Ethel Merman, Shelley Berman, Peter Gennaro

**Performance Notes:** Ethel trots out her first televised version of "Gee, But It's Good to Be Here," as well as "I Get a Kick Out of You." They are probably the best versions of both numbers Ethel ever televised.

When Ethel and Judy do their duet of numbers Merman made famous as duets, Judy charmingly stumbles and screams when she loses her way during "You're Just in Love." All in all, this is one of Ethel's best television appearances.

### The Bell Telephone Hour: A Salute to Cole Porter
**NBC, January 28, 1964 [60 minutes, Live, Color]**
**Cast:** Ethel Merman (host), John Raitt, Peter Nero, Martha Wright, Gretchen Wyler, Jillana

**Concept:** As the title suggests, this is a salute to the music of Cole Porter by these talented people.

**Performance Notes:** As one would imagine, Ethel is in incredible voice as she salutes her dear friend who is dying. Merman did a lot of television around this time. While she was almost always in incredible voice, it is interesting to note the great fluctuation of her weight from show to show. She seemed to gain and lose weight in just a few days and not just a few pounds, either.

*The Lucy Show*
**CBS, February 3, 1964 [30 minutes]**
**Written by Bob Carroll Jr., Madelyn Martin, Bob Schiller, Bob Weiskopf. Directed by Jack Donohue. Produced by Elliot Lewis**
**Cast:** Lucille Ball, Vivian Vance, Ethel Merman, Gale Gordon, Jimmy Garrett, Ralph Hart
**Concept:** Ethel Merman comes to Danfield incognito because Mr. Mooney has told her the price will go up on the purchase price of a house if people know who she is. Coincidentally, Jerry wants Lucy to get Ethel Merman to star in his Cub Scouts show. Lucy and Viv see Ethel at the bank, and thinking she is someone else, Lucy decides to teach her to sing like Ethel Merman.
**Performance Notes:** This is, without a doubt, one of the best television appearances Merman ever made. She is slender, chic, and very funny. Her song here is "I Got Rhythm," and she is magnificent.
**Interesting Sidenotes:** It is here that Merman sings her greatest recorded version of "Everything's Coming Up Roses". This show went so well that the writers decided to change it from a single episode to a two-part story. As originally written and shot, the last scene has Ethel singing "You're the Top," while Lucy acts out the phrases. Instead, they cut the last scene and signed Merman to come back in six weeks after her booking at the Persian Room in New York was finished.

At that time, they reshot the last scene of the first episode with different dialogue and then shot the second episode. While the two were aired back to back, one only has to watch the final scene of this episode to see what had happened. Lucy (who wore only wigs on this series) had changed the style of her wig in the intervening weeks. Vivian Vance's hair had grown out, and Ethel had her hair color lightened. From one shot to the next, it seems as though a magic hairstyling fairy had waved her wand and completely redid the three ladies' hair.

It has been said that this appearance was Lucille Ball's way of making it up to Ethel that the sitcom pilot she had shot several months earlier ("Maggie Brown") had not sold to CBS.

Although this show was filmed in color, it was originally broadcast in black and white.

*The Lucy Show*
**CBS, February 10, 1964 [30 minutes]**
**Written by Bob Carroll Jr., Madelyn Martin, Bob Schiller, Bob Weiskopf. Directed by Jack Donohue. Produced by Elliot Lewis**
**Cast:** Lucille Ball, Vivian Vance, Ethel Merman, Gale Gordon, Jimmy Garrett, Ralph Hart
**Concept:** Ethel Merman is starring in the Cub Scout show, and Lucy wants to get into the act.
**Interesting Sidenotes:** It was after this episode was shot that Lucille Ball threw Ethel a wedding shower for her upcoming nuptials to Ernest Borgnine.

Although this show was filmed in color, it was broadcast in black and white.

*Sunday Night at the Palladium*
**BBC, March 15, 1964 [60 minutes, Live]**
**Performance Notes:** This is another performance that has been lost to the ages.

*The Academy Awards*
**NBC, April 13, 1964 [120 minutes, Live, Color]**
**Performance Notes:** She did yet-another Irving Berlin medley.

*An Evening With Ethel Merman*
**BBC, October 1964 [60 minutes, Live]**
**Produced by Buddy Bregman**

**Cast:** Ethel Merman

**Concept:** A video version of Ethel's one-woman show.

**Performance Notes:** Wearing the same dress she had worn several months earlier on "The Judy Garland Show," Ethel does her entire one-woman show from start to finish with no breaks or editing. She is in much better voice than on her live-from-Vegas album in late 1962.

### *Kraft Suspense Theatre: 'Twixt the Cup and Lip*
**NBC, June 3, 1965 [60 minutes, Color]**
**Written by Don Brinkley. Story by Julian Symonds. Directed by Leon Benson**

**Cast:** Larry Blyden, Ethel Merman, Joan Blackman, Charles McGraw, Jean Hale, John Hoyt, Lee Patterson, Lane Bradford, John Harmon, William Tannen, Herb Barnett, Ken Lowry

**Concept:** This is an unusual entry for this dramatic anthology series. Larry Blyden is a mousy worker at an art gallery who enlists the aid of Ethel Merman to help steal a valuable scepter.

**Performance Notes:** This is one of only two dramatic television appearances Merman made in the 1960s. She is well directed, and her performance is both funny and touching.

**Interesting Sidenotes:** Talented Larry Blyden would work with Merman several more times in their careers, including singing with her at the 1972 Tony Awards. He died in an accident in 1975.

### *What's My Line?*
**CBS, June 22, 1965 [30 minutes, Live]**

**Cast:** Dorothy Kilgallen, Tony Randall, Arlene Francis, Bennett Cerf, John Daly, Ethel Merman (Mystery Guest)

**Performance Notes:** This appearance was timed so that Ethel could promote her latest film, *The Art of Love.*

### *The Dean Martin Show*
**NBC, November 4, 1965 [60 minutes, Color]**

**Cast:** Dean Martin (host), Ethel Merman, Leslie Uggams, Jack Carter, Joey Heatherton, Leonard Barr, the New Christy Minstrels, the Carlssons, Joe & Eddie

**Performance Notes:** In one of her best variety-show appearances, Ethel sings the Berlin medley of "All Alone"/"All By Myself" for the first time, as well as a medley of her hits with Dean. She is thin, wears a beautiful black dress with lovely diamonds, and is in incredible voice.

## The Mike Douglas Show
**Syndicated, December 17, 1965 [90 minutes]**
**Cast:** Mike Douglas (host), Ethel Merman, Dan Dailey, Benay Venuta, Billy De Wolfe, Cy Coleman
**Performance Notes:** This is one of the best talk-show appearances Merman ever did. Although she has done several stints with Steve Allen, Jack Paar, Johnny Carson, and Merv Griffin by this time (all of these dates and shows have been lost), here she was in such good spirits and voice that it is a shame this episode is not commercially available.
**Interesting Sidenotes:** Benay Venuta was Ethel's on-again, off-again pal for almost fifty years. Ethel shows her great deference here, going on and on about how talented she is. This is the only recorded moment of the two of them performing together.

It is sad to see how much Dan Dailey had aged in the eleven years since their last film together. He looked at least ten years older than she. Actually, she was the older of the two. Dan was discovered as a chorus boy in *Stars in Your Eyes*. He embarrassed Ethel by reminding her of the sumptuous meals that Sherman Billingsley used to send over to the theater for the entire cast.

Despite all this stellar talent, the showstopper was Billy De Wolfe's impression of a businesswoman coming home at the end of a long, hard day and removing her clothes to take a hot bath.

## The Ed Sullivan Show
**CBS, February 13, 1966 [60 minutes, Color]**
**Cast:** Ed Sullivan (host), Ethel Merman, the Rolling Stones, Wayne Newton, Sandy Baron, Hal Holbrook, Eddie Schaeffer
**Performance Notes:** Sporting her new, upswept hairstyle with

bangs and banana curls, Ethel sings a medley of songs from *Annie Get Your Gun*. She is joined by four chorus boys and performs about as much dancing as anyone ever saw her do on television.

**Interesting Sidenotes:** One of the chorus boys working with Merman that night was Lee Roy Reams, who went on to be a Broadway star and director. Two years later, Ethel repeated this medley during a Sullivan salute to Irving Berlin. This episode was repeated on June 10, 1966.

*The Hollywood Palace*
**ABC, March 13, 1966 [60 minutes, Color]**
**Directed by Grey Lockwood. Produced by William O. Harbach. Executive Produced by Nick Vanoff**
**Cast:** Fred Astaire (host), Ethel Merman, Marcel Marceau, Pat Morita, the Hardy Family, the Rogge Sisters
**Performance Notes:** It is on this show that Merman sings her new version of "Some People." Roger Edens arranged this number, writing a new introduction and interpolating a few bars of "People." It is the best she ever sang this number and would be in her act and concerts for the rest of her life.

The highlight of her appearance was her duet with Fred Astaire. As she was with Mary Martin in 1953, Ethel was on fire and in tremendous voice. She and Fred complemented one another perfectly. Not only were they in musical form, but they were both hysterically funny. It is a shame that this is the only time they worked together. They should have recorded an album or done a special together. Composer Richard Rodgers once said that the only regret of his long career was never having written a song for Ethel Merman or Fred Astaire. Gershwin, Porter, and Berlin wrote for them frequently.

*The Ed Sullivan Show*
**CBS, September 25, 1966 [60 minutes, Color]**
**Cast:** Ed Sullivan (host), Ethel Merman, Frank Fontaine, Diana Ross and the Supremes, Steve Rossi, Nipsey Russell
**Performance Notes:** In the first half of the show, Ethel sings her

medley of "All Alone"/"All By Myself." Both songs were written by Irving Berlin, and the arrangement is sensational. She wears a red chiffon dress that she will wear until she dies.

The second half featured the entire cast of the revival of *Annie Get Your Gun* performing "I Got the Sun in the Morning" with the costumes, scenery, and arrangements directly from the revival. As the tape of the 1967 television version has been erased, this is the only video extant of Ethel Merman performing a number from one of her shows in full costume while she was actually *in* the show. While Ethel is in top form vocally, watched today the number seems a little stilted and old-fashioned. It is priceless!

### The Ed Sullivan Show
**CBS, January 8, 1967 [60 minutes, Color]**
**Cast:** Ed Sullivan (host), Ethel Merman, Flip Wilson, the Serendipity Singers, Gordon MacRae, Jose Greco, Myron Cohen, the Malroe Girls
**Performance Notes:** Looking decidedly heavier than she had since the 1950s, Merman sports a new, shorter hairstyle while singing "Some People." She is not in particularly good voice. The *Annie Get Your Gun* revival had done damage to her throat. She also duets with Gordon MacRae on "You're Just In Love."

### The Gypsy Rose Lee Show
**Syndicated, January 1967**
**Performance Notes:** Sometimes, one has to wonder what Ethel was thinking. While Gypsy herself is thrilled to have Ethel as her guest on her birthday (and looks chic and youthful with her newly blonded hair), Ethel looks and acts like a tired old matron. Her hair is not freshly done, so she wears a mink hat to cover it. She slouches on the couch, giving Gypsy one-word answers to questions. The actual highlight of the appearance is home movies Gypsy's son, Erik Preminger, took during rehearsals for the eponymous musical.

## *Annie Get Your Gun*
**NBC, March 19, 1967 [120 minutes, Color]**
**Cast:** Ethel Merman, Bruce Yarnell, Jerry Orbach, Benay Venuta
See page 162 for all of the information about this special.

## *That Girl: Pass the Potatoes*
**ABC, September 7, 1967 [30 minutes, Color]**
**Cast:** Marlo Thomas, Ethel Merman, Ted Bessell, Lew Parker, Sandy Kenyon, Joy Harmon, Allan Emerson, Carolan Daniels, Renata Vanni
**Concept:** Ann Marie is a young struggling actress living in Manhattan. She has a handsome, caring boyfriend and an overprotective father. In this episode, Ann has a small part in a Broadway show starring Ethel Merman. Naturally, Merman ends up cooking dinner in Ann's apartment.
**Performance Notes:** Although Ethel handles the comedy beautifully, she neither looks nor sounds well. Singing a snatch of "Small World" and ending the episode with "Everything's Coming Up Roses," it is obvious that this show within a show is supposed to be *Gypsy*.
**Interesting Sidenotes:** The entire premise of this episode is bogus. No one ever revives a Broadway show for just one week. And Ethel Merman couldn't cook to save her life. Obviously, neither could the writers. Pearl onions in stuffed cabbage? Lew Parker had played Ethel's love interest all the way back in *Girl Crazy* in 1930.

## *The Ed Sullivan Show*
**CBS, September 15, 1967 [60 minutes, Color]**
**Cast:** Ed Sullivan (host), Ethel Merman, David Frye, the Lovin' Spoonful, Corbett Monica, Sandler & Young
**Performance Notes:** This is Merman's first public appearance since the death of her daughter a month earlier. Her songs are "Ridin' High" and "This Is All I Ask."

*Batman: The Sport of Penguins*
ABC, October 5, 1967 [30 minutes, Color]
Written by Charlie Hoffman. Directed by Sam Strangis. Produced by Howie Horwitz. Executive Produced by William Dozier
**Cast:** Adam West, Burt Ward, Yvonne Craig, Alan Napier, Neil Hamilton, Stafford Repp, Burgess Meredith, Ethel Merman, Horace McMahon, Lewis Charles, Herbert Anderson, Constance Davis
**Performance Notes:** Ethel portrays Lola Lasagne, girlfriend of the Penguin. This was a very unhappy time for Ethel. She was so emotional that the cast had to be reminded not to bring up the subjects of death or children in her presence. It is Burgess who takes Ethel under his wing and buffers her from anything that might upset her.

*Batman: The Horse of Another Color*
ABC, October 12, 1967 [30 minutes, Color]
Written by Charlie Hoffman. Directed by Sam Strangis. Produced by Howie Horwitz. Executive Produced by William Dozier
**Cast:** Adam West, Burt Ward, Yvonne Craig, Alan Napier, Neil Hamilton, Stafford Repp, Burgess Meredith, Ethel Merman, Horace McMahon, Lewis Charles, Herbert Anderson, Constance Davis

**Tarzan: Mountains of the Moon Part I**
ABC, December 1, 1967 [60 minutes, Color]
Written by Jackson Gillis. Directed by Harmon Jones
**Cast:** Ron Ely, Ethel Merman, Strother Martin, Harry Lauter, William Marshall, Harry Townes, Della Ross, Stanley Olson, Rockne Tarrington
**Performance Notes:** Ethel portrays the wife of a minister who is killed. Her performance is well paced and her acting very effective. She was thrilled to have a reason to get away from familiar surroundings and travel to Mexico, where these two episodes were filmed on location.

*Tarzan: Mountains of the Moon Part II*
**ABC, December 8, 1967 [60 minutes, Color]**
**Written by Jackson Gillis. Directed by Harmon Jones**
**Cast:** Ron Ely, Ethel Merman, Strother Martin, Harry Lauter, William Marshall, Harry Townes, Della Ross, Stanley Olson, Rockne Tarrington

*The Hollywood Palace*
**ABC, December 5, 1967 [60 minutes, Color]**
**Cast:** Jimmy Durante (host), Ethel Merman, Larry Bishop, Rob Reiner, the Grass Roots, Noel Harrison, Milt Kamen, the Lennon Sisters
**Performance Notes:** Her songs are "Walking Happy," "Something Stupid" (duet with Durante), and a medley with Durante and Harrison from *My Fair Lady*. It had been a while since Ethel and the Schnozolla had worked together. The magic was still there.
**Interesting Sidenotes:** Future sitcom star and film director Rob Reiner makes one of his earliest television appearances here. The sketch he does with Larry Bishop (son of comedian Joey) about twins about to be born is extremely well performed.

*That Girl: The Other Woman*
**ABC, February 1, 1968 [30 minutes, Color]**
**Cast:** Marlo Thomas, Ethel Merman, Ted Bessell, Lew Parker, Rosemary DeCamp
**Performance Notes:** Again playing herself, this time a newspaper article makes Ann's mother, Helen, think her husband is having an affair with Ethel. Although Merman does not sing in this one, it is a very funny show.

*The Dean Martin Show*
**NBC, February 15, 1968 [60 minutes, Color]**
**Cast:** Dean Martin (host), Ethel Merman, Lainie Kazan, Roger Miller, Carl Ballantine, John Barbour
**Performance Notes:** What a difference a few years made! As lovely

as Ethel looked on her last appearance with Dean, she now looks old and haggard. Her voice was in terrible shape as she sang a medley of "I Want To Be Happy"/"Make Someone Happy." That wobble was out of control. She does fare a little better in a medley with Dean and Lainie, and in a comedy version of "I've Still Got My Health."

### The Ed Sullivan Show
**CBS, May 5, 1968 [90 minutes, Color]**
**Cast:** Ed Sullivan (host), Ethel Merman, Bing Crosby, Kate Smith, Diana Ross and the Supremes, and others
**Concept:** A salute to Irving Berlin
**Performance Notes:** Every once in a while, Ethel would seem to shed decades of age and look and sing as if she were much younger. This is one of those times. Chic in white chiffon, she repeats the *Annie Get Your Gun* medley she had done two years earlier, but with much better results. She also joined Miss Ross and the Supremes for "You're Just in Love."

### Around the World of Mike Todd
**ABC, September 8, 1968 [60 minutes, Color]**
**Performance Notes:** Ethel is interviewed about her friendship with Mike on this retrospective special.

### That's Life: Moving In
**ABC, October 29, 1968 [60 minutes, Color]**
**Executive Produced and Created by Marvin Marx. Directed by Stan Harris. Musical Direction by Elliot Lawrence. The Tony Mordente Dancers**
**Cast:** Robert Morse, E. J. Peaker, Shelley Berman, Kay Medford, Ethel Merman, Terry-Thomas, Lou Jacobi
**Concept:** Morse and Peaker play a couple living in fictional Ridgeville, whose relationship is revealed in each weekly episode.
**Performance Notes:** Merman played the young couple's bossy interior decorator. Her songs included "Think Pink," "Everything's Coming Up Roses," "Class," and "You Owe It All to Us."

**Interesting Sidenotes:** Using a mixture of original music and show tunes, nearly everyone in show business from George Burns to Liza Minnelli to Rodney Dangerfield guested on this high-concept program. Although the series was a darling of the critics, it was not well received by the public.

*The Hollywood Palace*
**ABC, December 14, 1968 [60 minutes, Color]**
**Directed by Grey Lockwood. Produced by William O. Harbach. Executive Produced by Nick Vanoff**
**Cast:** Jimmy Durante (host), Ethel Merman, Vicki Carr, Bill Dana, Hendra and Ullott, Leland Palmer, Sugar Ray Robinson
**Performance Notes:** Ethel and the Schnozzola duet on "You Are Woman" from *Funny Girl*.

*The Mike Douglas Show*
**Syndicated, January 24, 1969 [90 minutes, Color]**

*The Mike Douglas Show*
**Syndicated, January 30 – February 4, 1969 [90 minutes, Color]**
**Performance Notes:** Ethel is Mike's cohost all week. Her grandchildren are brought on as a surprise.

*The Carol Burnett Show*
**CBS, March 3, 1969 [60 Minutes, Color]**
**Directed by Dave Powers. Produced by Joe Hamilton. Writing Supervised by Arnie Rosen. Written by Stan Burns, Mike Marmer, Hal Goldman and Al Gordon, Don Hinkley, Kenny Solms, Gail Parent, Buz Kohan, Bill Angelos. Choreographed by Ernest Flatt. Musical Direction by Harry Zimmerman. Special Musical Material by Artie Malvin**
**Cast:** Carol Burnett (host), Lyle Waggoner, Harvey Korman, Vicki Lawrence, Ethel Merman, Tim Conway
**Performance Notes:** Carol brings Ethel out at the top of the show to take questions from the audience. She tells the folks in atten-

dance that her favorite leading man was Jack Klugman from *Gypsy*. In response to how she remains so young and beautiful, Ethel quips that she lived right or that maybe she lived *wrong*. Her solo is a medley of "Elusive Butterfly" and "Gentle on My Mind." One cannot imagine why anyone would foist this sort of material on Ethel Merman. She did her best, but it would never be included among her finest moments.

Merman is much more successful in a sketch where Carol is an understudy trying to do harm to the leading lady so she can take her place. She and Carol also do a long medley of show tunes that is less than satisfactory. Whether it is simply a bad arrangement or Carol is nervous working with her admitted idol, Burnett seems intent on outshouting Merman. It is not a good collaboration, and Ethel is never again a guest on the one show it would seem she should have been on the most.

### The Tony Awards
**NBC, April 20, 1969 [120 minutes, Color]**
**Performance Notes:** After making a crack about directors she *wished* she could have given it to, Ethel presents Peter Hunt with the award for best director of a musical for *1776*.

### The Merv Griffin Show
**CBS, December 2, 1969 [90 minutes, Color]**

### The Mike Douglas Show
**Syndicated, January 22, 1970 [90 minutes, Color]**

### The Merv Griffin Show
**CBS, August 13, 1970 [90 minutes, Color]**

### The Tonight Show, Starring Johnny Carson
**NBC, September 9, 1970 [90 minutes, Color]**
**Cast:** Johnny Carson (host), Ed McMahon (announcer), Doc Severinsen (musical director), Joel Grey, Ethel Merman, David Merrick, Bernadette Peters

*The Merv Griffin Show*
**CBS, April 29, 1971 [90 minutes, Color]**
**Cast:** Merv Griffin (host), Ethel Merman, Ralph Edwards
**Performance Notes:** Looking dumpy (and with her eyebrows drawn on like a clown), Ethel did her two "extra" numbers from *Hello, Dolly!*—"World, Take Me Back" and "Love Look in My Window."
**Interesting Sidenotes:** Ralph Edwards had not done an episode of his classic series, "This Is Your Life," in a decade. Unknown to most people, he was mounting a new version for syndication. Merv asked Ralph how he would surprise a guest, and Edwards pulled out a scrapbook (as he used to on the old version), turned to Ethel, and told her that this was, indeed, her life!

*This is Your Life: Ethel Merman*
**Syndicated, May 20, 1971 [30 minutes, Color]**
**Performance Notes:** Taken directly from Merv's studio (see above) to Ralph's studio, taping had to be held up a half hour to give a crying Merman a chance to get a hold of herself.

*S'Wonderful, S'Marvelous, S'Gershwin*
**CBS, January 17, 1972 [90 minutes, Color]**
**Directed by Walter C. Miller and Martin Charnin. Written and Produced by Martin Charnin. Executive Produced by Joseph Cates. Music Directed by Elliot Lawrence**
**Cast:** Jack Lemmon (host), Leslie Uggams, Peter Nero, Larry Kert, Linda Bennett, Robert Guillaume, Alan Johnson, Fred Astaire, Ethel Merman
**Performance Notes:** The producers saved Ethel almost for last. Dressed in a beige sheath and her hair upswept in curls, this was Merman's first prime-time television appearance in almost three years. She sang the complete version of "I Got Rhythm," including the opening verse that she had never sung on television before or after. Alas, she looked bloated, and her voice had a distinctive wobble.

*The Tony Awards*
**CBS, April 23, 1972 [120 minutes, Color]**
**Performance Notes:** It is on this broadcast that Ethel is given her lifetime achievement award. See page 105 for all the details.

*The Merv Griffin Show*
**Syndicated, November 19, 1972 [90 minutes, Color]**

*The Tonight Show, Starring Johnny Carson*
**NBC, November 20, 1972 [90 minutes, Color]**
**Directed by Bobby Quinn. Written by Hank Bradford, Michael Barrie, Jim Mulholland, Eric Mark Cohen, Thomas Moore, George Tricker**
**Cast:** Johnny Carson (host), Ed McMahon (announcer), Doc Severinsen (musical director), Ethel Merman, Jennifer O'Neill, Charlie Callas, William Farrell
**Performance Notes:** She sings "It's DeLovely" to a prerecorded musical track from her new album, *Merman Sings Merman.*

*What's My Line?*
**Syndicated, September 1972 [30 minutes, Color]**
**Performance Notes:** Ethel is booked to promote her new album, *Merman Sings Merman.*

*Ed Sullivan's Broadway*
**CBS, March 16, 1973 [90 minutes, Color]**
**Cast:** Ed Sullivan (host), Ethel Merman, Jack Cassidy, Julie Harris, Lou Jacobi, Michele Lee, Marilyn Michaels, Frank Sinatra Jr., Melvin Van Peebles, Bobby Van, Gwen Verdon, Cyril Ritchard
**Performance Notes:** Her songs are "When the Lights Are On Again," "Heart," "Everything's Coming Up Roses," "I Got Lost in His Arms," and "Ridin' High."

*The Tonight Show, Starring Johnny Carson*
NBC, March 19, 1974 [90 minutes, Color]

*The Tonight Show, Starring Johnny Carson*
NBC, June 6, 1974 [90 minutes, Color]
**Directed by Bobby Quinn**
**Cast:** Johnny Carson (host), Ed McMahon (announcer), Doc Severinsen (musical director), Ethel Merman, Michael Caine, Karen Valentine, Bert Convy
**Performance Notes:** Her numbers are "Alexander's Ragtime Band" and "I Get a Kick Out of You." This is Ethel at a low point. She had just faced her father's heart attack as well as putting her mother's ashes in a mausoleum and then rushed to Burbank to do this show. She truly looks as though someone had beaten her up.

To add insult to injury, Doc started the band too early on "Alexander's Ragtime Band," so that Ethel wasn't even yet at the microphone when the song started. The same sort of thing happened at her second number, when Merman began to sing, but the engineer had forgotten to turn on the microphone. It really threw her, and she stumbled on some of the lyrics.

*The Tonight Show, Starring Johnny Carson*
NBC, October 22, 1974 [90 minutes, Color]
**Directed by Bobby Quinn. Written by Hank Bradford, Thomas Moore, George Tricker, Eric Mark Cohen, Pat McCormick, Ray Siller, Hal Goodman, Larry Klein**
**Cast:** Johnny Carson (host), Ed McMahon (announcer), Doc Severinsen (musical director), Ethel Merman, Tony Randall, Kip Adotta, James Dickey
**Performance Notes:** Her songs this time are "Someone to Watch Over Me" and "Some People" to promote her new album, *Ethel's Ridin' High*.

*Journey Back to Oz*
**SFM Holiday Network Syndicated, December 1974 [120 minutes, Color]**
**Produced by Norm Prescott, Lou Schimer, Preston Blair, Fred Ladd. Directed by Hal Sutherland. Written by Fred Ladd, Norm Prescott, Bernard Evslin. Songs by Jimmy Van Heusen**
**Cast:** Liza Minnelli, Ethel Merman, Milton Berle, Paul Lynde, Peter Lawford, Danny Thomas, Herschel Bernardi, Paul Ford, Margaret Hamilton, Jack E. Leonard, Mickey Rooney, Rise Stevens, Mel Blanc, Larry Storch, Bill Cosby
**Concept:** An animated version of the further adventures of Dorothy Gale in the Land of Oz.

The voice work for this turkey had been done in 1962. The animation was considered so abominable that the film was shelved and never released in the United States. In the late 1960s, limited television animation had become the norm, and it was decided to release the film directly to television.
**Performance Notes:** Her songs are "Keep a Gloomy Thought," "An Elephant Never Forgets," and "Be a Witch."


*The Tonight Show, Starring Johnny Carson*
**NBC, January 15, 1975 [90 minutes, Color]**
**Directed by Bobby Quinn. Written by Hank Bradford, Thomas Moore, George Tricker, Eric Mark Cohen, Pat McCormick, Ray Siller, Hal Goodman, Larry Klein**
**Cast:** Johnny Carson (host), Ed McMahon (announcer), Doc Severinsen (musical director), Ethel Merman, David Janssen, Bert Convy, Rosie Black, Jimmy Wynn
**Performance Notes:** Wearing a black pailleted gown (that she would wear on at least a dozen other television shows) and her hair in a shoulder-length flip, Merman stops the show with "Nothing Can Stop Me Now" and "They Say It's Wonderful."

*Dinah!*
**Syndicated, February 26, 1975 [90 minutes, Color]**
**Cast:** Dinah Shore (host), Ethel Merman, Michelle Lee, Phil Silvers, Robert Morse, Jack Cassidy
**Concept:** A salute to Broadway showstoppers.
**Performance Notes:** Looking about as thin as she ever would in the 1970s, Merman stops the show with her hits medley while wearing a semi-see-through dress.

*Dinah!*
**Syndicated, March 10, 1975 [90 minutes, Color]**
**Cast:** Dinah Shore (host), Ethel Merman, Bill Daily, Annette Funicello, Henry Mancini
**Performance Notes:** Not only does Merman sing "Alexander's Ragtime Band," she takes dictation from Dinah to prove what a wonderful secretary she had been!

*The Tonight Show, Starring Johnny Carson*
**NBC, March 25, 1975 [90 minutes, Color]**

*The Mike Douglas Show*
**Syndicated, May 12, 1975 [90 minutes, Color]**

*The Tonight Show, Starring Johnny Carson*
**NBC, June 12, 1975 [90 minutes, Color]**
**Directed by Robert Ostberg. Written by Pat McCormick, Sidney Green, Ray Siller, Norman Liebmann, Robert Hilliard, Hal Goldman, Larry Klein**
**Cast:** John Davidson (host), Doc Severinsen (announcer), Tommy Newsom (musical director), Ethel Merman, Charo, Carl Ballantine, Kip Adotta, Ralph Waite, Robert Goulet (cameo surprise appearance)
**Performance Notes:** Once again she sings "Some People," but the highlight of this show is a duet between Ethel and John Davidson of "You're Just in Love." It was deliciously bad! Davidson not only didn't know the words, he couldn't get into the tricky rhythm of the counterpoint song. Merman stopped the song to give him another

chance, but when he couldn't get it a second time, she looked up to heaven and just shook her head in disgust.

*Match Game '75*
**CBS, July 3, 4, and 9, 1975 [30 minutes, Color]**
**Cast:** Gene Rayburn (host), Johnny Olson (announcer), Bill Daily, Brett Somers, Charles Nelson Reilly, Ethel Merman, Richard Dawson, Fanny Flagg

*The Tonight Show, Starring Johnny Carson*
**NBC, August 29, 1975 [90 minutes, Color]**
**Directed by Robert Ostberg. Written by Pat McCormick, Sidney Green, Ray Siller, Norman Liebmann, Robert Hilliard, Hal Goldman, Larry Klein**
**Cast:** McLean Stevenson (host), Ed McMahon (announcer), Doc Severinsen (musical director), Ethel Merman, Barbara Bain, Martin Landau, Pat Martin Earnhardt, John Davidson, Rose Marie
**Performance Notes:** Her numbers this time were her hits medley and "I Get a Kick Out of You."

*The Merv Griffin Show*
**Syndicated, September 8, 1975 [90 minutes, Color]**

*The Tonight Show, Starring Johnny Carson*
**NBC, December 16, 1975 [90 minutes, Color]**
**Directed by Bobby Quinn. Written by Pat McCormick, Sidney Green, Ray Siller, Norman Liebmann, Robert Hilliard, Hal Goldman, Larry Klein**
**Cast:** Johnny Carson (host), Ed McMahon (announcer), Doc Severinsen (musical director), Shecky Greene, Ted Knight, Ethel Merman, Madlyn Rhue
**Performance Notes:** Once again she sings "Some People," still trying to push her album, *Ethel's Ridin' High.*

*Dinah!*
**Syndicated, January 31, 1976 [90 minutes, Color]**

*The Merv Griffin Show*
Syndicated, April 27, 1976 [90 minutes, Color]

*The Tonight Show, Starring Johnny Carson*
NBC, May 5, 1976 [90 minutes, Color]
**Directed by Bobby Quinn. Written by Pat McCormick, Sidney Green, Ray Siller, Norman Liebmann, Robert Hilliard, Hal Goldman, Larry Klein**
**Cast:** Johnny Carson (host), Ed McMahon (announcer), Doc Severinsen (musical director), Shecky Greene, Ethel Merman, Hoyt Axton, Dr. Thomas Tutko
**Performance Notes:** Miss Merman does "Gee, But It's Good to Be Here." By this point in her career, she does this song as often as possible because it falls well on her voice and is easy for her to sing.

*The Hollywood Squares*
Syndicated, May 1976 [30 minutes, Color]

*Match Game '76*
CBS, June 4-10, 1976 [30 minutes, Color]
**Cast:** Gene Rayburn (host), Johnny Olson (announcer), Avery Schreiber, Ethel Merman, Brett Somers, Charles Nelson Reilly, Richard Dawson, Joyce Bulifant

*Arthur Fiedler and the Boston Pops*
PBS, July 4, 1976 [60 minutes, Color]

*Dinah!*
Syndicated, July 8, 1976 [90 minutes, Color]

*Match Game '76*
CBS, August 2-10, 1976 [30 minutes, Color]
**Cast:** Gene Rayburn (host), Johnny Olson (announcer), Robert Hegyes, Brett Somers, Charles Nelson Reilly, Ethel Merman, Richard Dawson, Joyce Bulifant

### The Big Event
**NBC, September 27, 1976 [90 minutes, Live, Color]**
**Performance Notes:** After lip-synching to "Everything's Coming Up Roses" in the pouring rain in Shubert Alley in Manhattan, she enters Sardi's restaurant. She joins Marvin Hamlisch and sings "Ease on Down the Road," "All That Jazz," "Sweet Georgia Brown," and "What I Did For Love."

### The Tonight Show, Starring Johnny Carson
**NBC, October 6, 1976 [90 minutes, Color]**
**Directed by Bobby Quinn. Written by Pat McCormick, Ray Siller, Norman Liebmann, John Terry Hart, Hal Goodman, Larry Klein. Produced by Fred de Cordova**
**Cast:** Johnny Carson (host), Ed McMahon (announcer), Doc Severinsen (musical director), Ethel Merman, Abbe Lane, Bob Uecher, Dr. William A. Nolen
**Performance Notes:** Merman went from show to show trying to make both "What I Did For Love" and "Sweet Georgia Brown" associated only with her. She had sung both these numbers on "The Big Event."

### The Entertainment Hall of Fame
**CBS, October 26, 1976 [60 minutes, Color]**
**Performance Notes:** To induct George Gershwin, Cole Porter, and Irving Berlin, Ethel sings "I Got Rhythm," "I Get a Kick Out of You," and "There's No Business Like Show Business."

### The Ted Knight Special
**CBS, November 30, 1976 [60 minutes, Color]**
**Directed by Sid Smith. Musical Direction by Peter Matz**
**Cast:** Ted Knight (host), Ethel Merman, Ed Asner, Fred MacMurray, Rue McClanahan, Phil Silvers, Loretta Swit
**Performance Notes:** Completely miscast as Ted's old teacher, Ethel warbles "America" before she gets into "There's No Business Like Show Business."

*The Bobby Vinton Show*
**Syndicated, Fall 1977 [30 minutes, Color]**
**Performance Notes:** Her songs are "Alexander's Ragtime Band" and "There's No Business Like Show Business."

**The Muppet Show**
**Syndicated, September 1977 [30 minutes, Color]**
**Performance Notes:** Her numbers here include a medley with all the Muppets of her duets, as well as a production number version of "There's No Business Like Show Business." This is the first time Ethel is seen in her new, shorter hairstyle that she will wear for the rest of her life.

*From This Moment On: Steve and Eydie Salute Cole Porter*
**CBS, March 10, 1977 [60 minutes, Color]**
**Produced by Dwight Hemion and Gary Smith. Directed by Dwight Hemion**
**Cast:** Steve Lawrence, Eydie Gorme, Ethel Merman, Bob Hope, the Swingle Singers, the Yale Glee Club
**Performance Notes:** Her numbers include "I'm Throwing a Ball Tonight," "Make It Another Old-Fashioned," "I Hate Men," "My Heart Belongs to Daddy," and a duet with Hope of "It's DeLovely."
**Interesting Sidenotes:** During the taping of "DeLovely," the battery for Ethel's wireless microphone (which had been taped to the inside of her thigh) falls to the floor. Merman is very embarrassed to have caused the taping to stop. In the future, she will insist at all performances that two batteries be used at all times, taped to her ample bosom so that they could not fall out.

*The Merv Griffin Show: The Belters*
**Syndicated, March 10, 1977 [90 minutes, Color]**
**Cast:** Merv Griffin (host), Ethel Merman, Karen Morrow, Dolores Gray, Ann Miller

*Lifestyles with Beverly Sills*
**Syndicated, March 29, 1977 [30 minutes, Color]**

**Cast:** Beverly Sills, Ethel Merman, Mary Martin
**Performance Notes:** Ethel and Mary are on to promote their upcoming concert at the Broadway Theatre in May.

*The Tonight Show, Starring Johnny Carson*
**NBC, April 1, 1977 [90 minutes, Color]**
**Directed by Bobby Quinn. Written by Pat McCormick, Glenn Warren, Hal Goodman, Larry Klein, Norman Liebmann, Ray Siller, Bill Daley. Produced by Fred de Cordova**
**Cast:** Johnny Carson (host), Ed McMahon (announcer), Doc Severinsen (musical director), McLean Stevenson, Ethel Merman, Tom Dreesen, Ray Johnson
**Performance Notes:** Looking and sounding great, Ethel socks out "Ridin' High" and "This Is All I Ask."

*Match Game PM*
**Syndicated, April 29, March 2-5, 1977 [30 minutes, Color]**
**Cast:** Gene Rayburn (host), Johnny Olson (announcer), Don Sutton, Brett Somers, Charles Nelson Reilly, Ethel Merman, Richard Dawson, Fanny Flagg

*The Today Show*
**NBC, May 13, 1977 [120 minutes, Color]**

*You're Gonna Love It Here*
**CBS, June 1, 1977 [30 minutes, Color]**
See page 193 for the story of this show.

*The Ford 75th Anniversary Show*
**CBS, June 1977 [120 minutes, Color]**
**Performance Notes:** Ethel does a major production number singing "Before the Parade Passes By" in a circus setting.

*The Tonight Show, Starring Johnny Carson*
**NBC, June 16, 1977 [90 minutes, Color]**

**Directed by Bobby Quinn. Written by Pat McCormick, Glenn Warren, Hal Goodman, Larry Klein, Norman Liebmann, Ray Siller, Bill Daley. Produced by Fred de Cordova**

**Cast:** Johnny Carson (host), Doc Severinsen (announcer), Tommy Newsom (musical director), Angie Dickinson, Ethel Merman, Dr. Gerard O'Neill, San Francisco Bell Ringers

**Performance Notes:** By this point in her career, Merman's voice was not always as reliable as it once was. One day she might be perfection personified. Other times, she seemed to lack energy and have that annoying wobble in her voice. Singing "Nothing Can Stop Me Now," this was one of those times.

*Sha Na Na*

**Syndicated, September 1977 [30 minutes, Color]**

**Performance Notes:** Besides doing comedy sequences, her big moment here is a duet with Bowzer of "Anything You Can Do, I Can Do Better."

*Command Performance*

**CBS, January 13, 1978 [120 minutes, Color]**

**Produced by Bob Finkel. Written by Herb Baker. Directed by Tony Charmoli. Executive Produced by Bob Stivers**

**Cast:** Buddy Ebsen (host), Lynn Anderson, Jim Bailey, Victor Borge, Richard Burton, Red Buttons, Charlie Callas, Jack Carter, Bob Crosby, Phyllis Diller, Buddy Hackett, Elaine Joyce, Frankie Laine, Peggy Lee, Ethel Merman, Jan Murray, Ginger Rogers, Neil Sedaka, Bobby Short, Bobby Van

**Concept:** This was an attempt by CBS to do "The Ed Sullivan Show" without Mr. Sullivan.

**Performance Notes:** Ethel belted out "There's No Business Like Show Business" and "Alexander's Ragtime Band," although the latter number was cut from the final broadcast.

**Interesting Sidenotes:** Bringing to the television audience performers that they had "commanded," this special is one of the reasons why variety on television died. There was no audience (an applause track was used), and the performers were taped in bits and pieces and then edited together. And unlike Ed Sullivan's show, there was nothing here to appeal to young people.

### The Merv Griffin Show
Syndicated, May 15, 1978 [90 minutes, Color]

### The Tonight Show, Starring Johnny Carson
NBC, May 17, 1978 [90 minutes, Color]
**Directed by Robert Ostberg. Written by Michael Barrie, Jim Mulholland, Mickey Rose, Roy Teeclin, Ray Siller, Bill Daley, Larry Klein, Hal Goodman. Produced by Fred de Cordova**
**Cast:** Johnny Carson (host), Ed McMahon (announcer), Doc Severinsen (musical director), Jane Fonda, Ethel Merman, Charlie Callas, Carl Sagan
**Performance Notes:** Her big number was (once again) "Gee, But It's Good to Be Here."

### Bing Crosby: His Life and Legend
ABC, May 25, 1978 [120 minutes, Color]
**Performance Notes:** Merman does not sing in this retrospective special, but instead was interviewed (along with Mary Martin, Ella Fitzgerald, and a host of others) about making movies with him and her thoughts about him as a singer.
### The Merv Griffin Show
Syndicated, November 13, 1978 [90 minutes, Color]

### Christmas Eve on Sesame Street
CBS, December 3, 1978 [60 minutes, Color]
**Cast:** The characters and actors from "Sesame Street," Ethel Merman, Imogene Coca, Leslie Uggams
**Performance Notes:** It is interesting to watch Merman's 1970s television appearances. To save money, she often did her own makeup and hair. She wore and rewore the same dresses over and over. All of this money saving only served to make her look elderly and frumpy. She should have insisted on proper lighting and makeup,

and had her hair freshly done (especially for prime-time television). Her songs here were "Tomorrow" from the Broadway hit, *Annie*, and participation in a medley of Christmas carols.

Muppets creator Jim Henson was a huge fan of Merman's talent. This is her second of four appearances with the Muppets on television.

## *American Pop: The Great Singers*
**PBS, January 10, 1979 [120 minutes, Color]**
**Cast:** Tony Bennett (host), Ethel Merman, Sarah Vaughan, and others
**Performance Notes:** Her contribution here is her hits medley. She was gaining weight and had new dresses made. They were pailleted with cocktail-length pleated skirts with the same sash she had worn on dresses more than a decade earlier. They were blue and lavender, exactly alike, and she wore them in all of her concert work from this point forward.

## *The Tonight Show, Starring Johnny Carson*
**NBC, April 4, 1979 [90 minutes, Color]**
**Directed by Robert Ostberg. Written by Art McAloon, Michael Barrie, Jim Mulholland, Pat McCormick, Ray Siller, Mickey Rose, Larry Klein, Hal Goodman. Produced by Fred de Cordova**
**Cast:** Johnny Carson (host), Ed McMahon (announcer), Tommy Newsom (musical director), Angie Dickinson, Ethel Merman, Dr. Henry Heimlich, Richie Barathy
**Performance Notes:** Once again, Merman sings "Tomorrow," but the results are like night and day. She looks rested, is dressed and groomed properly, and has figured out how to sing the song for best possible effect.

During her interview with Johnny, she announces her forthcoming disco album. The studio audience cheered in appreciation.

## *Hee Haw*
**Syndicated, April 1979 [60 minutes, Color]**
**Cast:** Buck Owens, Roy Clark, Minnie Pearl, Grandpa Jones, Gunilla Hutton, Ethel Merman, and others

**Performance Notes:** While this might seem like an unlikely match, Ethel and this show hit it off like two hounds and a possum. Her broad comic delivery fit right in with the corn-pone comedy. Ethel's solo of "Doin' What Comes Nat'rally" is the only video extant of her doing this song in its entirety.

*The Merv Griffin Show*
**Syndicated, May 9, 1979 [90 minutes, Color]**

*The Muppets Go Hollywood*
**CBS, May 16, 1979 [60 minutes, Color]**

*The Love Boat: Third Wheel*
**ABC, May 12, 1979 [60 minutes, Color]**
**Written by Lee Ahronsohn, Ann Gibbs, Joel Kimmel. Directed by Gordon Farr**
**Cast:** Ethel Merman, Nanette Fabray, Barry Nelson, Beth Howland, Ken Berry, Bob Cummings, Michelle Tobin, Shelley Juttner
**Concept:** Each week, a luxury liner sets sail for romantic ports while the crew helps the passengers with their love lives.

**Performance Notes:** Ethel plays Roz, Gopher's bombastic mother. This is the first of several visits she pays to the series in this character. In this episode, she does not sing.

*Kids Are People, Too*
**Metromedia and Syndicated, July 1979 [120 minutes, Color]**
**Cast:** Michael Young (host), Ethel Merman
**Performance Notes:** This is not Ethel's finest moment. The host, Michael, is obviously a huge fan of hers, and she resents his fan worship. She does not want to talk about her career. She wants to plug her disco album! Ethel is almost nasty to him when he asks her to sing four bars of a duet with him.

Merman came across as an uncooperative old biddy to an audience of youngsters that might have bought her album had she been cool and played along. Sometimes, Ethel was her own worst enemy.

*The Tonight Show, Starring Johnny Carson*
**NBC, July 26, 1979 [90 minutes, Color]**
**Directed by Bobby Quinn. Written by Michael Barrie, Jim
Mulholland, Kevin Mulholland, Pat McCormick, Robert Smith,
Charles Lee, Ray Siller, Larry Klein, Hal Goldman. Produced by
Fred de Cordova**
**Cast:** Johnny Carson (host), Ed McMahon (announcer), Doc
Severinsen (musical director), Ethel Merman, Albert Brooks, Tom
Warren, Joan Embry
**Performance Notes:** It is here that Ethel tries to sing one of her
disco cuts live with a band. She does "Alexander's Ragtime Band,"
and the effect is strange. She is trying so hard to sell the song and
the arrangement, but it just does not come off right.
**Interesting Sidenotes:** This was Merman's final appearance with
Johnny Carson. He made a comment about her almost taking off on
the last note, and she took this as a knock. At the commercial, they
had words, and she was never invited back.

For those of you who are fans of the Carson DVD series, it is
from this episode that the producers chose the Albert Brooks clip
(with him stuffing a hot potato in his mouth to imitate Curly
Howard's woo-woo sound from *The Three Stooges*).

*Musical Comedy Tonight*
**PBS, October 1, 1979 [90 minutes, Color]**
**Produced and Written by Sylvia Fine Kaye**
**Cast:** Sylvia Fine Kaye, Ethel Merman, John Davidson, and others
**Concept:** Mrs. Kaye narrates and tries to reproduce moments from
great musicals with the original costumes and orchestrations.
**Performance Notes:** Ethel's numbers are "You're the Top" (with
Rock Hudson), "I Get a Kick Out of You," and "Anything Goes." It
is on this show that Merman first showed health problems that
might have been linked to her eventual brain tumor.

*Rudolph and Frosty's Christmas in July*
**CBS, November 25, 1979 [120 minutes, Color]**
**Directed by Arthur Rankin Jr. and Jules Bass**
**Cast:** Ethel Merman, Red Buttons, Mickey Rooney, Shelley Winters, Alan Sues, Jackie Vernon, Paul Frees
**Performance Notes:** This belatedly aired special gave Merman several cute numbers to sing, including the rousing "Don't Let the Parade Pass You By." Her songs had been recorded in the late 1960s, but the project had been shelved. When it was revived, she was asked to record "Rudolph the Red-Nosed Reindeer." The difference in vocal quality was amazing.

*The Love Boat: Not So Fast, Gopher*
**ABC, February 9, 1980 [60 minutes, Color]**

*The Merv Griffin Show*
**Syndicated, April 24, 1980 [90 minutes, Color]**

*Standing Room Only: Show Stoppers*
**HBO, June 22, 1980 [60 minutes, Color]**
**Performance Notes:** Her numbers are "I Get a Kick Out of You" and "There's No Business Like Show Business."

*The Merv Griffin Show*
**Syndicated, September 22, 1980 [90 minutes, Color]**

*The Palace*
**Syndicated, 1980 [60 minutes, Color]**
**Performance Notes:** Her numbers are her hits medley and a duet of "You're Just in Love" with Jack Jones.

*Great Performances: Beverly! Her Farewell Performance*
**PBS, October 27, 1980 [120 minutes, Color]**
**Cast:** Beverly Sills, Kitty Carlisle, Ethel Merman, Mary Martin, Dinah Shore, Carol Burnett, and others

**Performance Notes:** Her number is "There's No Business Like Show Business."

### *The Inaugural Celebration of Ronald Reagan*
**NBC, January 19, 1981 [120 minutes, Color]**
**Cast:** Johnny Carson (host), Ethel Merman, and others
**Performance Notes:** As she had done for John F. Kennedy exactly twenty years earlier, Merman belts "Everything's Coming Up Roses" to the newly elected president. She is bloated, and her hair does not look freshly done. She also wears an old dress. While she seems to be delighted to open this show, it seems odd that she put so little into her physical appearance.

### *100 Years of Popular Music*
**NBC, April 27, 1981 [60 minutes, Color]**
**Cast:** George Burns, Ethel Merman, John Davidson, Gordon MacRae
**Performance Notes:** This special had been shot in 1978 and held back for reasons unknown. Ethel does a very truncated version of her hits medley, as well as a duet with Gordon MacRae of "There's No Business Like Show Business."

### *The Monte Carlo Show*
**Syndicated, 1981 [60 minutes, Color]**
Hosted by Patrick Wayne
**Performance Notes:** Merman does her hits medley and "Gee, But It's Good to Be Here." Oddly, she sings the two numbers wearing the same dress, but made in two different colors.

### *The Love Boat*
**ABC, October 10, 1981 [60 minutes, Color]**

### *The Love Boat: The Love Boat Follies*
**ABC, February 27, 1982 [120 minutes, Color]**
**Cast:** Ethel Merman, Carol Channing, Della Reese, Van Johnson, Cab Calloway
**Performance Notes:** Her songs are "I'm the Greatest Star," "Everything's Coming Up Roses," and "What I Did For Love."

*Night of 100 Stars*
CBS, March 8, 1982 [180 minutes]
**Produced by Hildy Parks. Executive Produced by Alexander H. Cohen. Directed by Clark Jones. Written by Hildy Parks. Music Directed by Elliot Lawrence**

*The Merv Griffin Show*
**Syndicated, May 25, 1982 [90 minutes, Color]**

*Over Easy*
**PBS, June 1982 [30 minutes, Color]**
**Cast:** Mary Martin, Jim Hartz, Ethel Merman
**Performance Notes:** Her songs are "There's No Business Like Show Business" and a special-material version of "Anything I Can Do, You Can Do Better" with Mary.

*The Texaco Star Theater: Opening Night*
**NBC, September 11, 1982 [90 minutes, Color]**
**Cast:** Ethel Merman, Sammy Davis Jr., Carol Burnett, Bernadette Peters, and others
**Performance Notes:** Her songs are "Before the Parade Passes By" and "There Is No Tune Like a Show Tune."

*The Wonderful World of Musicals*
**BBC, November 8, 1982 [120 minutes, Live]**
**Cast:** Ethel Merman, Tim Curry, Howard Keel, Jack Jones, Millicent Martin, Topol
**Concept:** This is a BBC live telecast of a Royal Command Performance for the Queen Mother.
**Performance Notes:** Ethel is the final performer on the bill. Dressed in the last gown she ever bought (red underslip with long red and gold overcoat), she stops the show with "There's No Business Like Show Business." This is Ethel's final appearance in London.

*Broadway: A Special Salute*
**PBS, May 4, 1985 [120 minutes, Color]**
**Cast:** Ethel Merman, Mary Martin, Chita Rivera, Lee Roy Reams, Tom Bosley, and others
**Performance Notes:** This special, alternately called "That's Singing!," is actually a compilation of two different concerts shot for PBS and then pieced together. Aired after her death, Ethel's contributions of "Everything's Coming Up Roses" and "They Say It's Wonderful" had been taped in 1982.

# *The Films*

*The Cave Club*
**Warner Brothers Vitaphone, Released May 15, 1930, 9 minutes**
**Cast:** Frank Tinney, Ethel Merman, Ted Lewis, Marjorie Leach, Frank Pierlot, Harriet Harbaugh
**Plot:** Audiences are given a fictionalized view of prehistoric nightlife, and then through a mystic glass, get a glimpse of nightlife in 1930, showing that tastes have not changed.

*Her Future*
**Paramount, Released September 10, 1930, 11 minutes**
**Written and Directed by Mort Blumenstock**
**Plot:** A dejected woman contemplates her future.
**Merman's Songs:** "My Future Just Passed," "Sing You Sinners"

*Follow the Leader*
**Paramount, Released December 12, 1930, 76 minutes**
**Written by Gertrude Purcell and Sid Silvers. Directed by Norman Taurog. Songs by B. G. De Sylva, Lew Brown, Ray Henderson**
**Cast:** Ed Wynn, Ginger Rogers, Ethel Merman, Lou Holtz, Preston Foster, and others

**Plot:** A chorine with rough edges gets her big break when the star of the show is kidnapped and she has to go on in her place.
**Merman's Song:** "Satan's Holiday"

*Devil Sea*
**Paramount, Released February 27, 1931, 10 minutes**
**Written and Directed by Mort Blumenstock. Music Arranged by Al Siegel**

*Roaming*
**Paramount, Released November 27, 1931, 11 minutes**
**Written and Directed by Casey Robinson. Songs by Johnny Green**
**Plot:** Ethel and her father operate a traveling medicine show. Because of this, the man Ethel falls in love with thinks she is "easy" and breaks her heart.
**Merman's Songs:** "Hello, My Lover, Goodbye," "Shake Well before Using"

*Old Man Blues*
**Paramount, Released on March 18, 1932, 9 minutes**
**Directed by Aubrey Scotto. Written by J.P. Murray, Barry Travers, Ben Oakland**
This is Merman's strangest short. It is almost operetta in style, as Ethel tentatively sings "He Doesn't Love Me Anymore."

*Let Me Call You Sweetheart*
**Paramount, Released on May 19, 1932, 8 minutes**
**Produced by Max Fleischer. Directed by Dave Fleischer. Animation by James H. Culhane, David Tendlar. Songs by Beth Slater Whitson, Leo Friedman. Betty Boop's voice by Mae Questel**
**Plot:** Ethel sings the title song, which leads into a Betty Boop cartoon, followed by a bouncing ball sing-along with Ethel.

*Ireno*
Paramount, Released on June 30, 1932, 9 minutes
Directed by Aubrey Scotto. Written by Aubrey Scotto, Andrew Bennison
**Plot:** A woman is in a Reno, Nevada, gambling casino awaiting her divorce when her husband comes to reconcile.
**Merman's Songs:** "Wipe That Frown Right Off Your Face," "Shadows on the Wall"

*You Try Somebody Else*
Paramount, Released on August 1, 1932, 8 minutes
Produced by Max Fleischer. Directed by Dave Fleischer. Songs by De Sylva, Brown, and Henderson. Betty Boop's voice by Mae Questel
**Plot:** This is another sing-along that leads into a Betty Boop cartoon.

*Time on My Hands*
Paramount, Released on December 22, 1932, 10 minutes
Produced by Max Fleischer. Directed by Dave Fleischer. Animated by Willard Bowsky, Thomas Goodson. Songs by Harold Adamson, Mack Gordon, Vincent Youmans. Betty Boop's voice by Mae Questel
Another entry in the Betty Boop series.

*Song Shopping*
Paramount, 1933
Produced by Max Fleischer. Directed by Dave Fleischer. Animated by Willard Bowsky, Thomas Goodson
The last of Merman's Betty Boop cartoon sing-alongs.

*Be Like Me*
Paramount, Released on February 16, 1933, 10 minutes
Written and Directed by Casey Robinson
**Merman's Songs:** "Be Like Me," "After You've Gone"

*We're Not Dressing*
Paramount, Released April 26, 1934, 77 minutes
Produced by Benjamin Glazer. Directed by Norman Taurog.
Written by Horace Jackson, George Marion Jr. Based on a story
by Benjamin Glazer. Songs by Harry Revel, Mack Gordon
**Cast:** Bing Crosby, Carole Lombard, George Burns, Gracie Allen,
Ethel Merman, Leon Errol, Jay Henry, Ray Milland, John Irwin,
Charles Morris, Bill Hendricks, Ted Oliver
**Plot:** A group of people gets shipwrecked, and Bing Crosby
becomes their ruler. He teaches spoiled heiress Lombard how to
come down to earth and be a "regular guy."
**Merman's Song:** "It's Just a New Spanish Custom"

*Kid Millions*
United Artists, Released December 8, 1934, 90 minutes
Produced by Samuel Goldwyn. Directed by Roy Del Ruth.
Written by Arthur Sheekman, Nat Perrin, Nunnally Johnson.
Music Directed by Alfred Newman
**Cast:** Eddie Cantor, Ann Sothern, Ethel Merman, George Murphy,
Jesse Block, Eve Sully, Lucille Ball, Stymie Beard, and others
**Plot:** Three con artists try to do Eddie Cantor out of his inheritance.
**Merman's Songs:** "An Earful of Music," "Mandy"

*The Big Broadcast of 1936*
Paramount, Released September 26, 1935, 94 minutes
Produced by Benjamin Glazer. Directed by Norman Taurog.
Written by Ralph De Leon, Francis Martin, Ralph Spence
**Cast:** Bing Crosby, Amos 'n' Andy, Ethel Merman, George Burns,
Gracie Allen, Charlie Ruggles, the Nicholas Brothers, Jack Oakie,
Wendy Barrie, Ina Ray Hutton, Bill Robinson, and others
**Plot:** Jack Oakie's radio station is in trouble, and Bing Crosby and
others show what they can do on the air through an early version of
television.
**Merman's Song:** "It's the Animal in Me" (originally filmed for *We're Not Dressing*)

*Strike Me Pink*
United Artists, Released January 22, 1936, 104 minutes
Produced by Samuel Goldwyn. Directed by Norman Taurog.
Written by Frank Butler, Walter De Leon, Francis Martin,
Phillip Rapp. Songs by Harold Arlen, Lew Brown
**Cast:** Eddie Cantor, Ethel Merman, Sally Eilers, Harry Parke,
William Frawley, Brian Donlevy, Jack La Rue, and others
**Plot:** Eddie is a timid tailor who has the hots for nightclub singer
Merman.
**Merman's Songs:** "Shake It Off with Rhythm," "Calabash Pipe,"
"First You Have Me High, Then You Have Me Low"

*Anything Goes*
Paramount, Released on January 30, 1936, 92 minutes
Produced by Benjamin Glazer. Directed by Lewis Milestone.
Songs by Cole Porter, Leo Robbins, Richard Whiting, Ted
Fetter, Frederick Holland, Hoagy Carmichael, Edward Hayman
**Cast:** Bing Crosby, Ethel Merman, Charlie Ruggles, Ida Lupino,
Arthur Treacher, Margaret Dumont, and others
**Plot:** Merman loves Bing, who loves Lupino, who runs away on an
ocean liner and they both follow her.
**Merman's Songs:** "I Get a Kick Out of You," "You're the Top,"
"Shanghai-de-ho," "Anything Goes" (snippet)

*Happy Landing*
Twentieth Century-Fox, 1938, 102 minutes
Directed by Roy Del Ruth. Written by Boris Ingster, Milton
Sperling
**Cast:** Sonja Henie, Don Ameche, Jean Hersholt, Ethel Merman,
Billy Gilbert, Cesar Romero, and others
**Plot Outline:** Bandleader Romero and manager Ameche discover
skater Henie in Norway. They become rivals as they return to
America.
**Merman's Songs:** "Hot and Happy," "You Appeal to Me"

*Alexander's Ragtime Band*
**Twentieth Century-Fox, 1938**
**Directed by Henry King. Story by Irving Berlin. Adaptation by Richard Sherman. Written by Kathryn Scola, Lamar Trotti. Produced by Darryl F. Zanuck. Music and Lyrics by Irving Berlin**
**Cast:** Tyrone Power, Alice Faye, Don Ameche, Ethel Merman, Jack Haley, and others
**Plot Summary:** The story of a bandleader in 1911, how he becomes famous for his ragtime music, and his love life.
**Merman's Songs:** "Say It With Music," "Blue Skies," "A Pretty Girl Is Like a Melody," "Pack Up Your Sins and Go to the Devil," "My Walking Stick," "Everybody Step," "Marching Along with Time" (cut), "Heat Wave"

*Straight, Place and Show*
**Twentieth Century-Fox, 1938**
**Directed by David Butler. Written by M. M. Musselman, Allen Rivkin. Based on the play by Damon Runyon and Irving Caesar. Additional Dialogue by Lew Brown**
**Cast:** The Ritz Brothers, Ethel Merman, Richard Arlen, and others
**Merman's Song:** "With You on My Mind"

*Stage Door Canteen*
**Independent Production, 1943**
**Directed by Frank Borzage. Written by Delmer Daves**
**Plot Summary:** During World War II, a young soldier in Manhattan visits the famed Stage Door Canteen and falls for a pretty hostess while dozens of famous stage and film stars entertain.
**Cast:** Judith Anderson, Kenny Baker, Tallulah Bankhead, Count Basie, Ralph Bellamy, Edgar Bergen, Ray Bolger, Katharine Cornell, Xavier Cugat, William Demarest, Benny Goodman, Gracie Fields, Lynn Fontanne, Helen Hayes, Katharine Hepburn, Hugh Herbert, Jean Hersholt, Sam Jaffe, George Jessel, Gertrude Lawrence, Gypsy Rose Lee, Peggy Lee, Guy Lombardo, Alfred Lunt, Harpo Marx, Elsa Maxwell, Yehudi Menuhin, Ethel Merman, Paul Muni, Merle

Oberon, George Raft, Martha Scott, Cornelia Otis Skinner, Ned Sparks, Ethel Waters, Johnny Weissmuller, Dame May Whitty, Ed Wynn, and many others
**Merman's Song:** "Marching through Berlin"

*Call Me Madam*
**Twentieth Century-Fox, 1953**
**Directed by Walter Lang. Produced by Sol C. Siegel. Written by Arthur Sheekman. Based on the play by Russel Crouse and Howard Lindsay. Music and Lyrics by Irving Berlin**
**Cast:** Ethel Merman, George Sanders, Donald O'Connor, Vera-Ellen, Billy De Wolfe, Walter Slezak, and others
**Plot Summary:** Washington society hostess Sally Adams is sent to Lichtenbourg as the American ambassador. While she is there, she falls in love and manages to make mayhem in that country's politics.
**Merman's Songs:** "Hostess With the Mostes'," "Can You Use Any Money Today?," "The Best Thing For You," "The International Rag," "You're Just in Love"

*There's No Business Like Show Business*
**Twentieth Century-Fox, 1954**
**Directed by Walter Lang. Story by Lamar Trotti. Written by Henry and Phoebe Ephron**
**Cast:** Ethel Merman, Donald O'Connor, Marilyn Monroe, Dan Dailey, Mitzi Gaynor, Johnny Ray, and others
**Plot Summary:** The story of a theatrical family from the time of its vaudeville inception in the 1910s through World War II.
**Merman's Songs:** "When the Midnight Choo-Choo Leaves for Alabam'," "Play a Simple Melody," "A Pretty Girl is Like a Melody," "Alexander's Ragtime Band," "A Sailor's Not a Sailor," "There's No Business Like Show Business"

*It's a Mad, Mad, Mad, Mad World*
**United Artists, 1963**
**Produced and Directed by Stanley Kramer. Written by Tania and William Rose**
**Cast:** Spencer Tracy, Edie Adams, Milton Berle, Sid Caesar, Jimmy Durante, Buddy Hackett, Ethel Merman, Mickey Rooney, Dick Shawn, Phil Silvers, Terry-Thomas, Jonathan Winters, and a host of famous actors and comedians in smaller parts
**Plot Summary:** A man's car runs off a desert highway and throws him clear. As he is dying, he reveals the location of stolen loot to a group of divergent passers-by who try to rescue him. Buoyed by greed and avarice, each member of the group races the other to be the first to reach the stash. Unbeknown to them, their every move is being followed by the police.

*The Art of Love*
**Universal, 1965**
**Directed by Norman Jewison. Written by Carl Reiner. Story by Richard Alan Simmons and William Sackheim**
**Cast:** Dick Van Dyke, James Garner, Elke Sommer, Ethel Merman, Fifi D'Orsay, and others
**Plot Summary:** A starving American artist and his pal living in Paris stage his death in order to make his paintings valuable. They hide him in a bordello, where the artist falls for one of the courtesans while his pal makes a play for his fiancée.
**Merman's Song:** "You Just Have to Say the Word"

*Won Ton Ton, the Dog Who Saved Hollywood*
**Columbia, 1976**
**Directed by Michael Winner. Produced by David V. Picker, Arnold Shulman, Michael Winner. Written by Arnold Shulman and Cy Howard**
**Cast:** Bruce Dern, Art Carney, Phil Silvers, Madeline Kahn, and many famous actors and comedians in smaller roles including Ethel Merman

**Plot Summary:** In 1924, a woman comes to Hollywood to be a silent screen star, but the dog that follows her there becomes the star.

*Airplane!*
**Paramount, 1980**
**Written and Directed by Jim Abrahams, David Zucker, Jerry Zucker. Produced by Jon Davison and Howard W. Koch. Executive Produced by Jim Abrahams, David Zucker, Jerry Zucker**
**Cast:** Robert Hays, Julie Hagerty, Lloyd Bridges, Robert Stack, Leslie Nielsen, Peter Graves, and many others in small roles, including Ethel Merman
**Plot Summary:** On an ill-fated airplane flight, the only man who can fly the plane is afraid of flying.

This was Ethel Merman's final film role.

# *The Recordings*

There are two kinds of recordings listed here—those that were recorded for commercial release and those that were taken from film soundtracks and live radio sound checks, but not originally released commercially. I have endeavored to place all of these in chronological order to give a better vista of Ethel Merman's changing style and vocal quality through the years.

In many cases, songs have been rereleased on CD issues or compilations (sometimes more than once). I have listed here the first issue. The dates refer to the dates the songs were actually recorded.

**November 1930**
**"Satan's Holiday"**
This song from *Follow the Leader* was first released on an LP called *Merman in the Movies* (Encore Records ST-101).

**April 1931**
**"Wipe That Smile Right Off Your Face"**
This song from *Ireno* was first released on an LP called *Legends of the Musical Stage* (Take Two Records TT-104).

## October 1931
## "Life Is Just a Bowl of Cherries," "My Song," "Ladies and Gentlemen, That's Love"
These three songs from *George White Scandals of 1931* were record-ed by Ethel Merman at RCA Victor studios in New York City, but never released.

## September 28, 1932
## "I'll Follow You," "Satan's Lil' Lamb," I Gotta Right to Sing the Blues," "How Deep is the Ocean?" (Victor 24145 and 24146)
These were Ethel Merman's first commercially released studio recordings.

## December 16, 1932
## "Eadie Was a Lady" (Brunswick 6456)
This was the first of several recordings Ethel made for the Brunswick label from 1932-1935.

## October 8, 1934
## "An Earful of Music" (Brunswick 6995)
This was the studio version of the song Ethel sang in the film, *Kid Millions*.

## December 4, 1934
## "You're the Top," "I Get a Kick Out of You" (Brunswick)
These are Ethel's first studio recordings of songs from her hit show, *Anything Goes*.

## July 17, 1935
## "The Lady in Red," "The Animal in Me" (Brunswick 7491)
"Animal" is a studio version of the song Ethel filmed for *We're Not Dressing*, but was not used until *The Big Broadcast of 1936*. The other song was simply a pop number Ethel recorded to fill the other side of the record.

**November 6, 1936**
**"Down in the Depths on the 90th Floor," "It's DeLovely"**
**(Liberty Music Shop 206)**
**"Ridin' High," "Red Hot and Blue" (Liberty Music Shop 207)**
These songs from *Red, Hot and Blue* were recorded at the Liberty Music Shop in New York City and received limited release at the time. Eventually, they were released on an LP called *Ethel Merman Sings Cole Porter* (JJC Records M 3004).

**February 22, 1939**
**"A Lady Needs a Change," "I'll Pay the Check" (Liberty Music Shop 256)**
**"This Is It," "Just a Little Bit More" (Liberty Music Shop 257)**
These songs from *Stars in Your Eyes* were recorded at the Liberty Music Shop in New York City and received limited release at the time. Eventually they were released on an LP called *Ethel Merman Sings Cole Porter* (JJC Records M 3004).

**December 2, 1940**
*Ethel Merman in Songs From Panama Hattie*
**Decca Records**
**"Let's Be Buddies," "Make It Another Old-Fashioned, Please"**
**(Decca 23199)**
**"My Mother Would Love You," "I've Still Got My Health"**
**(Decca 23200)**
These four songs were released together as an album of songs. It is Ethel Merman's first recordings with Decca and is considered to be the first attempt at an original cast album.

**Spring 1944**
**V-Disc 368-A**
**"Why Do They Call a Private a Private?"**
**"Marching Through Berlin"**
**"Move It Over"**
These three songs were released as V-Discs during World War II. The first was transcribed from a live broadcast made just for people

in the service. The other two were recorded in the studio without an orchestra, as there was a union ban on using musicians for studio recordings.

**Summer 1944**
*Something for the Boys*
**Merman's Songs:**
**"Something for the Boys," "Hey, Good Lookin'," "He's a Right Guy," "I'm in Love with a Soldier Boy," "There's a Happy Land in the Sky," "By the Mississinewa"**
These recordings were made after the show *Something for the Boys* had closed. They are a combination of radio transcriptions and studio work done over a series of months. It is interesting that Decca did not think enough of the score to make an original cast album.

**May 26 and 28, 1946**
*Annie Get Your Gun Original Cast Album*
**Decca Records**
**Merman's Songs:**
**"Doin' What Comes Nat'rally," "You Can't Get a Man with a Gun," "There's No Business Like Show Business," "They Say It's Wonderful," "Moonshine Lullaby," "I'm an Indian Too," "I Got Lost in His Arms," "I Got the Sun in the Morning," "Anything You Can Do"**
This is Ethel's first official original cast album. Alas, complete studio recordings of her first nine shows, with original arrangements and performances, were never made. This album, originally released as a boxed set of 78-rpm records, sold very well for many years.

**Fall 1947**
*Songs I Made Famous*
**Decca Records**
**Arranged by Jay Blackton**
**"I Got Rhythm," "Life Is Just a Bowl of Cherries," "You're an Old Smoothie," "You're the Top," "I Get a Kick Out of You," "Blow, Gabriel, Blow," "It's DeLovely," "Eadie Was a Lady"**

This was Ethel's first attempt at a greatest hits album. Although the arrangements are, for the most part, dreary, the power of her vocals is impressive. This is the first time Merman recorded the entire version of "I Got Rhythm," seventeen years after she made it famous. This album was Ethel's first extended play 33-1/3 album.

**January 4, 1950**
**Decca Records**
**"A Little Girl from Little Rock," "Diamonds Are a Girl's Best Friend," "Dearie" (with Ray Bolger), "I Said My Pajamas" (with Ray Bolger)**
These are the first strictly pop songs that Ethel had recorded since the early 1930s. "Dearie" was a very big seller for its time, leading to the rest of the pop tries listed below.

**February 20, 1950**
**Decca Records**
**"It's So Nice To Have A Man Around the House" (with Ray Bolger), "I'd Have Baked a Cake" (with Ray Bolger)**
Decca thought they had hit pay dirt with "Dearie," so they desperately tried to make it happen again and again. That "Dearie" was a superior song, or that Bolger really couldn't sing, never seemed to occur to Decca. Rather than teaming Merman with other Decca superstars like Bing Crosby, Al Jolson, Judy Garland, or Mary Martin, they kept sticking her with Bolger and inferior songs. The result was less than atomic.

**May 3, 1950**
**Decca Records**
**"Calico Sal," "She's Shimmyin' on the Beach Again"**
Well, let's see. What is the most ridiculous type of music to ask Merman to sing? Hey . . . I know. Hawaiian music!

The folks at Decca must have still had the needles in their arms when they produced these sides.

May 17, 1950
Decca Records
"Hawaii," "Ukulele Lady"

May 19, 1950
Decca Records
"The Lake Song" (with Ray Bolger), "Don't Believe It" (with
Ray Bolger)

October 17 and November 20, 1950
*Ethel Merman Sings Songs From Call Me Madam*
Decca Records
Arranged by Gordon Jenkins
Merman's Songs:
"Washington Square Dance," "Marrying for Love," "The Best
Thing for You," "Something to Dance About," "Can You Use
Any Money Today?"
See page 109 for the story of this album. By the way, you will notice
that one song seems to be missing. That is because it was not includ-
ed in the original release. In 1955, when this album was rereleased
as a twelve-inch LP, Merman and Jenkins went into the studio again
and finally recorded "The Hostess With the Mostes' On the Ball."

February 22, 1951
Decca Records
"Once Upon a Nickel" (with Ray Bolger), "Oldies" (with Ray Bolger)

June 4, 1951
Decca Records
"Love Is the Reason," "The World is Your Balloon," "Make the
Man Love Me"

October 26, 1951
Decca Records
"You Say the Nicest Things" (with Jimmy Durante), "A Husband

– A Wife" (with Jimmy Durante), "If You Catch a Little Cold" (with Jimmy Durante)

It is a shame these songs never really caught on because the chemistry between Merman and Durante was always magical!

**March 1953**
*Call Me Madam Soundtrack Album*
**Decca Records**
**Merman's Songs:**
"Hostess With the Mostes' On the Ball," "International Rag," "You're Just in Love," "The Best Thing for You," "Can You Use Any Money Today?"

**May 1954**
*There's No Business Like Show Business Soundtrack Album*
**Decca Records/20th Century-Fox**
**Merman's Songs:**
"When the Midnight Choo-Choo Leaves for Alabam'," "Play a Simple Melody," "A Pretty Girl Is Like a Melody," "Alexander's Ragtime Band," "A Sailor's Not a Sailor," "There's No Business Like Show Business"

Ethel is not in good voice for these recordings. She sounds as though she is suffering from a head cold, and her voice begins to show the wobble that would evidence itself later in much of her work. For the original Decca version, Marilyn Monroe did not appear due to a conflict of contracts (Decca never learned), and Dolores Gray did her songs. When Fox rereleased the entire score on CD, everything recorded for the movie was released (except for the excised "Anything You Can Do," which was cut from the film).

**June 1955**
**Decca Records**
*The Hostess With the Mostes' On the Ball*
This is the recording that was added to the LP reissue of Decca's *Call Me Madam* studio album.

**Spring 1956**
*Ethel Merman Memories: 40 Great Songs from the "Gay Nineties" to the "Roaring Twenties"*
Decca Records
Medley One:
"Ta-ra-ra-boom-dee-ay," "The Band Played On," "The Bowery," "On a Saturday Night," "While Strolling through the Park One Day," "Hello My Baby," "Rings On My Fingers," "In My Merry Oldsmobile," "In the Good Old Summertime," "Sweet Rosie O'Grady," "Little Annie Rooney," "Waltz Me Around Again, Willie," "The Sidewalks of New York," "On a Bicycle Built for Two," "She'll Be Coming 'Round the Mountain," "Put On Your Old Grey Bonnet," "Mississippi," "Listen to the Mocking Bird," "You Tell Me Your Dream," "School Days," "Memories"

Medley Two:
"Way Down Yonder in New Orleans," "Somebody Stole My Gal," "Smiles," "Row Row Row," "I Want a Girl," "Sweet Georgia Brown," "Take Back Your Gold," "Frankie and Johnny," "A Bird in a Gilded Cage," "On Moonlight Bay," "By the Light of the Silvery Moon," "Shine On Harvest Moon," "That Old Gang of Mine," "Sweet Adeline," "Oh Johnny!," "Dear Little Boy of Mine," "Forty-Five Minutes from Broadway," "Mary's a Grand Old Name," "Give My Regards to Broadway"

As strange as it may seem, this unusual theme album is actually nothing short of magnificent. Each side of the LP was a long medley of old songs, sung by Ethel and a male chorus with sound effects and overdubbing. At one point, Merman sings three-part harmony with herself. She is in great voice, and this recording deserves a CD release.

**Summer 1956**
*Ethel Merman: A Musical Autobiography*
Decca Records
"I Got Rhythm" (new), "Embraceable You" (new), "Life Is Just a

Bowl of Cherries" (1947), "Eadie Was a Lady" (1947), "You're an Old Smoothie" (new), "Anything Goes" (new), "Blow, Gabriel, Blow" (1947), "I Get a Kick Out of You" (1947), "You're the Top" (1947), "It's DeLovely" (1947), "Ridin' High" (new), "Down in the Depths on the 90th Floor" (new), "This Is It" (new), "I'll Pay the Check" (new), "Do I Love You?" (new), "Friendship" (new), "Let's Be Buddies" (1940), "Make It Another Old-Fashioned" (new), "He's a Right Guy" (new), "Doin' What Comes Nat'rally" (1946), "Moonshine Lullaby" (1946), "You Can't Get a Man with a Gun" (1946), "I'm An Indian Too" (1946), "They Say It's Wonderful" (1946), "I Got Lost in His Arms" (new), "I Got the Sun in the Morning" (1946), "The Hostess With the Mostes'" (1950), "Washington Square Dance" (1950), "You're Just in Love" (1950), "The Best Thing for You" (1950), "Something to Dance About" (1950), "Alexander's Ragtime Band" (new), "Dearie" (1950), "How Deep Is the Ocean" (new)

Decca Records had been bought by MCA, and its main output became reissues of old recordings. Several of their biggest stars released these musical autobiographies, two-record sets that included reissues of old recordings plus narration and new recordings made by Buddy Cole and his small group. Included are many of the major recordings Ethel made for Decca from 1940 until 1955.

December 9, 1956
*Happy Hunting Original Cast Album*
RCA Victor Records
Merman's Songs:
"Gee, But It's Good to Be Here," "Mutual Admiration Society," "Mr. Livingstone," "This Is What I Call Love," "A New-Fangled Tango," "The Game of Love," "Happy Hunting," "I'm a Funny Dame," "This Much I Know"

Ethel may not have enjoyed doing this show, and the songs are not among her best, but boy is she in great voice for this recording! While "Mutual Admiration Society" was the only real hit from the show, Ethel just adored "Gee, But It's Good to Be Here." She sang it in clubs, concerts, and on television hundreds of times.

**May 24, 1959**
*Gypsy Original Cast Album*
**Columbia Records**
**Merman's Songs:**
"Some People," "Small World," "Mr. Goldstone, I Love You," "You'll Never Get Away From Me," "Everything's Coming Up Roses," "Together Wherever We Go," "Rose's Turn"
The only thing wrong with this album is that there is not more of it. At the time of the recording, they could not fit all of the verses to all of the songs on the LP format. It is a shame that they had not been recorded anyway so they could have been released on the CD reissue. There were extras on the CD, including the demo recordings of the score that Ethel made with Jule Styne.

**Spring 1961**
*Merman: Her Greatest*
**Reprise Records. Arranged by Billy May**
"I Got Rhythm," "This Is It"/"Do I Love You?" "I Get a Kick Out of You," "Sam and Delilah," "Life Is Just a Bowl of Cherries," "Blow, Gabriel, Blow," "Down in the Depths on the 90th Floor," "But Not for Me," "Friendship," "You're the Top"
This is easily Ethel's best album, a collection of her hits in the 1930s. She needed the exuberant and jazz-tinged arrangements of someone like Billy May to make her music come alive and sound vital. She is in near-perfect voice, and the engineering is top-notch.

Frank Sinatra signed Ethel to his Reprise Records in 1961. This was supposed to be the first in a series of studio albums, the next being those of her hits from the 1940s. That never happened because of the dismal failure of her next Reprise album.

**Fall 1962**
*The Return to Oz Soundtrack Album*

**Merman's Songs:**
"Be a Witch," "Keep a Gloomy Thought," "An Elephant Never Forgets"
See page 147 for the story behind this soundtrack recording.

**December 1962**
*Merman in Vegas*
**Reprise Records**
**Arranged by Billy May. Conducted by Eric Knight**
"Just a Lady with a Song," "I Got Rhythm," "This Is It," "A Lot of Livin' To Do," Hits Medley, "They Say It's Wonderful," "Make It Another Old-Fashioned," "You Can't Get a Man with a Gun," "Blow, Gabriel, Blow," "There's No Business Like Show Business"
Well, this album didn't kill Ethel's career, but it surely did not do it any good. Reprise thought for certain they would have a huge hit on its hands if they recorded the great Ethel live as Capitol Records had done with Judy Garland a year earlier.

What they did not count on was that while Judy had been a smash at Carnegie Hall in concert, Ethel laid an egg doing a night-club act at the Flamingo Hotel in Las Vegas. Judy had a thirty-piece orchestra behind her to make her arrangements sound lush. Ethel's was thirteen pieces plus twin pianos. Garland was a masterful manipulator of the hand microphone. Merman refused to use a hand microphone and instead used a chest mike. Uh-oh!

The recording was almost unusable due to the chest microphone either under- or overrecording Ethel's voice. So she was brought into the Reprise studios, and while they played back the tape of her performance, she sang the entire performance again in one take.

What they were left with was a muddy recording of Ethel in hoarse voice with two separate vocal renditions clearly heard on many of the tracks. The thing should never have been released and was a terrible embarrassment for Ethel. Reprise and Ethel parted company, and she did not make another pop album for ten years.

It is interesting that while her entire act was recorded at the time, only those tracks that fit on the LP format were rereleased on CD. The rest have been lost.

**Spring 1964**
**Piano Accompaniment by Goldie Hawkins**
Medley: "Just in Time," "I've Got a Crush On You," "At Sundown," "Manhattan," "My Funny Valentine," "The Most Beautiful Girl in the World," "But Not for Me"
Medley: "Star Dust," "My Funny Valentine," "Autumn Leaves," "September Song"
Medley: "Just One of Those Things," "The Party's Over," "I Can't Get Started," "Everything's Coming Up Roses," "Small World," "Smile"
What is a woman to do when her fiancé announces to the world that he has never heard his "baby" sing? She goes into a recording studio with a pianist pal and records medleys of love songs for him. These recordings were never meant to be commercially released. They were an engagement present to Ernest Borgnine from Ethel Merman!

**June 5, 1966**
*Music Theater of Lincoln Center Presents Ethel Merman in Annie Get Your Gun*
**Merman's Songs:** "Doin' What Comes Nat'rally," "You Can't Get a Man with a Gun," "There's No Business Like Show Business," "They Say It's Wonderful," "Moonshine Lullaby," "I'm an Indian Too," "I Got Lost in His Arms," "I Got the Sun in the Morning," "An Old Fashioned Wedding," "Anything You Can Do"
Ethel is in such high spirits and magnificent voice for this recording, it is a shame she did not record about 100 songs more! It is obvious that RCA knew how to engineer her voice. Perhaps they were the ones she should have signed with for her future recordings. Alas, it did not work out that way. This is the last truly splendid recording of the voice of Ethel Merman.

**February 12, 1967**
*Cole Porter – You're the Top: A Testimonial*
**Piano Accompaniment by Roger Edens**

**Merman's Songs:**
"Anything Goes," "I Get a Kick Out of You," "You're the Top," "Down in the Depths," "Make It Another Old-Fashioned," "Let's Be Buddies," "Friendship" (with Frank Sinatra, Fred Astaire, and Gene Kelly)

Ethel, Frank Sinatra, Fred Astaire, Gene Kelly, Roger Edens, Jimmy Stuart, and Garson Kanin joined forces in a special live symposium/performance to open the Cole Porter Library at USC. A private recording was made of the event and belatedly released on CD. Merman sang so loud, she blew out the microphone with her first notes!

**April 1970**
**"Love Look in My Window," "World Take Me Back"**

These are the recordings Ethel made of the extra songs from *Hello, Dolly!* Backed only by twin pianos and a bass, these songs were released as a 45-rpm record and sold at the theater where *Dolly* was playing. They have since been released on CD, as well.

**June 1972**
*Merman Sings Merman*
**London Phase 4 Records**
**Stanley Black conducting the London Festival Orchestra and Chorus**
**"You're the Top," "I Got Rhythm," You're Just in Love," "Alexander's Ragtime Band," "I Got Lost in His Arms," "Eadie Was a Lady," "There's No Business Like Show Business," "They Say It's Wonderful," "It's DeLovely," "I Get a Kick Out of You," "Everything's Coming Up Roses," "Blow, Gabriel, Blow"**

This album is of almost mythic proportions in the Merman mythos. In 1972, there were very few Merman recordings still available. Other than recent cast albums, there was almost nothing of Ethel's recorded work in record stores. This album, with arrangements mostly knocked off from those previously done by Billy May and Jay Blackton, was the only stereo version of Ethel's hits.

While the wobble in her voice is evident (especially in the ballads), her enthusiasm and incisiveness of notes still shine through.

This was supposed to be the first in a series of "Merman Sings" albums. The next one scheduled was *Merman Sings Kern*. However, the series was scratched after the next album.

**March 1973**
***Ethel Merman Sings Annie Get Your Gun***
**Stanley Black conducting the London Festival Orchestra and Chorus**
**Merman's Songs:**
**"Doin' What Comes Nat'rally," "You Can't Get a Man with a Gun," "There's No Business Like Show Business," "They Say It's Wonderful," "Moonshine Lullaby," "I'm an Indian Too," "I Got Lost in His Arms," "I Got the Sun in the Morning," "An Old Fashioned Wedding," "Anything You Can Do"**

This album was a total waste of time. Ethel's last *Annie* album had only been six years before and was much superior to this "quickie" effort. A new *Call Me Madam* album or even *Merman Sings Herman* would have been better than this.

**November 1973**
***Ethel's Ridin' High***
**Stanley Black conducting the London Festival Orchestra and Chorus**
**"Gee, But It's Good to Be Here," "Whispering," "Some People," "Sunrise Sunset," "What Kind of Fool Am I?" "Ridin' High," "Someone to Watch Over Me," "The Impossible Dream," "On a Clear Day," "Nothing Can Stop Me Now"**

One can complain about the choice of songs, but this is a superior Merman effort. She promoted it as an album of songs she did *not* make famous, but had always wanted to sing. That three of the songs were actually more of her old hits was overlooked. Through the years, Mighty Merman had sung many things on television and radio that she never recorded commercially. It is a shame that these were not included here instead of "Sunrise, Sunset" or "On a Clear Day."

**Spring 1979**
*The Ethel Merman Disco Album*
**A&M Records**
**Arranged by Peter Matz**
**"There's No Business Like Show Business," "Everything's Coming Up Roses," "I Get a Kick Out of You," "Something for the Boys," "Some People," "Alexander's Ragtime Band," "I Got Rhythm," "They Say It's Wonderful"**
It is not true that this album killed disco. Wounded it perhaps, but …

This album is pure camp, and despite its questionable contribution to disco, Ethel wisely squeezed enormous publicity from it. This was Ethel Merman's last recording.

# Broadway Appearances

## 29

*Girl Crazy*
Alvin Theatre, October 14, 1930 (272 Performances)
Produced by Alex A. Arons and Vinton Freedley. Music by George Gershwin. Lyrics by Ira Gershwin. Book by Guy Bolton and John McGowan. Staged by Alexander Leftwich. Choreographed by George Hale
**Opening Night Cast:** Ginger Rogers, Willie Howard, Ethel Merman, Lew Parker, and others
**Plot Summary:** A wealthy New York frat boy/socialite comes to a western college and is taken down a peg or two.
**Merman's Songs:** "Sam and Delilah," "I Got Rhythm," "Boy, What Love Has Done to Me!"

*George White's Scandals of 1931*
Apollo Theatre, September 14, 1931 (202 Performances)
Produced by George White. Music by Ray Henderson. Lyrics by Lew Brown. Book by George White and Irving Caesar
**Opening Night Cast:** Ethel Merman, Ray Bolger, Rudy Vallee, Ethel Barrymore Colt, Willie and Eugene Howard, Everett Marshall, the Gale Quadruplets, and others

**Plot Summary:** This is a vaudeville show done on a lavish, grand scale.

**Merman's Songs:** "Life Is Just a Bowl of Cherries," "Ladies and Gentlemen, That's Love," "My Song," "The Good Old Days"

*Take a Chance*

**Apollo Theatre, November 26, 1932 (243 Performances)**

**Produced by Lawrence Schwab and B. G. DeSylva. Music by Nacio Herb Brown and Richard A. Whiting. Lyrics by B. G. DeSylva and Roger Edens. Additional Songs by Vincent Youmans. Book by B. G. DeSylva and Lawrence Schwab. Additional Dialogue by Sid Silvers**

**Opening Night Cast:** Ethel Merman, Jack Haley, Sid Silvers, June Knight, Jack Whiting, Mitzi Mayfair, and others

**Plot Summary:** Originally written as a historical revue, the show became a loose collection of sketches with songs.

**Merman's Songs:** "Eadie Was a Lady," "You're an Old Smoothie," "Rise 'n' Shine," "I Got Religion"

*Anything Goes*

**Alvin Theatre, November 21, 1934 (420 Performances)**

**Music and Lyrics by Cole Porter. Book by Guy Bolton and P. G. Wodehouse, revised by Howard Lindsay and Russel Crouse. Produced by Vinton Freedley. Directed by Howard Lindsay. Dance and Ensembles by Robert Alton. Settings by Donald Oenslager. Gowns by Jenkins. Orchestra conducted by Earl Busby. Orchestrations by Russell Bennett and Hans Spialek. Choral arrangements by Ray Johnson**

**Opening Night Cast:** Ethel Merman, William Gaxton, Victor Moore, Bettina Hall, Vivian Vance, and others

**Plot Summary:** Reno Sweeney, an evangelist turned bar hostess, gets such a kick out of Billy Crocker that she boards a Europe-bound liner to dissuade him from pursuing Hope Harcourt. Although Billy dreams of Hope all through the night, Hope is determined to marry Sir Evelyn Oakleigh. Crocker has boarded without a ticket, so is forced to adopt a number of disguises. Also aboard is a wistful little man, the Reverend Dr. Moon, whom the FBI has branded "Public Enemy 13." Moon's ambition is to rise to the top of the list. On landing, Hope discovers she has become an heiress, drops her Englishman, and consents to marry Billy. Oakleigh turns his attention to Reno, and Moon, to his dismay, learns that he has been judged harmless and dropped from the FBI list.

**Merman's Songs:** "I Get a Kick Out of You," "You're the Top," "Anything Goes," "Blow, Gabriel, Blow," "Buddy Beware"`


*Red, Hot and Blue*
**Alvin Theatre, October 29, 1936 (183 Performances)**
**Music and Lyrics by Cole Porter. Book by Howard Lindsay and Russel Crouse. Produced by Vinton Freedley. Directed by Howard Lindsay. Dances and Ensembles by George Hale. Costumes by Constance Ripley. Set Design by Donald Oenslager. Orchestrations by Robert Russell Bennett. Musical Direction by Frank E. Tours**
**Opening Night Cast:** Ethel Merman, Jimmy Durante, Bob Hope, Vivian Vance. Paul and Grace Hartman, and others
**Plot Summary:** Former manicurist "Nails" Duquesne is now a wealthy widow determined to fill her time with philanthropic ventures. With the aid of her assistant, ex-convict "Policy" Pinkle, she takes up the case of lawyer Bob Hale, who lost the love of his life at age six when he shoved her into a waffle iron and branded her on the rear. When "Nails" starts a national lottery to find the girl, the Senate Finance Committee, hoping to use the contest money to balance the national budget, complicates an already messy situation.
**Merman's Songs:** "Down in the Depths on the 90th Floor," "You've Got Something," "It's DeLovely," "Ridin' High," "You're a Bad Influence on Me," "Red Hot and Blue"
**Note: When the production transferred to the 46th Street Theatre on September 30, 1935, the role of Reno Sweeney was played by Benay Venuta.**

*Stars in Your Eyes*
Majestic Theatre, February 9, 1939 (127 Performances)
Produced by Dwight Deere Wiman. Music by Arthur Schwartz. Lyrics by Dorothy Fields. Book by J. P. McEvoy. Directed by Joshua Logan. Choreographed by Carl Randall. Scenic Design by Jo Mielziner. Costumes by John Hambleton
**Opening Night Cast:** Ethel Merman, Jimmy Durante, Richard Carlson, Mildred Natwick, Tamara Toumanova, Mary Wickes, Maria Karnilova, Dan Dailey *and as a gentleman of the ballet*, Jerome Robbins
**Plot Summary:** A mishmash satire of intrigue in a Hollywood studio and socialist politics.
**Merman's Songs:** "This Is It," "A Lady Needs a Change," "Just a Little Bit More," "I'll Pay the Check," "It's All Yours"

*DuBarry Was a Lady*
46th Street Theatre, December 6, 1939 (408 Performances)
Music and Lyrics by Cole Porter. Book by Herbert Fields and B. G. De Sylva. Produced by B. G. De Sylva. Directed by Edgar MacGregor. Choreographed by Robert Alton. Costumes and Sets Designed by Raoul Pene du Bois. Lighting Designed by Albert A. Ostrander. Vocal Arrangements by Hugh Martin with the assistance of Ralph Blane. Orchestrations by Hans Spialek, additional orchestrations by Robert Russell Bennett and Ted Royal. Musical Direction by Gene Salzer
**Opening Night Cast:** Ethel Merman, Bert Lahr, Betty Grable, Charles (Chuck) Walters, Ronald Graham, Benny Baker, and others
**Plot Summary:** Louis Blore, attendant in the men's washroom of the Club Petite in New York, wins $75,000 in the Irish sweeps. Having long had his eye on the star of the floor show, May Daly, Louis seeks to win her away from Alex Barton, the young man to whom she is engaged. He tries to put Alex away with knockout drops, but mixes up the glasses and drinks the potion himself. During his delirium, Louis dreams that he is Louis XIV and that May Daly is DuBarry, his mistress. His unsuccessful pursuit of May

continues through the gardens and boudoirs of eighteenth-century Versailles. When he awakens, Louis realizes that he has no chance with May and will have to settle for her friendship.

**Merman's Songs:** "When Love Beckoned," "Come On In," "But in the Morning No," "Give Him the Oo-La-La," "Katie Went to Haiti," "Friendship"

**Note: When Merman took a leave of absence, her role was taken by Gypsy Rose Lee.**

*Panama Hattie*
**46th Street Theatre, October 30, 1940 (501 Performances)**
**Music and Lyrics by Cole Porter. Book by Herbert Fields and B. G. De Sylva. Produced by B. G. De Sylva. Staged by Edgar MacGregor. Choreography by Robert Alton. Costumes and Set Designs by Raoul Pene du Bois. Vocal Arrangements by Lyn Murray. Orchestrations by Robert Russell Bennett, Hans Spialek, Don Walker. Musical Direction by Gene Salzer**
**Opening Night Cast:** Ethel Merman, James Dunn, Phyllis Brooks, Rags Ragland, Betty Hutton, Arthur Treacher, Joan Carroll, Pat Harrington, Frankie Hyers, and others
**Plot Summary:** Hattie Maloney, a brassy nightclub singer in Panama, tries to fit into the upper-crust world of her fiancé, Nick Bullett, an officer in the armed forces and the divorced father of an eight-year-old child named Gerry. Hattie insists that he send for the girl before they are married. She eventually wins over both Gerry and Nick's boss, Whitney Randolph, by foiling a plot to blow up the canal.
**Merman's Songs:** "Visit Panama," "My Mother Would Love You," "I've Still Got My Health," "Let's Be Buddies," "I'm Throwin' a Ball Tonight," "Make It Another Old-Fashioned, Please," "You Said It"

*Something for the Boys*
**Alvin Theatre, January 7, 1943 (422 Performances)**
**Music and Lyrics by Cole Porter. Book by Herbert and Dorothy Fields. Working Title: Jenny, Get Your Gun. Produced by**

Michael Todd. Staged and Lighted by Hassard Short. Book Directed by Herbert Fields. Choreographed by Jack Cole, Lew Kessler. Costumes by Billy Livingston. Set Design by Howard Bay. Orchestrations by Robert Russell Bennett, Ted Royal, Hans Spialek, Don Walker. Musical Direction and Vocal Arrangements by William Parson

**Opening Night Cast:** Ethel Merman, Bill Johnson, Paula Lawrence, Betty Bruce, Betty Garrett, Allen Jenkins

**Plot Summary:** A defense worker (Blossom), a carnival pitchman (Harry), and a burlesque queen (Chiquita) inherit equal shares of a Texas ranch near Kelly Field. They successfully transform it into a boardinghouse for soldiers' wives, but Lieutenant-Colonel Grubbs, convinced that they're running a different sort of house, tries to put them out of business. Eventually, Blossom, aided by a Carborundum-coated tooth filling that allows her to hear radio signals, manages to clear the family name. Other characters include bandleader Sgt. Rocky Fulton (Blossom's love interest), Rocky's snobbish fiancée Melanie, squatter Tobias Twitch, and two of Rocky's admirers: Mary-Frances and Betty-Jean.

**Merman's Songs:** "Something for the Boys," "When We're at Home on the Range," "Hey, Good Lookin'," He's a Right Guy," "The Leader of a Big Time Band," "There's a Happy Land in the Sky," "Down by the Mississinewah"

*Annie Get Your Gun*
**Imperial Theatre, May 16, 1946 (1,147 Performances)**
Music and Lyrics by Irving Berlin. Book by Herbert and Dorothy Fields. Produced by Richard Rodgers and Oscar Hammerstein II. Directed by Joshua Logan. Musical Direction by Jay Blackton. Choreographed by Helen Tamiris. Scenic and Lighting Design by Jo Mielziner. Costume Design by Lucinda Ballard. Orchestrations by Philip J. Lang, Robert Russell Bennett, Ted Royal

**Opening Night Cast:** Ethel Merman, Ray Middleton, Harry Bellaver, Frances Baldwin, Marty May, and others

**Plot Summary:** All about female sharpshooter Annie Oakley—her triumphs and her romance with handsome Frank Butler.

**Merman's Songs:** "Doin' What Comes Nat'rally," "You Can't Get a Man with a Gun," "There's No Business Like Show Business," "They Say It's Wonderful," "Moonshine Lullaby," "I'm an Indian Too," "I Got Lost in His Arms," "I Got the Sun in the Morning," "Anything You Can Do"

*Call Me Madam*
**Imperial Theatre, October 12, 1950 (644 Performances)**
**Produced by Leland Hayward. Music and Lyrics by Irving Berlin. Book by Howard Lindsay and Russel Crouse. Directed by George Abbott. Dances and Musical Numbers Staged by Jerome Robbins. Musical Direction by Jay Blackton. Orchestrations by Don Walker. Costumes by Raoul Pene Du Bois. Miss Merman's Dresses by Mainbocher**
**Opening Night Cast:** Ethel Merman, Paul Lukas, Russell Nype, Galina Talva, Pat Harrington, Alan Hewitt, and others. Miss Merman's Standby: Elaine Stritch.
**Note: This play was suggested by the 1949 appointment of Washington hostess Perle Mesta as ambassadress to Luxembourg. However, the program announced "neither the character of Mrs. Sally Adams nor Miss Ethel Merman resemble any person living or dead."**
**Plot Summary:** Mrs. Sally Adams is appointed ambassador to the duchy of Lichtenbourg. While doing her duty, she falls in love with a diplomat and nearly sets diplomacy back a hundred years.
**Merman's Songs:** "The Hostess With the Mostes' On the Ball," "Washington Square Dance," "Can You Use Any Money Today?" "The Best Thing for You," "Something to Dance About," "You're Just in Love"

*Happy Hunting*
**Majestic Theatre, December 6, 1956 (412 Performances)**
**Produced by Jo Mielziner. Book by Howard Lindsay and Russel**

Crouse. Lyrics by Matt Dubey. Music by Harold Karr. Musical Direction by Jay Blackton. Orchestrations by Ted Royal. Directed by Abe Burrows. Costumes by Irene Sharaff

**Opening Night Cast:** Ethel Merman, Fernando Lamas, Virginia Gibson, Gordon Polk, Gene Wesson, Estelle Parsons, and others

**Plot Summary:** A brassy Philadelphia widow travels to Monaco during the wedding of Prince Rainier to Grace Kelly to find her daughter a husband. Instead, she finds love herself.

**Merman's Songs:** "Gee, But It's Good to Be Here," "Mutual Admiration Society," "Mr. Livingstone," "This is What I Call Love" (replaced by "Old Enough to Know Better" by Roger Edens and credited to Kay Thompson), "A New-Fangled Tango," "The Game of Love" (replaced by "Just a Moment Ago" by Roger Edens and credited to Kay Thompson), "Happy Hunting," "I'm a Funny Dame," "This Much I Know"

*Gypsy*
**Broadway Theatre, May 21, 1959 (702 Performances)**
**Produced by Leland Hayward and David Merrick. Book by Arthur Laurents. Music by Jule Styne. Lyrics by Stephen Sondheim. Directed and Choreographed by Jerome Robbins. Scenic and Lighting Design by Jo Mielziner. Costumes by Raoul Pene Du Bois. Based on the memoirs of Gypsy Rose Lee. Musical Direction by Milton Rosenstock**

**Opening Night Cast:** Ethel Merman, Jack Klugman, Sandra Church, Paul Wallace, Maria Karnilova, Marilyn Cooper, Lane Bradbury, and others

**Plot Summary:** The stage mother of all stage mothers is bound and determined to make stars of her two daughters. One turns out to be actress June Havoc, the other Gypsy Rose Lee.

**Merman's Songs:** "Some People," "Small World," "Mr. Goldstone," "You'll Never Get Away from Me," "Everything's Coming Up Roses," "Together, Wherever We Go," "Rose's Turn"

*Annie Get Your Gun* (Revival)
**Broadway Theatre, September 21, 1966 (78 Performances)**
**Produced by the Music Theater of Lincoln Center. Music and Lyrics by Irving Berlin. Book by Herbert and Dorothy Fields. Directed by Jack Sydow. Orchestrations by Robert Russell Bennett. Musical Direction by Franz Allers**
**Opening Night Cast:** Ethel Merman, Bruce Yarnell, Jerry Orbach, Benay Venuta, Harry Bellaver, and others
**Plot Summary:** An updated telling of the story of Annie Oakley.
**Merman's Songs:** "Doin' What Comes Nat'rally," "You Can't Get a Man with a Gun," "There's No Business Like Show Business," "They Say It's Wonderful," "Moonshine Lullaby," "I'm an Indian Too," "I Got Lost in His Arms," "I Got the Sun in the Morning," "Old Fashioned Wedding," "Anything You Can Do"

*Hello, Dolly!*
**St. James Theatre, March 28, 1970 (210 Performances)**
**Produced by David Merrick and Champion-Five Inc. Book by Michael Stewart. Music and Lyrics by Jerry Herman. Directed and Choreographed by Gower Champion**
**Merman's Cast:** Ethel Merman, Jack Goode, Russell Nype, June Helmers, Dany Lockin, Georgia Engel, and others
**Plot Summary:** Widow Dolly Levi, matchmaker supreme, schemes to make wealthy Horace Vandegelder her new husband.
**Merman's Songs:** "I Put My Hand In," "World Take Me Back," "Motherhood," "Dancing," "Love Look in My Window," "Before the Parade Passes By," "Hello Dolly," "So Long Dearie"

# Index

310